CONTEMPORARY RADICAL FILM CULTURE

Comprising essays from some of the leading scholars and practitioners in the field, this is the first book to investigate twenty-first century radical film practices across production, distribution and exhibition at a global level.

This book explores global radical film culture in all its geographic, political and aesthetic diversity. It is inspired by the work of the Radical Film Network (RFN), an organisation established in 2013 to support the growth and sustainability of politically engaged film culture around the world. Since then, the RFN has grown rapidly, and now consists of almost 200 organisations across four continents, from artists' studios and production collectives to archives, distributors and film festivals. With this foundation, the book engages with contemporary radical film cultures in Africa, Asia, China, Europe, the Middle East as well as North and South America, and connects key historical moments and traditions with the present day. Topics covered include artists' film and video, curation, documentary, feminist and queer film cultures, film festivals and screening practices, network-building, policy interventions and video-activism.

For students, researchers and practitioners, this fascinating and wide-ranging book sheds new light on the political potential of the moving image and represents the activists and organisations pushing radical film forward in new and exciting directions.

For more information about the Radical Film Network, visit www.radicalfilmnetwork.com.

Steve Presence is Senior Lecturer in Film Studies at UWE Bristol, UK. His research spans activist film culture, documentary and the UK film and television industries, and he is currently working on an AHRC-funded study of the UK's feature documentary film industry. He convened the Radical Film Network in 2013.

Mike Wayne is Professor in Film and Media Studies at Brunel University, UK. His research covers radical film practices, media and cultural studies, Marxist theory and questions of class inequality and its cultural impacts.

Jack Newsinger is Assistant Professor in Cultural Industries and Media at the University of Nottingham, UK. He has published widely on cultural and media policy, cultural labour and diversity, and has been involved in the Radical Film Network since 2015.

CONTEMPORARY RADICAL FILM CULTURE

Networks, Organisations and Activists

Edited by Steve Presence, Mike Wayne and Jack Newsinger

Routledge
Taylor & Francis Group

LONDON AND NEW YORK

First published 2021
by Routledge
2 Park Square, Milton Park, Abingdon, Oxon OX14 4RN

and by Routledge
52 Vanderbilt Avenue, New York, NY 10017

Routledge is an imprint of the Taylor & Francis Group, an informa business

British Library Cataloguing-in-Publication Data
A catalogue record for this book is available from the British Library

Library of Congress Cataloging-in-Publication Data
Names: Presence, Steve, editor. | Wayne, Mike, editor. |
Newsinger, Jack, editor.
Title: Contemporary radical film culture : networks, organisations and activists / edited by Steve Presence, Mike Wayne, and Jack Newsinger.
Description: London ; New York : Routledge, 2020. |
Includes bibliographical references and index.
Identifiers: LCCN 2020009745 (print) | LCCN 2020009746 (ebook) |
ISBN 9781138543607 (hardback) | ISBN 9781138543614 (paperback) |
ISBN 9781351006385 (ebook)
Subjects: LCSH: Motion pictures--Political aspects--History--21st century. |
Motion pictures--Social aspects--History--21st century. |
Documentary films--Political aspects--History--21st century. |
Experimental films--Political aspects--History--21st century. |
Film festivals--Political aspects--History--21st century. |
Politics in motion pictures. | Social problems in motion pictures. |
Radical Film Network (United Kingdom)
Classification: LCC PN1995.9.P6 C6685 2020 (print) |
LCC PN1995.9.P6 (ebook) | DDC 791.4309/05--dc23
LC record available at https://lccn.loc.gov/2020009745
LC ebook record available at https://lccn.loc.gov/2020009746

ISBN: 978-1-138-54360-7 (hbk)
ISBN: 978-1-138-54361-4 (pbk)
ISBN: 978-1-351-00638-5 (ebk)

Typeset in Bembo
by Taylor & Francis Books

This book is dedicated to Chuck Kleinhans (October 2, 1942–December 14, 2017). A towering figure in Film Studies, Chuck was a committed and inspirational teacher, activist and scholar. It is with love and respect that we dedicate this volume to his memory.

CONTENTS

FIGURES

ACKNOWLEDGEMENTS

This book would not exist without all the organisations and individuals who helped bring the Radical Film Network into being and push it along. Those that deserve particularly special thanks include Laura Ager, David Archibald, Holly Aylett, Hongwei Bao, Talat Bhat, Richard Bickle, Ursula Böckler, Elena Boschi, Violeta Bruck, Michael Chanan, Sue Clayton, Benjamin Cook, Paolo Davanzo, Jill Daniels, Shaun Dey, Margaret Dickinson, Tony Dowmunt, Gareth Evans, Debbie Freeman, Chris Garlock, Paula Geraghty, Lee Grieveson, Sarah Hamblin, Sylvia Harvey, Fran Higson, Patricia Holland, Sharon Hooper, Reuben Irving, Chris Jury, Anthony Killick, Chuck Kleinhans, Julia Lazarus, Julia Lesage, Franklin López, Kate Mara, Concha Mateos, Elizabeth Mizon, Pauline van Mourik Broekman, Laura Mulvey, Daniel Mutibwa, Clive Myer, Robert Navan, Heinz Nigg, Humberto Perez-Blanco, Michael Pierce, Dina Pokrajac, Sarah Redman, Duncan Reekie, Chris Reeves, Karen Ranucci, Chris Robé, Andy Robson, Marcy Saude, Steve Sprung, Rod Stoneman, Andrew Tilson, Hayley Trowbridge, Svetla Turnin, Vagabond, Maria Vélez-Serna, Richard Warden, Ezra Winton, Jan Worth and Andrea Luka Zimmerman.

We would also like to gratefully acknowledge the UK's Arts and Humanities Research Council, which funded some of the research in this book via the International Research Networking Scheme grant, 'Sustaining Alternative Film Cultures' (AH/M010600/1, 2015–18). Last, but not least, sincere thanks to our editors at Routledge, Natalie Foster and Jennifer Vennall, for their support and patience in seeing this project through to fruition.

CONTRIBUTORS

David Archibald is Senior Lecturer in Film and Television Studies at the University of Glasgow. His academic written work includes the monograph *The War That Won't Die: The Spanish Civil War in Cinema* (2012) and he has published widely on various aspects of film culture. David has worked on numerous practice research films, including the multi-award-winning *Govan Young* (2017), which he produced and co-directed, and, more recently, *Drifting with Debord* (2019), which he co-wrote and co-directed with his colleague, Carl Lavery. David regularly appears on stage alongside Lavery in the experimental performance project, Glasgow Glam Rock Dialogues.

Hongwei Bao is an associate professor in media studies at the University of Nottingham, UK, where he also directs the Centre for Contemporary East Asian Cultural Studies. He holds a PhD in Gender and Cultural Studies from the University of Sydney, Australia. His current research primarily focuses on queer film culture and political activism in contemporary China; it examines independent queer films and film festivals in China as a form of transnational and postsocialist cultural politics. He is the author of *Queer Comrades: Gay Identity and Tongzhi Activism in Postsocialist China* (NIAS Press, 2018) and *Queer China: Lesbian and Gay Literature and Visual Culture under Postsocialism* (Routledge, 2020). Together with Daniel Mutibwa, he co-organised 'Transnational Radical Film Cultures: An International Conference on Film, Aesthetics and Politics' (aka RFN Conference 2019) in Nottingham.

Elena Boschi is an independent scholar and film curator based in Genoa, Italy. After working at various universities in the north west of England as a lecturer and being a union rep for a few years, she realized that UK Higher Education wasn't sustainable anymore and decided to move on, looking for a new space for critical thinking and practice in a post-academic life. Her earlier research projects primarily focused on the role of popular music in the representation of sexuality, gender, and class in Italian, Spanish and British cinema. She has also published on visible playback technology in film and on the audiovisual style in the films of Wes Anderson (both co-authored with Tim McNelis), and she was co-editor of a special issue of the *Journal of British Cinema and Television* on *Gender, Ageing, and Sexuality in British Cinema After Thatcher* with Christine Geraghty. Elena's more recent research on alternative screening practices has informed her curation of interrupted screenings, in which participants discuss films in small groups during scheduled breaks rather than just at the end to promote a radical film experience. She has curated screenings in England, Scotland and Italy, working primarily with film festivals, charities and occupied spaces.

Haim Bresheeth is a filmmaker, photographer and film studies scholar. His books include the best-selling *Introduction to the Holocaust* (with Stuart Hood, two reprints since 1997; also published in Turkish, Croatian and Japanese. Edited volumes include *The Gulf War and the New World Order* (1991), *Cinema and Memory: Dangerous Liaisons* (Hebrew, 2004) and *The Conflict and Contemporary Visual Culture in Palestine & Israel* (2007), special issue of *Third Text on Palestinian and Israeli Art, Literature, Architecture and Cinema*. His films include the widely shown *State of Danger* (1989, BBC2), *London is Burning* (2013) and *Convivencia at the Turnpike* (2015). Recent films include the feature documentaries, *The Last Honeymoon in Europe* (2018) and *The Mind of the Occupier* (forthcoming, 2020). His book, *An Army Like No Other: How the IDF Made Israel*, will be published by Verso in May 2020.

Nick Cope is Senior Lecturer and Program Manager, Digital Film and Video at RMIT University, Vietnam, and a filmmaker who has worked in the higher education sector since 1995, following eight years working in the creative and media industries. He has been a practising film, video and digital media artist since 1982, and completed a PhD in October 2012. This locates a contemporary visual music practice within current and emerging critical and theoretical contexts and tracks back the history of this practice to initial screenings of work as part of the 1980s British Scratch video art movement, and later collaborations with electronic music pioneers Cabaret Voltaire and others. He continues to screen older work and new, and present papers, at conferences, cinemas, concerts, galleries and festivals; nationally and internationally. A personal website and archive is online at www.nickcopefilm.com.

Jens Eder is Professor of Dramaturgy and Aesthetics of Audiovisual Media at Film University Babelsberg 'Konrad Wolf' in Potsdam, Germany. His research focuses on theories of narration, aesthetics, and reception of audiovisual media, as well as their current developments and their relations to society. He has written books and papers on characters, emotion, narrative and politics in films and other visual media. Among others, he has co-edited the publications *Image Operations. Visual Media and Political Conflict* (with Charlotte Klonk, 2017), *Characters in Fictional Worlds* (with Fotis Jannidis and Ralf Schneider, 2010) and the issue *#Emotions* of the journal *NECSUS* (with Julian Hanich and Jane Stadler, 2019). Together with Britta Hartmann and Chris Tedjasukmana, he is pursuing the research project 'Attention Strategies of Video Activism on the Social Web'.

Ieuan Franklin is Lecturer in Media and Cultural History at Bournemouth University, where he undertook his PhD (awarded in 2010). Between 2010 and 2014 he was post-doctoral research assistant on the AHRC-funded 'Channel 4 and British Film Culture' project at the University of Portsmouth. He has published widely on media history topics, and was lead editor (with Hugh Chignell and Kristin Skoog) of *Regional Aesthetics: Mapping UK Media Cultures* (Palgrave, 2015). His research interests include documentary, community media and youth culture.

Mette Hjort is Chair Professor of Humanities and Dean of Arts at the Hong Kong Baptist University, Affiliate Professor of Scandinavian Studies at the University of Washington, and Visiting Professor of Cultural Industries at the University of South Wales. Mette's monographs include *Small Nation, Global Cinema* (2005). Her interest in the politics of talent development, including 'twinning' projects on a North/South basis, is reflected in the two-volume *The Education of the Filmmaker* (ed., 2013) and *African Cinema and Human Rights* (edited with Eva Jørholt, 2019). Mette holds an Honorary Doctorate in Transnational Cinema Studies from the University of Aalborg. She has served on the Board of the Danish Film Institute (appointed by the Danish Ministry of Culture) and on Hong Kong's University Grants Committee (appointed by the Chief Executive of Hong Kong).

Eamonn Kelly is Senior Lecturer teaching Film and Cultural Studies at the University of South Wales. He is a long-time activist in the University and Colleges Union, and a Director of Bristol Radical Film Festival.

Anthony Killick is a Lecturer in Media, Communication and Culture at Liverpool John Moores University. His recent work at the University of Leeds and the Centre for Understanding Sustainable Prosperity (CUSP) has focused on the role of arts and cultural practices in contributing to more socially and ecologically sustainable communities.

Shweta Kishore lectures in Screen and Media at RMIT University. She is a documentary practitioner and author of *Indian Documentary Film and Filmmakers: Independence in Practice* (2018). Shweta's research on Indian documentary, documentary ethics, feminist film and activist film festivals has appeared in *Camera Obscura, Feminist Media Studies, Third Text, Bioscope, Studies in Documentary Film* and *Senses of Cinema*. Her current practice-based research project, 'In Art as in Life', examines the interrelation between contemporary art, gender and documentary filmmaking towards the construction of feminist knowledge and research methodologies.

Chuck Kleinhans (1942–2017) was Associate Professor of Film Studies at Northwestern University in Illinois for thirty-two years. In 1974, with Julia Lesage and John Hess, he co-founded the non-sectarian left, feminist, anti-racist and anti-imperialist journal, *Jump Cut: A Review of Contemporary Media*. In addition to his many Jump Cut publications, Kleinhans published more than sixty peer-reviewed articles and book chapters on subjects ranging from Marxism, documentary, experimental and avant-garde filmmaking, Hollywood blockbusters, pornography and the LA Rebellion. In additional to his writing, Kleinhans was also an inspirational and innovative teacher who taught generations of scholars, activists, makers and critics. For his services to film education, the Society for Cinema and Media Studies awarded Kleinhans its first Outstanding Pedagogical Achievement Award in 2007.

Julia Lesage is Professor Emerita in the Department of English at the University of Oregon, which she joined in the late 1980s. She co-founded and is the editor of *Jump Cut: A Review of Contemporary Media*, and has published several books and more than thirty essays and peer-reviewed journal articles, in addition to numerous essays and articles in *Jump Cut*.

Jack Newsinger is Assistant Professor in Cultural Industries and Media at the University of Nottingham, UK. He has published widely on cultural and media policy, cultural labour and diversity, and been involved in the Radical Film Network since 2015.

Steve Presence is Senior Lecturer in Film Studies at the University of the West of England in Bristol (UWE Bristol). He is the convenor of the Radical Film Network and co-founder of the Bristol Radical Film Festival, and has published widely on activist film culture and the UK film and television industries. He is currently Principal Investigator on 'UK Feature Docs', a three-year AHRC-funded study of the UK's feature-length documentary film industry.

Andy Robson is Screen Heritage Producer at Film Hub North, overseeing a four-year screen heritage exhibition programme across the BFI Film Audience Network. He co-founded the Marc Karlin Archive in 2010, leading to the publication, *Marc Karlin – Look Again* (2015) that focused on the radical filmmaker's work broadcast on Channel 4 and the BBC between 1982 and 1999. He has recently completed a collaborative PhD with the University of Sunderland and the Newcastle-based Amber Film and Photography Collective investigating Amber's production, exhibition and distribution strategies underpinned by the Workshop Declaration (1982–1989).

Ana Rodríguez Granell holds a PhD in Art History (Universitat de Barcelona, 2012), entitled 'Film Theory and Practice as a Critical Dispositive: The Achievement of Modernism and the Shape of Politics in the Cinema of the Thirties'. She is Associate Professor in the Arts and Humanities Department at the Universitat Oberta de Catalunya where she coordinates MA and BA courses related to Cultural History, Film Studies, History of Cinema and Art History. Since 2006 she has been a member of several research groups and R+D projects funded by the Spanish Ministry of Economics, working on the relationships between culture and society, cinema and Spanish History, and also researching cinema and digital media. In 2013 she joined the editorial team of the indexed journal *Artnodes: Journal on Art, Science and Technology* as executive manager. Her latest research articles and papers have been focused on cultural history of modernism; on fascist studies; and on political agency and oppositional aesthetics in social documentary and film.

Chris Tedjasukmana (Dr. phil.) is a film and media scholar at the University of Bonn, Germany. He is principal investigator of the research project 'Attention Economies of Video Activism on the Social Web' (funded by the Volkswagen Foundation) and co-editor of the German journal *Montage AV*. In 2014, his book *Mechanical Vitalization: Aesthetic Experience in Cinema* was published in German. His research focuses on digital publics, media theory, film theory, political theory, philosophical aesthetics, and gender and queer studies.

Christo Wallers is a film-programmer, filmmaker and founding member of the Star & Shadow Cinema, and its predecessor, Cineside, at the Side Cinema, Newcastle upon Tyne. He has been involved with DIY culture in the North East since 2001, playing in bands, making films, producing zines and building the various editions of the Star and Shadow. He co-founded Film Bee, an experimental film cooperative, which has screened work internationally at festivals in New York, Melbourne, Brussels, Paris, Edinburgh and London. He founded and edits *Filmo#*, a zine for the Kino Climates network of alternative cinemas. He lives in rural Northumberland and runs an annual film retreat, 'Losing the Plot'. He is an SWW DTP-funded PhD candidate at Reading University, researching a DIY model of film exhibition since the mid-1990s. He is a member of Co-op Early Research Network (CERN), and teaches on a number of MA modules around the country.

Mike Wayne is a Professor in Film and Media Studies at Brunel University. His most recent book is *Marxism Goes to the Movies* (Routledge, 2020) and he has also made three feature length documentary films, most recently *The Acting Class* (2017). His research covers radical film practices, media and cultural studies, Marxist theory and questions of class inequality and its cultural impacts.

Ezra Winton holds a PhD in Communication from Carleton University and is currently a Visiting Scholar at the Reimagining Value Action Lab (RiVAL) at Lakehead University. His monograph, *Buying In to Doing Good: Documentary Politics and Curatorial Ethics at the Hot Docs Film Festival*, will be published by McGill-Queen's University Press in 2020. He is also working on a book about *Kanehsatake: 270 Years of Resistance*, the ground-breaking film by Abenaki director, Alanis Obomsawin, as well as an international curatorial-research project that looks at the construction of settler identity and society across five settler cinemas (Britain, Canada, Australia, New Zealand, United States) called 'Settler Frames'. Ezra is the co-founder and Director of Programming of Cinema Politica, the world's largest campus and community-based documentary screening network. He tweets occasionally as @ezrawinton.

INTRODUCTION

Steve Presence, Mike Wayne and Jack Newsinger

In October 2019, the largest protests in Chile in three decades erupted in Santiago and quickly spread across the country. Initially triggered by a fare increase on Santiago's subway system, a mass fare-dodging movement escalated into a nation-wide uprising demanding dramatic changes to Chile's political and economic system. The protestors' objections are familiar: low wages, long hours and wealth inequality in a country ruled in the interests of the rich; unequal access to education, privatised social services, inadequate healthcare and a lack of social security. As we write this introduction, Chile's billionaire conservative president, Sebastián Piñera, has declared a state of emergency, while the protestors' demands that the Pinochet-era constitution be scrapped look set to be put to a vote.

In early December 2019, activists involved with the protests sent a message to the Radical Film Network (RFN) mailing list, appealing for films that could be shown as part of a weekly screening series they had set up in Valdivia, a city in Southern Chile. In response, activists from Bombozila, an online exhibition plat-form in Rio de Janeiro dedicated to 'social struggle' films from Latin America and the Caribbean, replied to help curate a selection of their films for the series in Chile. Bombozila had affiliated to the RFN in the previous summer, on the recommendation of an Argentinian filmmaker affiliated with Contraimagen, a longstanding radical production collective and RFN member based in Buenos Aires. We mention this story as just one of many examples of how the RFN has, from its initial base in the UK, become a global network of organisations and individuals working at the intersection of radical politics and film culture. Like most organisations affiliated to it, the RFN is unfunded and its operation is largely decentralised and non-hierarchical, and yet the network continues to grow in unpredictable and exciting ways that are testament to the energy and dynamism of contemporary radical film culture.

This book is the first collection of texts to have emerged from the RFN since its foundation in 2013. Currently comprised of almost 200 organisations from twenty-nine countries across four continents – as well as several more hundred individual members – the RFN has become the largest network for activist and experimental film culture in the world.[1] *Contemporary Radical Film Culture: Networks, Organisations and Activists* is an attempt to capture some of the immense geographic, political and aesthetic diversity represented within the network and in global radical film culture more generally. The book interrogates some of the key political and practical issues, histories and practices with which this culture is concerned and which, indeed, have defined the history of Left film practice and politics since at least the 1920s. These fundamental topics range from issues of organisation, sustainability and funding (or lack thereof) – which are intimately connected to questions regarding the state and cultural institutions, and the Left's engagement with them – to matters of film form and aesthetics, and of the myriad challenges and affordances involved in different modes of distribution and exhibition.

The book is organised into four parts. Part I explores some of the perennial challenges facing radical film culture, and the ways in which strategies for engaging with and overcoming these challenges are evolving in the digital era. In Chapter 1, Steve Presence, the convenor and co-founder of the RFN, reflects on the genesis and development of the network to date. Recalling some of the historical precedents for progressive film networks and the ways in which these inspired the RFN, Presence explores the conceptual and practical difficulties involved in creating a decentralised, unfunded network in the digital era, and considers how the RFN might develop as it moves into its second decade. Chuck Kleinhans' Chapter 2 is an edited version of the keynote address he delivered at 'Radical Film Network NYC: A Global Gathering', a three-day conference organised by Steve Presence and Mike Wayne in Manhattan in May 2017 in association with the Workers Unite! Film Festival. Chuck provides a typically masterful analysis of the key trends in the evolution of political and experimental film in North America, from the Workers Film and Photo League to *I Am Not Your Negro* (2017), yet never loses sight of the infrastructural challenges involved in building and maintaining radical film cultures, or of the importance of passing on radical histories across generations. Chuck's last point takes on special resonance here, as he sadly passed away shortly after sending us the written version of his keynote, which he planned to develop into his chapter. We are honoured to publish Chuck's text here and hope his chapter, and the book as a whole, helps pass on his passion and knowledge of the radical film tradition to future scholars and activists.

In Chapter 3, Julia Lesage reflects on four decades of feminist documentary production, distribution and exhibition. The chapter explores key changes in feminist documentary since the 1970s – from overcoming scarcity in feminist filmmaking to problems with abundance and the 'flattening out' of previously pronounced differences between radical and mainstream media texts – and makes clear that, while in some respects feminist documentary is more accessible than ever, this history is not one of straightforward progress. With detailed reference to key organisations, including Women Make Movies, and filmmakers from Michelle

Citron to Irene Lusztig, the chapter also analyses the critical historical and contemporary function of canon formation. In the era of streaming and subscription-on-demand platforms, Lesage argues, the curatorial and promotional role that teachers, writers and others play in securing the life-span of feminist and other kinds of radical filmmaking is more important than ever.

Chapter 4 turns to video activism, one of the most pervasive forms of radical film in circulation today. Jens Eder and Chris Tedjasukmana provide an overview of contemporary video activism on the Social Web – a term that underscores the interactivity and exchange that marks current Internet usage – and places it in the context of radical film cultures historically. Tracking the development of the form from the 1920s' agit trains in Soviet Russia to contemporary platform-based 'social videos', the chapter also explores the range of interdisciplinary research approaches to video activism in fields ranging from film studies to social movement studies. Eder and Tedjasukmana investigate current strategies to aid contemporary video activists in the battle for attention on social media.

In Chapter 5, Ieuan Franklin explores the relationship between radical filmmakers and broadcast television – a relationship which he argues is typically characterised by a continuum between two poles: 'enter or subvert'. Analysing key theoretical approaches to alternative media, the first section of the chapter shows how video art has often functioned as an embodiment of radical critiques of mass culture, such as those developed by the Frankfurt School. The second section explores the role that artists and filmmakers have played in influencing media policy through campaign groups. Drawing on examples from Amsterdam and the United States as well as the UK, Franklin argues for the importance of working both within and against dominant institutions and the risks involved in imposing rigid ideological frameworks for conceptualising the diverse range of practices which fall under the rubric of 'alternative media'.

The chapters in Part II provide accounts of historical and contemporary radical interventions in film practice and policy around the world. In Chapter 6, David Archibald reflects on the development of RFN Scotland between 2015 and 2019. The principal focus of the chapter is the 'Radical Film Network Festival and Unconference', which took place in Glasgow in 2016. Reflecting on his experience as one of the organisers of that event, Archibald explores the principles and practices that underpinned the Unconference (a non-hierarchical mode of event organising in which participants co-create the schedule collectively) and the decentralised approach they adopted to coordinate the accompanying city-wide film festival – a major event that drew on the combined efforts of over forty organisations and was attended by almost two thousand people, making it one of the largest radical film events organised in Scotland.

In Chapter 7, Ana Rodríguez Granell explores the affordances of Information and Communication Technology (ICT) – including Creative Commons licenses and participatory profit distribution – for the production and circulation of militant documentary. Focusing on *Ciutat Morta/Dead City* (2015), a film about police brutality and corruption in Barcelona by the radical audiovisual platform, Metromuster, Granell shows how the producers' deep involvement in the anti-austerity 15-M Movement and strategic use of various social media platforms saw a crowd-sourced film that premiered in a squatted cinema go on to win awards at several major Spanish film festivals and be broadcast on TV3. Chapter 8 also discusses issues of distribution but in a very different context, as Shweta Kishore explores the circulation of radical documentaries in India and the ways in which different kinds of regulation – from censorship and vigilante forces to gate-keeping NGOs – impact on the films, the audiences they reach, and how they reach them. Developing the notion of 'tactical circulation' to examine how some of the country's leading radical filmmakers and organisations are countering these regulatory forces, Kishore provides a valuable analysis of contemporary radical film practice and culture in India.

In Chapter 9, Mette Hjort prefaces her discussion of activist film practices in Africa by emphasising that the immense diversity of the continent – over a billion people in fifty-four countries – renders the very concept of African filmmaking problematic. Yet, as she argues, 'some generalisations do have a legitimate role to play', not least in helping to 'pinpoint certain tendencies [and] describe shared challenges, solutions and goals'. Hjort's central contention, that much filmmaking by African filmmakers can be understood as in some senses 'activist', is explored through several analyses of key filmmakers and organisations, including Zanzibar International Film Festival (Tanzania); the film school, IMAGINE (Burkina Faso); and a detailed case study of Cameroonian filmmaker, Jean-Marie Teno.

In Chapter 10, Haim Bresheeth explores the political film cultures in Israel and Palestine after the 1993 Oslo Accords. Tracing the growth of film in Palestine under the Palestinian Liberation Organization (PLO) from the late 1960s, Bresheeth argues that after the 1993 agreements, support for filmmaking was largely abandoned because of the Palestinian National Authority's failure to see the relation between cultural and political struggle. While the decade or so following 1993 saw Israeli and Palestinian filmmakers alike access support from liberal funders both within and beyond Israel, the current Israeli regime has worked hard to hinder any critical cultural production. Nevertheless, echoing a sentiment found in many chapters in the book, Bresheeth argues that films such as *5 Broken Cameras* (2011) demonstrate how a lack of support has ironically resulted in greater cultural independence and creativity.

Chapter 11 and Chapter 12 focus on two key interventions in British radical film history. Nick Cope revisits Scratch video, the radical video-art movement of the early 1980s that exploited new editing technologies to oppose and 'détourn' broadcast television. Cope re-evaluates the history of Scratch's development, including its initial rejection by many critics and its swift recuperation into mainstream aesthetics. Shedding new light on the history of Scratch, Cope shows how key aspects of the movement have been overlooked – often as a result of the London-centric focus of critics and exhibitions – and how it anticipated the creative possibilities of digital technologies and, as a kind of audiovisual music, embodied an original aesthetic mode. In Chapter 12 Andy Robson focuses on The Workshop Declaration (1982–89), the extraordinary attempt to nurture a permanently funded regional network of community-based film and video workshops across the UK. Dismissed at the time and largely overlooked since, Robson's detailed history explores the emergence and untimely demise of this 'profoundly radical agreement', and how it fostered 'some of the most politically provocative films ever broadcast in Britain'. While the Declaration is in many ways unthinkable by today's standards, Robson teases out some of the many lessons this moment holds for those engaged in building alternative film cultures today.

Part III comprises five chapters that encapsulate some of the diverse practices and approaches within a key sector of contemporary radical film culture: exhibition. In Chapter 13, Elena Boschi explores the ideas behind 'interrupted screenings', a model of exhibition in which participants 'discuss film during breaks within, not just after the screening'. A major historical reference point for the interrupted screening, Boschi reminds us, comes from Solanas and Getino's landmark film, *The Hour of the Furnaces* (1968), and their reflexive essay on the experiences of making and screening that film, 'Towards a Third Cinema'. Combining insights from this key reference point with recent research on film studies, anxiety and militancy, and her own experiences running interrupted screenings, Boschi argues that the 'interrupted' mode of viewing, antithetical to the dominant modes of consumption, could open up a more radical and participative engagement with film.

Anthony Killick explores the politics of radical film exhibition in Chapter 14 via an analysis of the ways in which film festival organisers produce spaces of resistance to neoliberalism from within neoliberal cities. Noting how terms such as 'activism' and 'human rights' are increasingly delineated and assimilated by neoliberalism – and that Western human rights festivals often focus on abuses overseas while ignoring issues such as economic violence at home – Killick outlines an internationalist, class-conscious conception of human rights that understands austerity as a human rights issue. Focusing on Liverpool Radical Film Festival as a case study, he argues that radical film festivals must consider how such global human rights issues manifest in local contexts and provide spaces through which the working class can participate in resisting them.

Ezra Winton's Chapter 15 addresses the politics of programming and curation. While film studies courses around the globe continue to prioritise textual analysis, the ways in which films are valued, chosen and contextualised receive nothing like the same level of critical scrutiny. And yet, as Winton argues, the age of media abundance is also, by necessity, an age of curators – as audiences we depend on curation and curators to help us navigate the vast flows of culture swirling around us. Developing a curatorial model based on two opposing tendencies – capital programming and community programming – and critiquing Toronto International Film Festival as an example of the former, Winton urges us to focus our critical energies on politics, power and 'counterpower' underpinning film festival programming. Hongwei Bao discusses similar themes in his discussion of Beijing Queer Film Festival (BJQFF) in Chapter 16. In an era in which the radicalism of many queer film festivals has been diluted by their incorporation into capitalism's 'pink economy', BJQFF stands out not only as one of the longest running identity-based film festivals in China but also one that has maintained a radical outlook both in terms of its programming and organisational practices. Bao's chapter focuses on the history of the festival, the various ways in which it embodies a prefigurative politics based on principles of egalitarianism and direct democracy, and the challenges of running a radical queer film festival in a hostile, heteronormative environment.

In Chapter 17, Christo Wallers shifts attention to the bricks and mortar of film exhibition in his study of the Star and Shadow Cinema in Newcastle in the North East of England. The Star and Shadow grew out of both continuities and transformations in Left cultural politics during the 1990s and 2000s, notably the anti-World Trade Organisation protests and the growth of autonomous radical media groups but also underground culture, environmentalism and the post-punk spirit of party and protest. Wallers – one of the Star and Shadow's founders – places his insider account in this context and demonstrates the emergence of a national network of radical exhibition groups throughout the period. In doing so, the chapter provides the connection between the history of the UK workshop movement and contemporary radical exhibition practices, providing a detailed account of what goes into establishing and maintaining a radical cinema in the twenty-first century.

Part IV, the final part of the book, comprises five interviews with different filmmakers, activists, and artists from around the world that represent elements of the contemporary radical film culture less documented in the chapters outlined above. The first interview focuses on artists' film and video – represented here by Oliver Ressler, the Austrian video-artist whose work addresses issues from climate change and migration to alternative economics and labour struggles. European radical feature docs are represented here by Moviemienta (formerly Infowar Productions), the Greek production company behind films such as *Debtocracy* (2011), *This Is Not a Coup* (2016) and *Make the Economy Scream* (2019). Reel News, the longest-running video-activist collective in British film history, are the subject of the third interview. Paolo Davanzo and Lisa Marr, co-founders of Los Angeles' Echo Park Film Center – a 'media arts center, cinema, and film school in the belly of the Hollywood beast' – are our fourth interviewees, while the final word goes to Nadir Boumouch, the Moroccan filmmaker and former member of Guerrilla Cinema – one of many film collectives that emerged during the so-called 'Arab Spring' – who discusses his experiences working in the Third Cinema tradition and the challenges involved in building radical film culture in North Africa.

Note

1 To find out more about these organisations explore the Directory of affiliated groups at https://radicalfilmnetwork.com/directory/

PART I

Issues in radical film culture, past and present

1

'ADMIN WILL MAKE OR BREAK THE REBELLION'

Building the Radical Film Network

Steve Presence

This chapter provides a history of the Radical Film Network (RFN) and its development to date. The network was founded in 2013 and since that time has expanded rapidly, in several exciting and unpredictable directions, and looks set to expand further, with iterations of the network developing in India, Nigeria and Sweden. This chapter is written partly in response to questions regarding the formation of the RFN that activists and academics from these countries asked at the RFN conference in Nottingham in 2019, as they considered how to build the RFN in their own countries. While the chapter is therefore partly a 'how-to' guide from one of the network's founders, this does not, of course, mean those building versions of the network in their parts of the world should necessarily follow suit. Indeed, part of what I want to do here is to show how the RFN developed from a specific context in the UK, and to offer an account of the challenges involved in using the particular approaches to network-building that we have adopted so far. This is intended to record this history and to help others who follow in our footsteps to learn from our mistakes and make the RFN a stronger, more resilient network in the future.

Writing the history of the RFN is important partly because – as David Archibald notes in his chapter in this volume – so few activist initiatives manage to reflect on their development *and* do the work they were set up to do. Frequently unfunded and dependent on volunteer labour, it is often simply not possible for radical cultural organisations to document the processes involved or explain why things occurred in the way that they did, at the same time as organising a film festival, for example, or building a production collective. As a result, it is all too often the case that, as Julia Knight and Peter Thomas found in their history of alternative film promotion and distribution, 'new generations of … practitioners and distributors … remain unaware of historical precedents… strategies and models that are now being heralded as new and [are] therefore unable to benefit from lessons learnt in the past' (Knight and Thomas 2011, 27).

Moreover, the digital culture myth that everything is readily available online is simply not the case, especially when it comes to already marginal cultures. In a digital context, when so much work is done online via email and social media – and so little produced by way of a paper trail for future researchers – stepping back to record and analyse what happened and why becomes even more important. This is perhaps especially the case when it comes to the building of counter-cultural infrastructures such as the RFN, which inevitably require sometimes dull administrative work and are thus less glamorous than the cultures they seek to support. Consequently, as Simeon Blanchard has argued in relation to the Independent Filmmakers Association (IFA) in the 1970s and 1980s, while much of the work of the IFA was about making independent film 'visible', much of that work itself was 'often barely visible' (Blanchard and Holdsworth 2017, 294). And yet that infrastructural, administrative labour is crucial – without it, long-term initiatives simply cannot function effectively. As Extinction Rebellion (2019) put it, 'admin will make or break the rebellion'.

The chapter is organised into four sections: the first three explore the genesis of the RFN; the conceptual framework on which it is based; and the practical steps involved in building the network and how it operates on a day-to-day basis. The final section poses some thoughts on the future of the network and suggests three ways in which its contribution to activist and experimental film culture could be bolstered in the next decade or so of its existence.

Genesis

The RFN was founded in London in September 2013, but its origins really begin in Bristol several months before. I had completed my PhD thesis in the spring: a study of activist documentary filmmaking in the UK from 1990 onwards (Presence 2013). In 2012, partly to provide a platform for the work I and other colleagues at my university were researching, and partly in response to the lack of political film screenings in Bristol at that time, I and a handful of others co-founded the Bristol Radical Film Festival, which quickly became an annual event following the consistently large audiences it attracted (Ager 2016, 205–40). Several things became apparent as a result of the festival and the research that underpinned it.

First, radical film culture in Britain was alive and kicking – albeit significantly under-resourced – with organisations up and down the country making, showing and sharing political and/or experimental film of all shapes and sizes. Second, while some groups active in the culture were in touch with one another, there were many gaps where organisations with clear affinities or aligned interests were unaware of their contemporaries in other parts of the country. Third, while some of these groups were conscious of the more recent history of activist filmmaking in the UK, these were the exception rather than the rule, and there was often little awareness of the deeper tradition of radical film, in the UK (Hogenkamp 1986, 2000; MacPherson 1980; Dickinson 1999; Burton 2005) or elsewhere (Waugh 1984; Eshun and Gray 2011; Dickinson 2018). Fourth, as indicated by the striking number of international relationships we formed from the film festival, similar film cultures were thriving all over the world – though again, there was little sense that those involved felt part of a global community.

Yet the history of radical film culture is also in part a history of various attempts to coordinate and network at regional, national and international levels. In the UK, the nearest historical predecessor to the RFN – indeed, in many ways the inspiration for it – was the Independent Filmmakers Association (IFA, 1974–1990). I have written about the formative influence of the IFA on the RFN elsewhere (Presence 2019), but there are many other examples from different epochs and other parts of the world. The Workers' Film and Photo League was active in the United States (Campbell 1977) and the UK (Hogenkamp 1976) in the 1930s, for example. In the late 1960s and 1970s, SLON and the Medvedkine Groups in France (Lupton 2005, 110–18; Hennebelle 1972, 15–17) overlapped with the IFA in Britain and the various Newsreel groups in the United States (Renov 1987), which also sought to connect with the revolutionary film movements taking place across much of Africa and Latin America.

Indeed, several efforts were made to formalise international relationships throughout this history (though sustaining them beyond initial conferences – major achievements in themselves – proved difficult). The Independent Cinema Congress, held in September 1929 in La Sarraz, Switzerland, and attended by Alberto Cavalcanti, Walter Ruttmann, Ivor Montagu and Sergei Eisenstein, among others, is probably the earliest example (Lenauer 1929/1980, 168–9). A Third World Filmmakers Meeting took place in Algiers in December 1973 and was attended by leading filmmakers from across Africa (Ousmane Sembène, Med Hondo) and Latin America (Manuel Perez, Jorge Silva) as well as members of Third World Newsreel in the United States (Young 2006, 180; Bakari and Cham 1996, 17–24). In August 1978, the European Federation for the Progressive Cinema was founded in Utrecht, but appears to have faltered soon after (IFA 1978, 7–11). Yet, while these and other precedents existed, in 2013 there was no network for radical film culture in Britain or anywhere else, despite the clear need for one, and despite the opportunities presented by the Internet for network-building.

Conceptual framework

The core conceptual framework for the RFN was established in the first stage of the RFN's development, which stretches from that spring/summer in 2013 to the inaugural conference in February 2015. In part, the framework was based on an analysis of the factors that contributed to the splintering of activist and experimental film culture in the UK since 1990. Margaret Thatcher's brutal de-funding of cultural organisations in the latter half of the 1980s, for example, wiped out much of the independent film culture of the time – including the IFA itself. As a result, experimental filmmakers gravitated towards the art world and gallery space, where funding could still be found, while the more militant, activist-oriented organisations were largely left 'out in the cold' (Chanan 2015, 28) – surviving on meagre self-generated funds and exhibiting in squats, pubs and community and social centres. By the 2010s, while the 'two avant-gardes' – political and aesthetic – still existed, they were no longer in dialogue with one another, or even particularly aware of each other's existence.

The notion of the two avant-gardes – first posited by Peter Wollen (1975) to explore shades of difference in art and experimental cinema, and later articulated in the political and aesthetic senses by Robert Stam (1998) and others – was therefore a key concept for the RFN. However, while the political and aesthetic avant-garde was and remains a useful conceptualisation of two historical tendencies in radical film culture, its relative obscurity outside of film history scholarship meant it was inappropriate as an everyday organising tool. The term 'radical' provided a useful – if more ambiguous and provocative – alternative and was eventually embedded in the title of the network for several reasons. The notion of 'radical film' has been explored in detail elsewhere (Presence 2019), so instead I want to focus on two further ideas that were key to the RFN's development.

The first was that the RFN should be comprised of and aim to serve not just filmmakers but also all the groups and individuals involved in radical film activity of other kinds. This idea was adapted from the IFA, which quickly expanded its remit from a focus on 'makers' to 'all those involved in producing film meaning [...] not only independent film producers but also distributors, exhibitors, film teachers, critical workers and film technicians' (IFA 1976, 8). For the RFN, this was expressed as all those 'involved in radical film *culture*' (my emphasis) – a similar attempt to emphasise that film cultures need all kinds of participation, and that the network was for everyone interested or active in radical film regardless of the nature of their participation. Indeed, though current measures to support film culture in the UK do not support cross-sector initiatives (Presence 2019, 444–5), fostering interaction across production, distribution and exhibition – something the IFA referred to as 'integrated practice' (see Robson's Chapter 12 in this volume) – is a critical part of building any kind of non-mainstream film culture.

The second key idea was ensuring that the RFN reached out to those artists, activists and academics from previous generations, making clear the network was keen to learn from their successes and mistakes and to build a sense of continuity for those more recently involved. Again, the IFA was a key reference point here, both as a way of conveying what we were aiming to do to those who were involved in the earlier organisation but also as a way of sign-posting younger filmmakers and activists back into what is often viewed as a 'golden era' of radical film in Britain (Kidner 2013, 18). Enlisting the involvement of former IFA members meant that the RFN benefitted from their experience and advice and embedded the notion of the new network as a historically conscious one. As ex-IFA Michael Chanan later observed:

> One of the notable features at the inaugural conference of the Radical Film Network in Birmingham last weekend was the mix of generations, from new blood to survivors from the days of the IFA ... in the 1970s. Speaking as one

of the latter, it was pleasing to find that what the comrades did back then has not been entirely forgotten, but more important, that this new initiative has a genuine sense of history, of historical inquiry, and is disposed to look to past experience both in order to commend what was achieved and to mull over its weaknesses.

(Chanan 2015, n.p.)

Finally, the RFN's focus on 'film' and its description of itself as a 'network' (rather than an 'organisation' or 'association') provided important conceptual boundaries. 'Film' is of course intended to encompass all kinds of audio-visual work, but we could have opted to build a radical *media* network and open it up to artists and journalists working print and photography as well as film, for example. This has occasionally been raised at the RFN's various conferences (discussed below) and it is an issue about which I feel ambivalent. On one hand, why intentionally exclude media-makers with whom we would have a natural affinity, and thus miss opportunities to foster relationships, facilitate communication and build a broader radical media culture? On the other hand, organising around 'film' provided a more manageable constituency (albeit still one that includes several hundred organisations spanning all kinds of film-related activity) and finding a strong shared foundation was important. At the time, with building the RFN something of an experiment, I think we made the right decision – but maybe that should change in the future, as the network develops. Similarly, building a network rather than an organisation was another important distinction: with most radical film groups already chronically under-funded, the last thing the culture needed was another organisation to run. In that context, aspiring to simply provide the connective tissue between already existing organisations was a key theoretical distinction.

Practicalities

These conceptual considerations continue to shape the practical activities of the RFN in many respects. In the early phases, the practical work of building the RFN involved initiating a multitude of conversations with many individuals and organisations from the various sectors the network was designed to support. Focusing on the UK at first, this typically took the form of email 'pitch' that explained the idea, asked if it was something the stakeholder would support, and outlined possible next steps. After receiving much enthusiasm and 'buy in' from UK organisations, the scope spread overseas – and the RFN very quickly became an international endeavour.

Having held countless individual discussions with different organisations, a meeting was convened to explore the network proposal in more detail with those involved, develop a sense of shared ownership of the project and discuss the next steps. An initial meeting, held in September 2013 at the MayDay Rooms in central London, turned into two subsequent meetings – one during Bristol Radical Film Festival in March 2014 and another at London's Open City Documentary Festival in June. It was then decided that a larger-scale conference was needed and that this should be held in Birmingham – home to a few different groups in the RFN as well as several sympathetic staff members at Birmingham City University's School of Media, who hosted the event in February 2015.[1] We discuss this and other events and activities the RFN has carried out to date in the introduction to this volume, but one of the key outcomes of that inaugural conference was the decision to adopt a structure based on the radical environmentalist group Earth First!, in which voluntary, self-organised working groups comprise the basic organisational units to carry out particular tasks. Working groups have emerged to manage communications and social media output, coordinate exhibition initiatives, liaise with external organisations and to organise subsequent RFN conferences, for example. This approach has its limitations – (see Presence 2019, 441–2) – but is nevertheless suited to such a large, decentralised and unfunded network as the RFN.

Another unanticipated outcome of the inaugural conference was the extent to which subsequent events would respond and react to one another. As detailed in David Archibald's Chapter 6 in this volume, at the close of the Birmingham conference, a group of filmmakers, producers, activists and academics from Glasgow volunteered to host a subsequent event the following year. The 'Unconference and Film Festival' they organised – which ran for four days, drew on the combined efforts of over forty organisations and was attended by 1,745 people – was a response to the overly academic tone of the first event, and subsequent conferences have in turn reacted to perceived limitations or gaps identified in the others. The Nottingham conference, in 2019, sought to build upon the participation of RFN members from the Global South at the Dublin conference in 2018, for example.

The conferences in turn have been critical to building the RFN's sense of itself as a community. Outside of the conferences, the network exists largely online, via its website, mailing list and social media channels. This is appropriate for a network which, outside of a project-specific grant from the Arts and Humanities Research Council in 2015, receives no core funding, and charges no membership fees.[2] As noted above, with no resources or income of its own on which to draw, it is essential that the RFN remains predominantly a network – in the sense of a structure of connections linking other organisations – rather than an organisation itself. As a network, the RFN can sustain itself with a minimum amount of administrative oversight. This intentionally 'light-weight' infrastructure also means the RFN can sometimes feel quite intangible, which compounds the importance of the conferences as the moment when the network 'touches down' and becomes something more concrete. The conferences provide a key opportunity for RFN members to meet each other in person, share work, discuss issues and ideas and plan activities. Indeed, the conferences have proven to be the crucible from which many RFN collaborations and activities have sprung.

Outside of the conferences and the day-to-day activities of the affiliated organisations, the RFN itself is a largely virtual entity. Most interaction and exchange takes place online via the mailing list or its social media accounts on Facebook and Twitter. The website then acts as the shop window for the RFN and a portal through which interested parties join the mailing list and follow the network on Facebook and Twitter – effectively how people 'join' the RFN. As a shop window, a key feature of the website is the Directory of affiliated organisations – a searchable database organised both by the country in which the organisation is based and its primary area of activity: production, distribution or exhibition (or as many as apply). Indeed, the Directory has become a unique resource: as the largest record of radical film organisations in the world, it is a valuable record of contemporary radical film culture. Outside of the Directory though, the rest of the site is designed to be fairly static. Like the network itself, the website must require the minimum amount of oversight and input – an essential characteristic for an initiative designed to survive in the long-term with a minimum amount of resources.

Problems, limitations and future directions

This chapter has provided an account of the genesis of the RFN and its development so far. In the space I have left, I want to outline what I see as some of the problems and limitations that derive from this approach to network building, and how it might develop in the future.

In 1977, reflecting on the difficulties of running the IFA, its organisers wrote that 'the major problem remains where it has always been: at the bank' (IFA 1975). Then, as now, and wherever one happens to be in the world, a lack of resources is the key problem from which most others stem in experimental/activist film culture. For this reason, I have mixed feelings about the decision not to attempt to secure core funding for a network administrator or some similar position. However, I also accept that – given the current context of cultural funding in the UK and a key lesson learned from the IFA's experience: that accessing funding can quickly erode organisations' ability to survive when that funding is withdrawn – this may be the most sensible approach for the long-term sustainability of the network. So, while there are several potential sources of funding the RFN could explore – be it through the British Film Institute (BFI), the trade union movement, the Labour Party in the UK or the RFN's international academic constituency, or even self-generated funds from a membership subscription scheme – I will limit my discussion here to three ideas that can be achieved on a volunteer basis alone, without funding.

The first concerns the RFN's capacity to promote its members' work and facilitate debate and discussion within the international radical film community. Over the past seven years, an infrastructure has been built that connects a large constituency of stakeholders from across the culture, but the main platforms through which that constituency communicates – the RFN mailing list, primarily, its social media, secondarily, and its annual conferences – are inadequate tools for fostering sustained dialogue. Any topics needing wider discussion that emerge on the mailing list, for example, must be taken elsewhere or risk quickly overtaking people's inboxes and forcibly involving all members in the discussion. Yet this also means that those initiatives which do go on to develop elsewhere are largely invisible to the rest of the network.

Indeed, as several authors in this book attest, the absence of visible and long-term exchange and debate is a key limitation of contemporary radical film culture, and not just in the West. The level of debate and discussion is nowhere near where it was in the pre-digital era. So, as the Moroccan filmmaker, Nadir Boumouch, puts it in his interview in this volume, 'we need critical magazines, debates, spaces!'. A quarterly or biennial newsletter or zine produced by the RFN could thus be a major contribution to the culture: it would provide a record of the incredible diversity of activities produced by members of the network; a space for constructive criticism and reflection; and could promote future conferences, film festivals and calls for collaboration. Once released, the publication would not only provide the means through which RFN members could better engage with one another but could be easily shared across networks of other politically committed and mainstream organisations and institutions. It would act as a regular ambassador for everyone involved in the network and significantly enhance awareness of and engagement with contemporary radical film culture from those not already directly involved.

Members have mixed feelings about film competitions for obvious reasons (see the interview with the LA-based Echo Park Film Center in this volume for a sensible critique of the concept) but this would also provide a means through which the RFN could support makers in the network to get their work seen by a wider audience. There are several film festivals and exhibition groups in the RFN – Alternative Film/Video Festival in Belgrade; Chicago Feminist Film Festival; Mawjoudin Queer Film Festival in Tunis; the Nordic Labour Film Festival in Malmö; the Tolpuddle Radical Film Festival in Dorset, to name but a few – many of which also run competitions of their own. An annual 'best of the best' competition, judged by a panel of RFN members from around the world and perhaps with a high-profile guest judge each year, would provide the means through which a selection of films from the RFN community could break through into mainstream film culture.

Finally, the RFN has yet to stage a serious attempt to intervene in film policy, despite the considerable skills and experience that exist within the network in this area, and the fact that policy is the field in which long-term change is most powerfully effected. As Toby Miller (2000) has provocatively argued: 'resistance goes nowhere unless it takes hold institutionally ... [so] getting to know film policy and intervening in it is an important part of participating in film culture' (37). What kind of policy initiatives would the RFN develop? In the UK, the context with which I am most familiar, a good starting point would be to lobby existing organisations for independent and so-called 'specialised film' for coordinated, sector-wide support. Likewise, pressuring the BFI's Film Audience Network (FAN) – an initiative which in many ways parallels the RFN – for acknowledgement and support would also be productive. While there was an (unsuccessful) attempt to liaise with BFI FAN early in the network's history, a significant and sustained effort to secure support from this and other institutions has yet to be made. This support would not have to be financial: such organisations could significantly assist the RFN simply by virtue of their major role in the UK's broader independent film culture, providing links to the RFN on their sites, offering passes to conferences and events and so on. A policy working group could take this work forward and, moreover, liaise with radical policy experts overseas to develop and spread their ideas elsewhere.

Conclusion

I hope these last remarks convey the extent to which the RFN remains a live and unfinished endeavour. Just as we did not know if or how the network would develop when it was set up, we cannot know what directions it will take in the future – that will be determined by the energy and enthusiasm of those involved, some of whom may not even be aware of the network's existence at the time of writing.

Moreover, as noted in the Introduction, the approach we adopted to building the RFN was shaped by several factors specific to the UK, and there are of course many ways of building networks that differ from our approach. However, several issues discussed in this chapter will surely be faced by those who wish to develop similar networks, wherever they may be. Administrative labour – including who will do it, or how to minimise it – is a key consideration, for example, as are questions of conceptual frameworks, practical operations and historical awareness. In setting down this account of the RFN's development, I hope current and future participants in radical film culture will be encouraged to join the RFN and participate in shaping its future as they see fit.

Notes

1 The minutes of the initial meetings and programmes from all RFN conferences to date are available on the RFN website at www.radicalfilmnetwork.com
2 That said, this grant was significant. It afforded a small amount of administrative time to be spent on the network at a critical moments (immediately after the 2015 conference, for example), and facilitated the organisation of four events – in addition to the annual conferences – between 2015 and 2018. For a more thorough discussion of the funding and its significance, see Presence (2019).

References

Ager, Laura. 2016. *Universities and Film Festivals: Cultural Production in Context*. PhD diss., University of Salford.

Bakari, Imruh, and Mbye B. Cham, eds. 1996. *African Experiences of Cinema*. London: British Film Institute.

Blanchard, Simon and Claire M. Holdsworth. 2017. 'Organising for Innovation in Film and Television: The Independent Filmmakers Association in the Long 1970s'. In *Other Cinemas: Politics, Culture and Experimental Film in the 1970s*, edited by Sue Clayton and Laura Mulvey, 279–298. London: I.B. Tauris.

Burton, Alan G. 2005. *The British Consumer Co-operative Movement and Film, 1890s–1960s*. Manchester: Manchester University Press.

Campbell, Russell. 1977. 'Film and Photo League: Radical Cinema in the 30s'. *Jump Cut: A Review of Contemporary Media* 14: 23–25.

Chanan, Michael. 2015. 'Common Endeavours'. In *Marc Karlin: Look Again*, edited by Holly Aylett, 25–33. Liverpool: Liverpool University Press.

Dickinson, Kay. 2018. *Arab Film and Video Manifestos: Forty-Five Years of the Moving Image Amid Revolution*. London: Palgrave Macmillan.

Dickinson, Margaret, ed. 1999. *Rogue Reels: Oppositional Film in Britain, 1945–90*. London: BFI.

Eshun, Kowdo and Ros Gray. 2011. 'The Militant Image: A Ciné-Geography, Editors' Introduction'. *Third Text* 25 (1): 1–12.

Extinction Rebellion. 2019. Bristol In-office Rebellion Support Call-out. November 2019.

Hennebelle, Guy. 1972. 'SLON: Working Class Cinema in France'. *Cinéaste* 5 (2): 15–17.

Hogenkamp, Bert. 1976. 'Film and the Workers' Movement in Britain: 1929–39'. *Sight and Sound* 43 (2): 68–76.

Hogenkamp, Bert. 1986. *Deadly Parallels: Film and the Left in Britain, 1929–39*. London: Lawrence and Wishart.

Hogenkamp, Bert. 2000. *Film, Television and the Left, 1950–1970*. London: Lawrence and Wishart.

IFA. 1978. *IFA Newsletter Spring 1978*. Source: IFA archive, Adsetts Centre, Sheffield Hallam University.

IFA. 1977. *IFA Regional Digest* no. 2, November. Source: IFA archive, Adsetts Centre, Sheffield Hallam University.

IFA. 1976. Independent Filmmaking in the '70s: An introductory discussion paper from the Organising Committee for the IFA Conference held in May 1976. IFA Archive, Adsetts Centre, Sheffield Hallam University.

Kidner, Dan. 2013. 'There and Back Again'. In *Working Together: Notes on British Film Collectives in the 1970s*, edited by Petra Bauer and Dan Kidner, 17–18. Southend-on-Sea: Focal Point Gallery.

Knight, Julia and Peter Thomas. 2011. *Reaching Audiences: Distribution and Promotion of Alternative Moving Image*. Bristol: Intellect.

Lenauer, Jean. 1929/1980. 'The Independent Cinema Congress'. In *Traditions of Independence: British Cinema in the Thirties*, edited by Don MacPherson, 168–169. London: BFI.

Lupton, Catherine. 2005. *Chris Marker: Memories of the Future*. London: Reaktion Books.

MacPherson, Don, ed. 1980. *Traditions of Independence: British Cinema in the Thirties*. London: BFI.

Miller, Toby. 2000. 'The Film Industry and the Government: "Endless Mr Beans and Mr Bonds"?' In *British Cinema of the 90s*, edited by Robert Murphy, 37–47. London: BFI.

Presence, Steve. 2019. 'Organising Counter-Cultures: Challenges of Structure, Organization and Sustainability in the Independent Filmmakers Association and the Radical Film Network'. *Screen* 60 (3): 428–448.

Presence, Steve. 2013. The Political Avant-garde: Oppositional Documentary in Britain since 1990. PhD diss., University of the West of England (UWE Bristol).

Renov, Michael. 1987. 'Newsreel: Old and New, Towards an Historical Profile'. *Film Quarterly* 41 (1): 20–33.

Stam, Robert. 1998. 'The Two Avant-gardes'. In *Documenting the Documentary: Close Readings of Documentary Film and Video*, edited by Barry Keith Grant and Jeanette Sloniowski, 254–268. Michigan: Wayne State University Press.

Waugh, Thomas, ed. 1984. *Show Us Life: Towards a History and Aesthetics of the Committed Documentary*. Metuchen, NJ: Scarecrow Press.

Wollen, Peter. 1975. 'The Two Avant-Gardes'. *Studio International* 190 (November/December): 171–175.

Young, Cynthia, A. 2006. *Soul Power: Culture, Radicalism, and the Making of a U.S. Third World Left*. Durham, NC: Duke University Press.

2

IMAGINING CHANGE

A history of radical film in the USA

Chuck Kleinhans

Editor's note: This chapter is an edited version of the keynote address Chuck Kleinhans gave at 'Radical Film Network NYC: A Global Gathering', a three-day conference held in Manhattan in May 2017 in association with the Workers Unite! Film Festival. Chuck sadly passed away on December 14 2017, shortly after sending us the written version of his talk, which he planned to use as the basis for his chapter in this book. We are privileged to publish the text below, and hope Chuck's passion for and knowledge of the radical film tradition continues to inspire generations of scholars and activists to come.

Introduction

I want to thank Steve Presence, Mike Wayne, Andrew Tilson and the other organisers of this wonderful event for inviting me to talk to you today. It's great to be back in New York City, a sanctuary city, which on Monday, May Day, the international worker's day, held a number of number of rallies and demonstrations for immigrant workers – as did other US cities. Obviously, we now live in interesting times and an energised discussion is taking place among activists in the wake of recent electoral events. I don't want to address that discussion here. I think we will all be referring to it both formally and informally during the conference, and we can learn from each other.

Instead, I want to address three large topics today. One is to take a longitudinal look, an historical survey, of radical film. Second is to take a latitudinal look, to move from the usual focus on specific films and makers to include other agents in the much larger process of funding, production, distribution, exhibition, political organising, curating, archiving and teaching. Third is to consider the role of new and changing technologies in radical media opportunities in the past, present and future.

History

Reviewing the Lumière's *Workers Leaving the Factory* (1895), we are reminded that the working class has been present from the very start of cinema, although usually without a voice or without their perspective (it is worth noting that many of the workers in the film are women).

The power of moving image photography, adding to a previous activist practice of using photography for social and political reform, was seen as an important tool by reformists, both liberal and radical. And, we might remember, even by conservatives, as in D. W. Griffith's *A Corner in Wheat* (1909), which contrasts the opulence of the rich with the misery of the poor caused by a capitalist speculator in the grain market. By apparently divine justice, he dies buried in wheat.

The potential of filmmaking as effective propaganda for social and political campaigns inspired early efforts in the US and UK, for issues such as women's suffrage, healthcare reform, poverty, and so forth. Early in the twentieth century, we see film used for documentation, and for dramatic narration of important issues. In other words: to show and to persuade.

And let me remind us of the importance of visual evidence: of showing in a way that earlier was conveyed through the filter of words, of journalism within the framework of the capitalist press. The footage of Jack Johnson, the famous boxer, itself was considered so potent for showing a black man beating a white boxer, that it was often censored by cities and by states, and the man himself was attacked by white opinion (at the same time as he and the film provided a powerful image for African Americans). Thus, it's not always the precise *intention* of moving images that accounts for everything. We also have to understand the history of how films were seen and used by the audience. In addition to actuality presentations and social reform efforts, we know that throughout the 1910s and 1920s entertainment cinema appealed to the working class. While I won't get into that here, I want to note that comedy, particularly in the figure of Chaplin's Little Tramp in films such as *The Immigrant* (1917) and *Modern Times* (1936), stood for and gave an empathetic validation to the dispossessed, picturing Charlie as clever, resourceful and an active agent in facing opposing forces.

Two other moments from the 1920s should be mentioned here: the full flowering of a radical film movement in the Soviet Union, with innovative directors seizing the opportunity to build on earlier developments in film form and narrative for a directly politically informed body of work (though it would become better known in the West in the 1930s). And, typically without the resources of state sponsorship, independent artists working in the Surrealist and Dada movements in New York, Berlin, Paris and elsewhere created the first examples of an artisan cinema that often addressed political topics.

Both of these movements inspired people in the United States in the 1930s to develop the Film and Photo League (FPL) and begin the production of working-class activist films. The FPL worked with labour organising, led by the Communist Party, and in that framework also showed Soviet films. It was thus an important starting point for directly political filmmaking, and supported not only the documentation of strikes and protests from a ground-level point of view, but contributed to international efforts, including the Spanish Civil War, with films such as Joris Ivens' *The Spanish Earth* (1937).

This period marks the start of a sustained social documentary movement in the United States (see Barnouw, 1974, and Ellis, 1989) that is often linked to liberal-progressive films of the era, such as Roosevelt administration policy promotions for rural electrification and water resource management. I think it's worth noting that we have often looked at many films of this era, and in this tradition, as 'liberal' or 'mildly progressive' rather than truly class-consciously radical. But looking back from the current neoliberal shredding of the social contract and the destruction of public goods such as clean drinking water, and the capitalist takeover of such essentials as healthcare and education, we might want to reconsider those films as promoting basic rights.

These films and their filmmakers showed that cinema could be a powerful force for influencing public opinion, for showing otherwise hidden events and situations, and adding to the visual imagination of political understanding. And World War II accelerated media use in the service of national policy and practice. For military training, for industrial education, for propaganda film production – all of which was outside of the Hollywood studio system – there was a vast expansion of filmmaking, particularly in 16 mm. After the War, this also produced a huge surplus of film technology: projectors went to school classrooms, cameras and discount film stock were available for independent filmmaking, and new markets appeared for educational film, television journalism, advertising and industry films.

That change in the infrastructure provided the basis for a new wave of politically motivated radical film in the 1960s. The fiercely militant film, *Columbia Revolt* (1968), by New York Newsreel, could come into being precisely because of earlier work by a wide variety of progressive filmmakers: some of them artists, some of them journalists and some of them people with something to say who realised that it really was now within their grasp to make a film. Here I want to note the Lithuanian artist, immigrant and anti-war activist, Jonas Mekas, whose film *The Brig* (1964) interpreted the last outlaw performance of the Living Theatre's production of the anti-military play by Kenneth Brown, at the start of the US escalation of the Vietnam War. And, earlier, the journalist Edward R. Murrow's report on migrant farm labour, *Harvest of Shame* (1960), was shown on Thanksgiving evening on a major network. Individuals and local groups were also active at this time, such as Edward Bland et al., who made an amazing polemic about African American culture in *The Cry of Jazz* (1959).

The 1960s also marked an important change in the US radical film scene as international films brought new topics and ideas into public discussion in the United States. Italian Neorealism and the French New Wave, for example, gave younger audiences new ways of imagining the world, their place in it, and how to understand it. These challenging films became part of a common core of this generation's intellectual development, and often the most compelling way to consider ethics, politics, personhood and being engaged in the world. New work from

Poland, Czechoslovakia, Yugoslavia and Hungary opened eyes to another view of socialist society. And films such as *The Battle of Algiers* (1965) presented a compelling understanding of colonial repression and national liberation.

Most significantly, films produced by, for, and in the Third World became available. Films from Cuba, Latin America and Africa presented a new political militancy, boosted the growing native US opposition to the Vietnam War, and expanded anti-imperialist consciousness. The presence of these new voices broadened the audience and spoke in new ways to emerging political movements: Black Civil Rights, Chicano farm labour organising, the student movement, the anti-war movement and the beginnings of Second Wave feminism. And younger radicals often began the important task of recovering the lost and repressed histories of earlier militant activism by recovering and exhibiting films such as *Salt of the Earth* (1954), by blacklisted makers, and films about the militant past such as *Union Maids* (1976) and *The Life and Times of Rosie the Riveter* (1980).

This movement changed in the 1970s – partly because of changing politics and conditions, and partly because of new faces and new perspectives. New work continued to be made, but often under different circumstances, and this transition was complicated. For example, while initially broad-based and shaped by socialist feminists, the Women's Movement was often weakened by domination by white liberal feminists who tied it to the Democratic Party, and who ignored women of colour or rejected cultural lesbian feminism. It took time, and 'the long way around' to bring this diversity back together. The actual history and politics of this are complicated, and I don't want to get into a contest about it. But it is important to note that movements change. The gay liberation movement, for example, went from being a relatively simple civil-rights and cultural hub to becoming increasingly political with the AIDS crisis. Similarly, the films made in, with, and by emerging forces also changed, such as the Black Movement after the end of the Black Panthers, and so on.

Throughout the Reagan and Bush Era (1980–1992), radical filmmaking continued but in a broadening stream. This partly reflected new social and political movements, but also resulted from hard-won advances in the representation women and minorities, and from newer technologies that made production and distribution easier, quicker and cheaper. The shift to video in broadcast and professional making as well as in alternative- and grass-roots media allowed for vastly different shooting ratios and a quicker turn around for news production. We might remember the Vietnam War that appeared on US dinner tables in the 1960s was shot on film and shipped to the United States for processing and editing. When combined with satellite transmission, video allowed for real time coverage of events. And the new delivery system of videocassettes grew through the 1980s to allow radical 'film' to be seen easily in many new spaces: the home, the workplace, the school, the community centre, the gathering of friends.

With this understanding, let me underline the title of my talk: imagining change. I think this is a useful way to think about the 'radical' in 'radical film': as that which helps us and others imagine that change is needed, that it is possible, and what it might look like. Thus radical film should be understood as a spectrum of possibilities and examples. During the darkest days of Bertolt Brecht's exile from Nazi Germany, he wrote about what people within Hitler's realm could do to resist within a totalitarian dictatorship: talk about change. Against the 'Thousand Year Reich', the playwright said simply reminding people of dialectics, of contradiction and inevitable change, broke the power of the dictator.

We can use the same idea to form an encompassing view of radical media today. What works to help people imagine change? Certainly it's easy to see how short militant works targeted at specific campaigns such as the fight for a higher minimum wage, or against a pending change to environmental policy should be included here. But it is also the case that within the weekend multiplexes, in the past few years we can find films that point to the necessity for change and the possibility of change: Academy award winner *Moonlight* (2016) and box office hit *Get Out* (2017) are cases in point. Indeed, we are living in a remarkable period of media that recognises black America. Consider *Hidden Figures* (2016), *Loving* (2016), *Fruitvale Station* (2013), *Tangerine* (2015), *O.J.: Made in America* (2016), *Selma* (2014), *13th* (2016) and *I Am Not Your Negro* (2017). But as you can see, I've already moved beyond my initial longitudinal survey of notable films into my ideas about the larger context of the world surrounding the individual film and about technological change. So let me pivot to that.

Observing the process: funding, distribution and exhibition

The dominant tendency in thinking about radical film is to concentrate on the work itself as an aesthetic and communicative object, and usually on the filmmaker, the auteur and his/her achievement as genius. This is understandable: it is what most often gets attention when a new film is released. It starts the publicity ball rolling. It fits the need that film has to justify itself in relation to what are often more highly regarded fields of serious writing, investigative journalism and traditional arts. Filmmakers are artist-creators too!

But this tendency also obscures the essential parts of the process, from funding to exhibition. Consider funding. Gathering the resources to begin to make creative work takes time, talent and money, money, money. Where does this money come from? How can we find it? Beyond the first step of finance, assembling the creative and craft talents to begin production involves training, experience and learning to work together. It means organising a complex process that must be continually reassessed and guided on the fly. And then, when we get to a finished product, how do we get the work distributed and exhibited? All these stages of filmmaking are essential and often difficult, sometimes stopping projects before they are finished. And it's even more complicated with radical political film. The inevitable ebb and flow of real world politics changes the media world. Projects begun under one set of circumstances can be sidelined as conditions change, different forces emerge, or events overtake initial projections.

I want to emphasise this because to focus too much on the individual film and filmmaker can lead to failing to anticipate the difficulties of the process. How many of us older folks can remember projects that went on for years without reaching completion, or which were functionally dead on arrival due to changing political situations? And how many younger folks saw a Kickstarter that got out of the starting gate but failed to complete the race? Or works which failed to speak effectively to an intended audience? I say this not to scold, but to ask us, all of us, to wisely manage our projects. Dreams and good intentions are not enough. Hard shell realism needs to balance the hopes. So, we need to think of the whole process, to take the wide view of radical film projects.

To get films seen, noticed and talked about requires distribution and exhibition. In most cases in the United States, those functions must be conducted as a business, even if a nonprofit business. That makes it a volatile sector, but over the years a fairly stable network of festivals has developed, such as the Worker's Unite Festival beginning Friday night here in New York City. For decades now, a wide range of other festivals covering feminist film, black and African film, LGBTQ film, Latino and Latin American film and social justice issues, have expanded both as independent projects and sometimes tied to multifaceted organisations.

Progressive distributors have managed to find and maintain a place. Some, such as Icarus, aimed at the education market, and Sut Jhally's Media Education Foundation, which makes media criticism videos targeted to classrooms. Others such as New Day, Women Make Movies, Frameline (LGBTQ issues) and Third World Newsreel and California Newsreel also have had long legs, continuing for decades. And a salute to Chicago's Kartemquin Films, which just celebrated fifty years of producing films on political and social issues.

Another dimension of distribution should be considered: the deliberate screening and discussion model of a targeted political campaign. Perhaps the best model for this in the United States was Al Gore's *An Inconvenient Truth* (2006). While essentially a flashy illustrated lecture on man-made global warming, the finished film was shown theatrically, but more importantly in local and community-based venues. In Chicago, where I lived at the time, there were dozens upon dozens of screenings in churches sponsored by social justice committees, in community centres and schools, and so forth. By widespread DVD distribution, a small group screening with a discussion afterwards educated viewers and enlisted them in appropriate neighbourhood action: 'Think Globally, Act Locally' in practice. From finance to end-point activism, the project was conceived and executed thoughtfully and effectively.

And following the US propensity for DIY (Do It Yourself) independent institutions, we also have a variety of projects ranging from the more recently expanded and evolved Flaherty Film Seminars to important local spaces and programmes, such as UnionDocs here in New York City, as well as venues such as Anthology Film Archives, film exhibition by MoMA, the Whitney, and other museums. Similar exhibition spaces exist across the United States, many run as a labour of love or in the precarious world of indie funding. Related to this, in the past two decades we've seen the development of two new models, often called 'nomads and settlers'. This refers to the practice of independent artist/makers regularly touring with their new work, finding venues and helpers/supporters across a wide geographic spectrum, and also the practice of local micro-cinemas, pocket-sized exhibition spaces in a home, loft, or studio, storefront or gallery that bring together and bond intimate viewing and discussion, often with the makers present.

And it is also important to recognise the work of writers who and publications which attend to radical films. A film may be shown, but knowledge of it needs to be spread, amplified, by journalists and critics writing about it, explaining and evaluating it, and letting others know about it (see Julia Lesage's Chapter 3 in this volume). Since the 1960s, that role has often been taken up by writers for the weekly papers (now in a state of decline) or more recently by online publications. Special mention should go to two publications that have sustained attention to radical media for decades: *Cineaste*, now fifty years old, and my own publication, *JUMP CUT*, for which all issues are available free online at www.ejumpcut.org. Reading back issues of both is one of the best ways to understand the rich and varied history of radical media in the United States.

Fortunately for all of us, some people do that: media curators, archivists, preservationists, historians, and teachers organise and maintain at their best, the vital knowledge of past achievements and failures. They help move forward without reinventing the wheel. And I'd like to recommend to all of us here, and especially the younger people, that it can be refreshing and inspiring to learn from the dynamic past of radical film. I've suggested some starting points for your own exploration in my references below.

So, with that attempt to open-up our field to not only time and history, but also expand it laterally, beyond just films and filmmakers, to account for the broad network which is necessary for radical film to exist and thrive, I want to pivot back. But first, an aside now that will become important later. We need to remember that the 'radical' in radical film is always pertinent to a context and contingent on history. Something not originally intended as political can become so. A classic example: Hollywood made a fast-paced thriller in 1979, *The China Syndrome*, in which a nuclear power plant begins a crisis meltdown. The film wasn't made to be radical (though it clearly marks the villains as big energy corporations that short-cut safety regulations for a buck, and it starred Hollywood progressives Jane Fonda, Jack Lemon and Michael Douglas). But it became radical in the activist sense when, twelve days after release, there was a nuclear energy plant incident at Three Mile Island, Pennsylvania. Suddenly an entertainment film became the focal point for the public imagination of disaster, and anti-nuke activists were able to effectively leaflet at screenings and get their message across.

The point I want to make here is that a specific work can become unexpectedly politicised. But the reverse is also true: an intentionally political project can self-sabotage if it can't change with the time. When a project takes years and years, the fundamental situation on the ground may change and thus the completed work may no longer be topical or even very relevant. For radical media, 'windows open, and windows close'.

New forms, new technologies, new makers

If we can say that neoliberalism became the dominant aggressive form of capitalist exploitation and governance beginning in the Thatcher–Reagan era, we can also say that moment marks a new direction in the world of radical media. The arrival of consumer format video, of digital media, Internet and streaming has changed the game. On the one hand, neoliberalism wants to invade the commons and monetise it, to shred the social net and privatise it, to make everyone an individual consumer in order to sell more, extract more value. On the other hand, by giving individuals more tools and more chances, a new basis emerges for grass-roots activity.

We see the results of these changes in some dramatic ways. For example, ten years into the introduction of the home video camera, we have the footage of Los Angeles police beating motorist Rodney King captured and replayed again and again on the news (1991).

The resulting trial of the officers resulted in their acquittal and following that the four-day Los Angeles Riots. Subsequently, the O. J. Simpson murder trial took place and was broadcast in its entirety by a new cable channel, Court TV, and the networks followed suit. These events mark a new era in media use to document politically charged moments, and to make previously obscured government processes suddenly open. Of course, we now know where that takes us: to cell phone cameras that allow widespread capture of challenging images, of personal communication devices that allow for rapid mobilisation of opinion and gathering for action. (The cop-watch activity of organisations such as El Grito de Sunset Park, as presented by founder Denis Flores at the RFN: NYC conference, is an excellent example of this, and one could point to many others.)

It also opens new possibilities for youth and community media, several examples of which – such as Echo Park Film Center in LA – were also present at the conference. The tools of media production are now potentially in the hands of many more people who can bring their own perspectives and issues to the fore. I point at this change as something we need to understand, not because I think that new media is going to remake political reality: the optimistic projections of the 'Arab Spring' have now settled down to sober estimations of practical power and the force of repression on citizens. But the diversity we see as a result of many new voices, and new makers, is apparent in radical work from the 1990s on. Sometimes this takes the form of dramatic narrative film, the most familiar type of storytelling, but it can also take performative shape, with mediated versions of music, dance, visual art, spoken word and embodied action.

Formerly, the main line of radical film development was the model of the classic social documentary, with a sobriety of investigation, a modelling of clarity through organised persuasion, and a point-of-view – if not an omniscient narrator – guiding us along. That changed in the 1990s in the wake of Michael Moore's *Roger and Me* (1989), which investigated a serious (and still present) issue: the disastrous decline of the General Motors factory town of Flint, Michigan, with a goofy host whose own personality was much of the centre of attention. As a full-length theatrical success, it became a model for many aspiring documentary filmmakers.

Today, Internet distribution and streaming delivery have created new possibilities for delivery of radical content. Particularly with video blogs, new voices have been empowered to add their issues and creativity to important issues. Much of this is in flux and varies with degrees of access and quality of service, but we are definitely in a time where interactive media is an active presence that radicals can use. Interactive documentaries, for example, can expand the range of voices speaking to an issue, voices which often come from activists who use a website based on the documentary as a resource for collective social action.

Conclusion

I want to reflect on an earlier point I made, the one about the need to understand radical media in terms of a broad production concept and also to think about actual effects and political efficacy and impact. When new work appears, all the attention is on the film itself and understandably the maker. But there's little discussion of projects that are never completed, or which fail to find an audience, or which don't serve an ongoing real-world political campaign. But we need to do post mortems. We see that often painful task proceeding in the wake of our Presidential election, and in the UK, post-Brexit. It is not easy to analyse and discuss failure, but it is necessary if we are going to move forward, to learn from our mistakes and losses, and find a new and better strategy to succeed next time, to make new work to rise to the challenge, and to actually have a career, to have a long-term commitment to radical change that we can live with and live through. That's not easy, but learning from the past can help us imagine change in the future.

References

Barnouw, Eric. 1974. *Documentary: A History of the Non-Fiction Film.* New York: Oxford University Press.

Ellis, Jack C. 1989. *The Documentary Idea: A Critical History of English-Language Documentary and Video.* Englewood Cliffs, NJ: Prentice Hall.

Ellis, Jack C. and Betsy A. McLane. 2005. *A New History of Documentary Film.* New York: Bloomsbury.

Field, Allyson, Jan-Christopher Horak, and Jacqueline Najuma Stewart. 2015. *L.A. Rebellion: Creating a New Black Cinema.* Berkeley: University of California Press.

Pioneers of African-American Cinema. 2016. [DVD boxset]. New York: Kino Lorber.

3

FEMINIST DOCUMENTARY

Distribution, exhibition and interactive platforms

Julia Lesage

Introduction: reflections on the expansion of the field

In the last ten years, I have begun to mix criticism with autobiography.[1] Certainly the topic of this chapter refers to a trajectory in Film Studies in which I have been a participant, since I have critically defended feminist realist documentary as well as written about more modernist work, often focusing on stylistically innovative documentary (Lesage 1978a; 1978b). As Diane Waldman and Janet Walker note, in Film Studies in the 1980s and 1990s, debates around realism led many feminist scholars to neglect documentary studies in general (Waldman and Walker 1999).[2] In the same period, more and more women began making video, myself included, and often chose to make both documentaries for social activism and auto-biographical work.

As with many of my peers, the 1970s and 1980s were a ferment of activism for me. In those years I taught at the University of Illinois at Chicago where, with other women, faculty and staff and undergraduates, we fought for, founded and collectively taught a women's studies introductory course and then a women's studies programme with a socialist feminist orientation. In later years, for over a decade I taught video production as well as film theory and criticism at the University of Oregon, where I also made activist documentaries, both in experimental and realist modes.[3] My enduring critical interest has been in alternative media and political subcultures, and from 1976 on I worked with Chuck Kleinhans and John Hess to bring the sensibility of the alternative press to film scholarship with the founding and ongoing publication of *Jump Cut: A Review of Contemporary Media*. Now with the death of John and Chuck, I am its sole managing editor. It is with all these 'hats' that I come to reflect on what has happened to feminist documentary since the 1970s.

One of the things that has changed in terms of women's filmmaking is that in the 1970s and 1980s many more women's works were seen at feminist conferences or women's film festivals than were available anywhere else. In 1974, at the first women's film festival in Chicago, the planning committee, which included B. Ruby Rich and Laura Mulvey, had to work hard to generate a list of women directors of documentary, fiction, and experimental work. We found so few. For several decades after that, a grassroots organisation, Women in the Director's Chair, put on an annual Women's Film and Video Festival with assistance from two other Chicago alternative media institutions, the Center for New Television and Chicago Filmmakers. It was at these events that I saw many works that later would be the foundation for my courses on women and film: including Carolee Schneemann's *Fuses* (1965), Cecelia Condit's *Possibly in Michigan* (1983) and Ayoka Chenzira's *Secret Sounds Screaming: The Sexual Abuse of Children* (1986). Film screenings played a big role in the early years of Second Wave feminism in that they gave viewers, often in mainly women's gatherings, a common basis on which to discuss social issues and to explore women artists' aesthetics, sometimes phrased then as searching for 'new languages' in video and film. In such festivals, the experimental, the documentary and the autobiographical converged.

Of particular importance for my understanding of women's documentary film-making was attending an international feminist film and video conference held in Amsterdam in 1981.[4] I discovered for the first time how widely the parameters of women's media making and issues of social concern varied internationally, and from region to region. Some of the filmmakers spoke of trying to get into national film schools and to get women-oriented thesis projects approved; others, especially in Europe, customarily had their films funded by national television, usually in advance of production. Filmmakers from Francophone Africa told us how they had to send all footage back to France for processing. In some countries there were lively feminist subcultures; in others, little outlet for feminist scholarship and teaching, indeed for teaching about film or popular culture at all. What became clear to me was the relation between political activism, money and cultural possi-bilities, and how unique that constellation is from country to country. In addition, as this conference evidenced, I saw how international gatherings could promote border crossings and exchange: among filmmakers, scholars, aesthetics and ideas. Participants expanded their professional and personal identities and forged new relations that shaped their future media-making and critical work (Hammer 2010, 112).[5] Because of the insights I gained there, I focus my discussion here mainly on developments and institutions in the United States, where a specific combination of social and economic circumstances has shaped the development of both feminist film theory and feminist film/video making, distribution and viewing platforms.

In 1980s and 1990s, film festivals, even the expanding circuit of women's film festivals, took on a different function and attracted a different audience from those at early women's film events. For many, going to a festival indicates what Pierre Bourdieu (1984) would call *distinction*: it marks the viewer as someone who can afford the tickets, perhaps even travelling to see the event; it also marks him/her as someone with elite taste. Currently, cinephiles who can afford it make it a point to attend festivals, and broadcasters and distributors send representatives to see new work. At the same time, with much more anxiety, directors go to festivals with newly completed films to find an outlet for their work. When they do, they discover that getting into a festival is the funnel to an even narrower bottleneck: few will net a distributor or a spot on TV.

Thus, my concerns in this chapter are not just about feminism and documentary but about some problems that alternative media generally face, especially in terms of distribution, reception and use. In a parallel way, both feminism and documentary have undergone developments and dispersals. In the United States, both have relied on educational institutions and, now, on the Internet and streaming television to remain visible and to flourish. In each case, that of feminism and that of documentary, the issue arises of how something comes to 'count', of making sure it does not disappear shortly after entering its public life. One of the main reasons that some feminist documentaries have had prolonged use is that they fit feminist or media scholars' concerns and have had academic essays explicating them that makes them ideal for college classroom use.

Creating a canon: teaching and writing as promotion and gatekeeping

Feminist film criticism, like other critical tendencies in literature and the arts, has favoured certain kinds of women's media and theoretical approaches in order to promote new frames of knowledge, new ways of theorising gender in film, and the discovery of new or lost women artists. In the 1980s, film theory needed a more Brechtian style of documentary. Certain women's documentaries, then, were the right film at the right time. Earlier, in the women's movement in the 1970s in the United States, often-seen films included realist documentaries such as *Growing Up Female* (1971), *The Woman's Film* (1971) and *I Am Somebody* (1970),[6] which served a consciousness-raising function. In the 1980s, in the midst of debates around key critical issues framed within terms drawn from Marxism, feminism, psychoanalysis and semiotics, more favour was granted to modernist, mixed-genre documentaries such as *Daughter Rite* (1980), *Reassemblage* (1983) and *Thriller* (1979),[7] films which Women Make Movies distributor Debra Zimmerman calls 'evergreens', because they still produce substantial revenue from sales and rentals. In the 1990s, changes in feminist theory across all academic fields drew from developments in queer, postcolonial and critical race theory. More media production and criticism by women of colour has led to an expanded canon of media works regularly taught in classes dealing with women's issues. Nevertheless, few women's documentaries have had the distribution success of those select 1980s modernist works. In that sense, a small number of film texts became a kind of feminist documentary canon (Staiger 1985, 4).

Scholars of documentary, the avant-garde and feminist film (these are overlapping categories) have reason to celebrate and critique the works they admire so as to keep them in circulation. Several female scholars have indicated to me that they regularly write about a film because they want it to be used more broadly, and they take pleasure in keeping some films in active circulation for a longer time. Although I would not attribute too much power to the scholar and her ability to give a film a big viewership, if only among feminist teachers, it is important to understand that the writer is also a gatekeeper. The most common practice in Film Studies pedagogy in general is to teach a film along with an accompanying essay or book chapter, and films without essays written about them can languish on distributors' shelves. Since the advent of inexpensive digital production and streaming platforms, gatekeepers – including festivals, distributors, critics, bloggers and scholars – are playing a more important role than ever in bringing a plethora of work to our attention. In addition, media artists have the option of publishing their own work on the Internet. There is an excessive amount of film and video available to be seen, much less written about, and documentaries compete for our attention along with television and fiction film, now coming to us in a digital form from all over the world. I would argue that both scholars and media-makers will rely even more on gatekeepers, much as they may bemoan the elitism and restrictiveness that those figures seem to embody. A new form of gatekeeping has arisen with what we might call the 'Netflix phenomenon', which refers to viewers solely watching streamed TV and Internet video, even dropping cable subscriptions. This has led to a plethora of offerings and list-keeping as viewers track what to watch next. Internet sites have sprung up that promise to help viewers navigate the sea of material, offering 'best of —,' lists and 'ten documentaries about —' recommendations. All of this is another form of curation (Horeck, Mareike, and Kendall 2018).

For several decades now, I have wondered how many and what kind of films a film scholar should see, and under what circumstances? The same for television and streaming viewing. Does it matter if we see things on a small or big screen, on a computer or cell phone, or via an aficionado's Blu-ray? What orchestrates our narrative attention, our desire to watch? My own experience is that my personal media viewing now has a generally global reach, expanded by digital video recorders, Internet streaming and multiregional DVD players. Watching DVDs and streaming films give me a certain kind of control in selecting what I will watch, but they have also clearly led to a levelling and flattening out of my seeming 'choices', universalising the works because of the way they get to my living room and onto my HDTV. Especially when I am alone, keeping a list of documentaries I might like to see and picking one from the streaming selections on my Roku box seems like I'm just choosing a high-culture viewing option among a myriad of other entertainment offerings. Furthermore, as a peculiarity of the neighbourhood where I live, my Internet service is so slow that using a Wi-Fi connection to watch YouTube leaves me frustrated: even a short video keeps stopping and restarting. I think it important to keep up with Internet video as a cultural phenomenon but cannot easily do so. Also, because I pay so much for a cable TV subscription along with premium channels, I am often reluctant to add to my bill by renting a documentary via VOD (video on demand), where independent documentaries often land. What is important to note about all these media platforms is that far fewer artistic and socially committed productions by women come to me by these means than those by and about men. Gatekeepers impose an implicit, politically inflected point of view, and here those gatekeepers are the competing players in the entertainment industry.

Women Make Movies and the US educational film market

Both now, when we have a plethora of media that might potentially interest us to write about or teach, and earlier, when a far narrower range of documentaries was available, documentary films have been profitably distributed in the United States through the educational film market, in which schools typically purchase films for $200–$500. Many educational distributors have come and gone since the 1970s, but some have persisted throughout these years and maintain an active catalogue of many progressive social issue films, works by people of colour, documentaries from international perspectives, queer and feminist documentaries and experimental works.[8] The distributors vary in the degree to which they promote and market their films, across platforms and to targeted audiences. And they function in parallel, if not in competition, with streaming digital media platforms aiming to go directly to the viewer. In particular, feminist film criticism has flourished in the United States partly because a feminist distribution company, Women Make Movies (WMM), has flourished along with it.

Founded in 1972 mainly as an organisation dedicated to teaching media-making skills to women in New York City, by the 1980s WMM changed its mission to be a market-driven, non-profit distributor carrying films by and about women. This focus partly derives from identity politics.[9] But it is also a very smart marketing move, branding WMM as the place to turn to first for documentaries about women's issues, especially for teaching or organising campaigns in arenas such as rape prevention or health. WMM, like other educational distributors, defends the high 'institutional pricing' charged for its collection, saying that many people get to see each work and that this kind of pricing allows more money to be returned to the filmmakers. In fact, the educational market has kept these distributors in business. Of all the educational distributors in the United States, however, WMM is also the smartest about marketing. It has gotten its holdings on to television and into festivals, and has developed strategies to help each work find the most interested users. Indeed, its website frequently gives links under a film's listing not only to the maker's site but to other sites that deal with the issue at hand or to essays that analyse the film, thus reinforcing the tie between written critique and film screening, so important in distribution.

Beyond that, the organisation and its holdings bear the stamp of director Debra Zimmerman's curatorial savvy. As Patricia White (2000) notes, if early holdings built up the canon of 'evergreens', of critically hailed modernist works, 'acquisitions throughout the 1980s and 1990s … followed shifts in cultural thinking about identity toward issues of exile, displacement and hybridity – the works of Tracey Moffat, Ngozi Onwurah, Pratibha Parmar, Mona Hatoum'. The collection has broadened in this way because Zimmerman travels to many women's and documentary film festivals around the world, so that now almost half the catalogue comes from outside the United States. And these films follow the international spread of feminist activism around specific women's issues – especially around culture, health, globalisation and violence – so that an attentive viewer can trace the historical trajectory of how an issue has been dealt with: in film, in feminist theory and in public policy.

For instance, WMM's films on female genital cutting (FGC) and infibulation[10] include *Warrior Marks* (1993), a film that was vehemently denounced on its release but which nevertheless circulated widely (Grewal and Kaplan 1996), *The Day I Will Never Forget* (2002), *Mrs. Goundo's Daughter* (2009), *Sarabah* (2011) and *Africa Rising: The Grassroots Movement to End Female Genital Mutilation* (2010). These films vary widely in terms of film form and thematic approach, and demonstrate the range of perspectives and approaches taken towards this critical issue over the past three decades. Significantly, the links on the WMM website for the latter film link-out to activist websites; information from the World Health Organization; personal accounts, news and an online documentary from the UN around this issue; and grassroots websites from the countries where the film was shot.

I mention this collection of films and links to show a shift in the relation between feminist film scholarship and films of potential interest to women. All the films mentioned above have women directors who are feminist activists but not African, although many African activists are featured in them. It is this latter aspect that merits investigation by those interested in the relation between feminism and documentary: how films on FGC, even when directed by those from outside the cultures that continue this practice, might contribute to local and national activism and assist changes in civil policy and 'tradition'. Furthermore, the group of films itself demonstrates the increasing number of films one might write about or teach, films that add complexity to debates within transnational feminism, but still films most of us have never heard of. The links presented by WMM are also worth teaching, since they demonstrate the kind of branching out that activist media can and should generate. Moreover, the degree to which we know, or more likely do not know, about this small collection on the topic of FGC leads to the issue of how we, in fact, learn about new work.

Currently, in this age of digital filmmaking and distribution, most documentaries will garner a viewership of no more than a few hundred people. It's become inexpensive to make documentaries, but is somewhat more costly to submit work to and attend festivals. Even if the works do get into festivals, even fewer films get a distributor, and only a miniscule number achieve theatrical release or purchase for TV. The alternative, do-it-yourself route is to try to use the Internet to build an audience and prolong a film's life. The Internet can reach a potentially large viewership and specific communities, but it takes money to build and maintain an effective website, and not many filmmakers want to limit themselves to just one issue, to which they devote all their efforts. Most filmmakers make a film and then move on to other projects. In the United States, filmmakers or distributors some-times get a grant to build a website, but often the links and references are not updated after the grant runs out. The US public television network, PBS, used to maintain excellent websites for the films it bought rights to, with extended inter-views, sometimes streaming, and links to many kinds of social outreach. But in recent years, since PBS itself has become a streaming site, its website has been redesigned to attract viewers in a way that lets it compete with Netflix, with much less focus on outreach or extended information.

Feminist documentary online: production, distribution and exhibition

Internet marketing and distribution, or the use of the Internet itself as an exhibition platform, depends on a whole new kind of media and business savvy. As I prowl around the Internet looking for things I might like to see, especially if considering a DVD purchase, I particularly assess the 'quality' of the maker's website. This includes the attractiveness and emphasis of the site design, what tools it contains that would be useful to potential users/viewers, and the kinds of communities of which it is part of (for example, women's studies, cinephiles, activists or the avant-garde). As mentioned, teachers often want an essay to teach with a film, so it is especially useful to have PDFs available, including essays written about a work or interviews with the filmmaker. Regrettably, few distributors' or filmmakers' sites offer this feature. The avant-garde lesbian filmmaker, Su Friedrich, is an exemplary exception to this rule, yet in contrast to the kind of amplification that Friedrich's site provides, distributors' sites are usually less useful in terms of providing and updating links, addressing potential groups of users, or incorporating PDFs by the filmmaker or essays about the film.[11]

When documentary filmmakers create websites, get festival exposure, or provide opportunities for online viewing, knowledge about their work crosses national boundaries. The website opens up exposure and sales to a worldwide marketplace and many potential communities of viewers and users. Understanding this, Canadian Filmmakers Distribution Center of Canada and V Tape, two major Canadian dis-tributors of independent media, have received funding from the Canada Council of the Arts to create 'Fringe Online',[12] a collection of distinct websites by both film-makers and web artists. Found here is the unique Internet artwork of Midi Onodera, who has available on her site such video collections as *Movie of the Week*, or *A Movie A Day* (365 videos from 2006–2007), as well as PDFs of essays and interviews. Much of Onodera's work is also available as DVD from various distributors in Canada and the United States, but she is distinctive in the way she makes her extensive work available online, including monthly videos for the last ten years.

One major new form through which contemporary multimedia artists commu-nicate is the interactive documentary, or 'i-Doc'.[13] I-Docs usually feature multiple voices and perspectives, often on aspects of a single issue. Sometimes the works are biographical or autobiographical. Sometimes they take on an important social issue. They almost always involve 'co-creation' between filmmaker or director, web designer and coder, and various contributions by other people who are often filmed or themselves add content to the project.[14] In addition, the user creates a personal experience from the project as she chooses among various navigation choices. I-Docs differ from traditional linear filmmaking practices in that they are agglomerative, often see various iterations, and may have in place procedures for users to add material.

The i-Doc format makes visible two interrelated dimensions of documentary that have long defined the genre: ethics and aesthetics. On the ethical level, makers often use democratic production processes and try to assess what true 'interactivity' might mean for the eventual user, so that the process of creation and the control of the Internet platform remains dispersed among its participants. For example, Brenda Longfellow, an accomplished Toronto i-Doc producer, likes i-Docs for their slow, agglomerative creative process, which gives time for building relationships, listening, gathering information, and letting participants' ideas and feedback shape the project. She is currently working on *Inside/Out*, an i-Doc with formerly incarcerated women; together they are deciding how the participants want to present themselves, either with a public face or more anonymously.[15] On camera, the women discuss their experiences of jail, the justice system, drugs, getting out and healing. Longfellow says she has been inspired to make the film by the concept of talking circles, especially as used in restorative justice.

Longfellow is building *Inside/Out* from the ground up, with an emphasis on equitable process rather than final product. However, in most cases the costs of producing a largescale, growing i-Doc and its website must also meet the needs of funders who have their own vision of a final online documentary product. Furthermore, the i-Doc's shaping, site maintenance and site design, also mutable, usually remain in the hands of institutionally hired specialists. The kind of democratic input that marks the beginning process can easily become narrowed down in its final digital iteration.

Concerning aesthetics: the i-Doc design must draw users to a site and keep them there because it intrigues and attracts them. I am writing this chapter as a low-budget solo documentarist who believes only one person can make the decisions in the editing room and have control over the site design if the documentary is to have aesthetic cohesion. I have little faith in the possibility of a collectively edited whole. Thus, and again this is a personal preference, I am attracted to i-Docs that are strongly shaped by an authorial voice, such as *The Worry Box Project: A Collective Archive of Maternal Worries* [16] by Irene Lusztig and *Queer Feast* by Michelle Citron, discussed below. These intrigue me most because they are philosophically and socially complex.

Lusztig's seemingly very simple i-Doc lures me back repeatedly. Onscreen, in a wooden box, little rolls of paper appear. When I click on a roll, I see a close-up of Lusztig's hands writing out a worry or fearful dream sent in by a pregnant woman or mother. Some of the worries are realistic, others relate dreams of monstrous mothers, monstrous children. On one side of the frame, a tape measure unspools, and viewers can choose worries by type. On the other side of the frame, buttons allow viewers to send their own worries and dreams. The temporal and ontological dimensions of this site are fascinating. The moving hand writes out the worry in longhand and in real time. That act and its duration give a tangibility to the worry, a kind of careful 'listening' through the handwriting. Furthermore, both 'realistic' worries and 'outrageous' dreams are accorded the same status as real, the reality of a mother or mother-to-be's mind, and these minds here are given an audience. As Lusztig (2013, 2) writes about her piece: 'The transformation of invisible anxiety into material object articulates a polyvocal narrative space of women's experiences that is both intimate and communal.'

Digital decay online?

One problem with *The Worry Box Project* – a repository of worries submitted by the project's users – follows many i-Docs: decay and potential unavailability. Lusztig constructed it with the software Adobe Flash and now fewer and fewer computers, as they upgrade, allow Flash projects to play. Writ large, unplayability is a problem endemic to interactive media, and consequently some of the most important early feminist i-Docs are no longer available. This is the case, for example, with Australian Debra Beattie's pioneering autobiographical *The Wrong Crowd*, dealing with police brutality in Queensland and its traumatic impact on Beattie's family and her own growing up. In 2002, it was seen originally as a virtual reality CD-ROM and on the Australian Broadcasting Corporation's website. As with many successful large-scale interactive projects, the work had outside funding (here Screen Australia), but it became unavailable because of the discontinuance of its software platforms.[17]

This kind of digital decay has also plagued the career of Michelle Citron, director of *Daughter Rite*, who has moved across media platforms, from filmmaking to i-Docs to literary authorship, back to filmmaking. She hoped to settle into building a complex interactive narrative site on the web, partly autobiographical and partly about lesbian lives. Tellingly, she faced major economic and technical issues in moving away from documentary film production marketed to a well-established niche. Thus, her autobiographical book, *Home Movies and Other Necessary Fictions* (Citron 1998), won a number of major literary prizes; it clarifies events suggested in *Daughter Rite* but has never been used as frequently as her film, perhaps because the original essays about the film are so often photocopied and reproduced in course packets. For the next fourteen years, Citron worked on a major multimedia project, a series of CD-ROMs and DVDs, put online cumulatively as *Queer Feast*, also largely in an autobiographical mode. In these works, she mixed production platforms – including Polaroids, video with an old DV camera, fake home movies shot with 16 mm Bolex, super 8 film from her and other lesbians' lives, photographs, documentary archive footage – and this work also mixes documentary and fiction. Her aesthetic and political goal in making *Queer Feast* was to use her own family history and social context to trace the kinds of complex intersections of identity and social history that might characterise many queer lives, a phenomenology of identity, as it were. However, Citron was plagued by technical problems that resulted from competition between media giants and software problems that have led to the rapid disappearance of many artists' multimedia works. Although Citron worked with a software expert to translate her digital works to HTML5, a more stable code, only one of the quartet of works, *As American as Apple Pie* (1999), functions properly on the Internet.[18]

If Debra Beattie and Midi Onodera were pioneers in using the Internet as an outlet for extensive individual artistic production, other established feminist film and videomakers in the United States have also developed Internet sites to present and expand the scope of their work. Videomaker and installation artist Lynn Hershman Leeson's documentary, *!Women Art Revolution*, traces relations between the US feminist art movement and 1970s anti-Vietnam War activism, the civil rights movement and the women's movement, and the film features images of artwork, video clips of performances and protests and interviews with many of the feminist art movement's participants.[19] Hershman Leeson's work in general stands as an example of how feminist works by women known in the *experimental* film/ video community often have not made their way into the feminist film canon described above. Partly there is a kind of academic ghettoization of what gets shown in what kind of classes, and certainly a frequent exclusion of avant-garde media in the educational film/video market, but there is also an insularity of the avant-garde media world itself, which maintains its own canon of frequently seen, and taught, works (Zyrd 2006).

Working in a way more attuned to popular culture, starting in 2007, Alex Juhasz taught a number of college classes exclusively using YouTube and then wrote *Learning from YouTube* (2011), an online-only academic book with many video clips, perhaps unique in academic publishing.[20] Juhasz has been a pioneer in the feminist documentary community, taking leadership in teaching how to use the Internet in activist, open access and non-commercial ways.[21] In the case of the YouTube web book and her current *#100hardtruths-fakenews* project, she has developed a discursive form for feminist documentarians that is a blend of the i-Doc and the older hypertext form, perhaps needing the newer term 'video-book'. *#100hardtruths-fakenews* is, according to Juhasz, a critical digital-media-literacy primer. Such projects, which straddle i-Docs and analytic prose and, in the case of *#100hardtruths-fakenews*, promote activism, are a new form of documentary and point in the direction that digital platforms for documentary might fruitfully take.[22]

Conclusion

I mention these specific feminist multimedia artists because I esteem their work and the scope of their production, actual and planned. Yet they all face a number of similar problems. One is the issue of platform. The other is the issue of visibility. Some forms of putting media on the Internet will be successful. Some artists will build a viewership, some sites or platforms will endure, others will not. As editor of *Jump Cut*, I wonder about this as I get older. We bought the domain name ejumpcut.org for 100 years in a grand gesture of hope, but what platforms will

Jump Cut migrate to after we can no longer tend to it? Filmmakers had to decide what to do about video, then about CD-ROM, then about DVD, and now about the web. So did distributors. Lots has been lost. Right now, the DVD endures, perhaps a cinephile platform, cheap to reproduce, perhaps as an *aide memoire* for scholars and an item to be checked out of libraries or taught in class.

With more use of streaming media platforms and with the branching out of feminisms and feminist activism, how is current and future feminist media to be found? Once we move past the canonised feminist works, it is hard to keep up with feminist films we might like to see. We are in the same position as most viewers in the way we find out about the film and television programmes we plan to watch. Feminist documentaries come to our attention via reviews, festival roundups, the screening schedules we find on cable or satellite TV, the kinds of film information we choose to pursue on the Internet, or word of mouth. In neoliberal culture, democracy goes hand-in-hand with marketing, as do most aspects of the public sphere. We rely on often-restrictive gatekeeping practices to select from an overabundance of potential viewing material. After that, our own writing makes us curators of the work we hope others will see.

Notes

1 This is a revised, expanded version of an essay originally written in 2010 (Lesage 2013). In preparing it, I had several conversations with the following people who helped me better understand the state of feminist documentary, especially in terms of distribution and reception. In this sense, this chapter has been a collaborative effort. Thanks to Jacqueline Bobo, Michelle Citron, Gary Crowdus, Mary Erickson, Christine Holmlund, Chuck Kleinhans, Alexandra Juhasz, Kate Kane, Lynn Hershman Leeson, Brenda Longfellow, Irene Lusztig, Cornelius Moore, Mandy Rose, Janet Staiger, William Uriccio, Diane Waldman, Janet Walker, Janet Wasko, Patricia White, Linda Williams, Sarah Wolozin and Debra Zimmerman.
2 Janet Walker and Diane Waldman give an excellent overview of this history in their introduction to *Feminism and Documentary*, Minneapolis: University of Minnesota, 1999, pp. 1–35.
3 These works, along with those of Chuck Kleinhans, are available on the Internet on Vimeo: https://vimeo.com/julialesage
4 This conference was put on by the feminist film organisation, Cinemien. As I recall, other US attendees included Barbara Hammer, Frances Reid and Michelle Citron.
5 Barbara Hammer, *HAMMER! Making Movies Out of Sex and Life*, NY: Feminist Press, CUNY, 2010, p. 112.
6 *Growing Up Female*, dir. Julia Reichert, James Klein, 1971. *The Woman's Film*, dir. Judy Smith, Louise Alaimo, Ellen Sorin, 1971. *I Am Somebody*, dir. Madeline Anderson, 1970.
7 *Daughter Rite*, Michelle Citron, 1979. *Reassemblage*, Trinh T. Minh-ha, 1982. *Thriller*, Sally Potter, 1979.
8 Major US distributors of educational media who carry feminist documentaries include Women Make Movies, Cambridge Documentary Films, Third World Newsreel, California Newsreel, Frameline, Icarus, Cinema Guild, Zeitgeist. Video Data Bank and Canyon Cinema distribute independent experimental work.
9 'Women Make Movies is devoted exclusively to films that are by and about women, which to this day continues to irk, confuse, confound, puzzle, and make men mad' (Debra Zimmerman in a lengthy interview with Pat Aufderheide, 2004).

10 Because of debates around the cultural disdain implied by the term 'mutilation', most advocacy groups in the United States now use the more neutral term, 'cutting'.

11 Friedrich's website provides PDFs of many essays written about each of her films as well as her own writings on filmmaking and film art. Her site also is a promotional vehicle for a fourteen-DVD set of her work, remastered from film negatives, which she sells at a relatively modest home-viewing price of $109 (the educational price for the 14-DVD set is $695). See www.sufriedrich.com

12 From the site: 'Fringe Online is the largest online publication project in the Canadian media arts. It features a wide range of writings, stills and clips from sixteen Canadian media artists. Hundreds of never seen before documents have been made available for the first time, assembled into a suite of virtual libraries which we invite you to explore.' www.fringeonline.ca/

13 For more work on i-Docs, see: Aston, Gaudenzi and Rose (2017) and Zimmerman (2019).

14 The Co-Creation Studio is the name of an MIT Open Documentary Lab Project devoted to i-Docs. Its manifesto is a useful place to start when thinking about the potential advantages of the i-Doc as a political advocacy platform or as a platform for making a multifaceted or collective art project.

15 Longfellow is also co-editor of *Gendering the Nation: Canadian Women Filmmakers* (Armatage et al. 1999) and maker of environmental i-Doc, *Offshore*, about extreme-depth oil drilling in the oceans, such as that which led to the Deepwater Horizon Disaster. http://offshore-interactive.com/

16 See Lusztig (2013) and visit http://worryboxproject.net/

17 *The Wrong Crowd* was, and perhaps may be yet again, of particular use in college classes because the creative work was part of Beattie's doctoral thesis, the entirety of which is still available as a PDF for download. Beattie's study theorises both 'buried' national/family history and the structure and functioning of online documentary. '*The Wrong Crowd*: an Online Documentary and Analytical Contextualization,' thesis, Faculty of Creative Industries, University of Queensland, December 3, 2008 http://eprints.qut.edu.au/15874/

18 The last project in Queer Feast has now been remade as two 16 mm films, *Lives: Visible* (2017) and *Leftovers* (2018), made from a box of 2,000 snapshots of a couple who documented Chicago's working-class butch/fem life in the pre-Stonewall era. Citron herself has turned to making short YouTube videos for local environmental activism in Wisconsin.

19 See: https://exhibits.stanford.edu/women-art-revolution. The film's website is http://www.womenartrevolution.com/

20 See: http://vectors.usc.edu/projects/learningfromyoutube/

21 Alexandra Juhasz's expansive website is at http://alexandrajuhasz.com/. Juhasz has placed her *Women of Vision* series and the documentary *Scale* to be viewed for free on SnagFilms at http://www.snagfilms.com. I would note, in this regard, that documentary viewing, free or inexpensive, is becoming more available on small screen devices. I suspect that the social issue documentary, with its strong argumentation, might appeal to small-screen viewers because it is compelling and easy to follow and does not generally rely on spectacle for its appeal as much as fiction film does. Here, too, as with most exhibition platforms, smart-phone and tablet viewers have access to more works directed by men than by women.

22 *#100hard truths* can be found at http://scalar.usc.edu/nehvectors/100hardtruths-fake-news/index. This and many other valuable video-book projects have been developed using the open source platform Scalar, developed and maintained by the University of Southern California (https://scalar.me/anvc/scalar/). A useful description of how Scalar works is 'How to Read this Scalar Project', by Nicholas Mirzoeff, as part of his activist project, '*We Are All Children of Algeria': Visuality and Countervisuality 1954–2011* (http://scalar.usc.edu/nehvectors/mirzoeff/index).

References

Armatage, Kay, Kass Banning, Brenda Longfellow, and Janine Marchessault. 1999. *Gendering the Nation: Canadian Women's Cinema*. Toronto: University of Toronto Press.

Aston, Judith, Sandra Gaudenzi, and Mandy Rose, eds. 2017. *i-Docs: The Evolving Practices of Interactive Documentary*. London: Wallflower Press.

Aufderheide, Pat. 2004. 'From A to Z: A Conversation on Women's Filmmaking'. *Signs: Journal of Women in Culture and Society* 30 (1): 1455–1472.

Bourdieu, Pierre. 1984. *A Social Critique of the Judgement of Taste*. London: Routledge.

Citron, Michelle. 1998. *Home Movies and Other Necessary Fictions*. Minneapolis: University of Minnesota Press.

Gardiner, Judith Kegan. 2008. 'What Happened to Socialist Feminist Women's Studies Programs? A Case History and Some Speculations'. *Feminist Studies* 34 (3): 558–583.

Grewal, Inderpal and Caren Kaplan. 1996. 'Warrior Marks: Global Womanism's Neo-Colonial Discourse in a Multicultural Context'. *Camera Obscura* 13 (3): 4–33.

Hammer, Barbara. 2010. *HAMMER! Making Movies Out of Sex and Life*. New York: Feminist Press.

Horeck, Tanya, Mareike Jenner, and Tina Kendall. 2018. 'On Binge Watching: Nine Critical Propositions'. *Critical Studies in Television: The International Journal of Television Studies* 13 (4): 499–504.

Juhasz, Alexandra. 2011. *Learning from YouTube*. Cambridge, Massachusetts: MIT Press [online only].

Lesage, Julia. 1978a. 'The Political Aesthetics of the Feminist Documentary Film'. *Quarterly Review of Film Studies* 3 (4): 507–523.

Lesage, Julia. 1978b. 'JoAnn Elam's Rape: Disarming Film Rape'. *Jump Cut* 19: 14–16.

Lesage, Julia. 2013. 'Feminist Documentaries: Finding, Seeing and Using Them'. In *The Documentary Film Book*, edited by Brian Winston, 266–274. London: Palgrave Macmillan.

Lusztig, Irene. 2013. 'The Worry Box Project: An Archive of Maternal Worries: An Ongoing Participatory Archiving Project'. *Studies in the Maternal* 5 (2): 1–3.

Staiger, Janet. 1985. 'The Politics of Film Canons'. *Cinema Journal* 24 (3): 4–23.

Walker, Janet and Diane Waldman. 1999. 'Introduction'. In *Feminism and Documentary*, 1–35. Minneapolis: University of Minnesota.

White, Patricia. 2000. Feminist Independents. Paper presented at Console-ing Passions, Indiana, May 11–14.

Zimmerman, Patricia R. 2019. *Documentary Across Platforms: Reverse Engineering Media, Place and Politics*. Bloomington IN: Indiana University Press.

Zyrd, Michael. 2006. 'The Academy and the Avant-Garde: A Relationship of Dependence and Resistance'. *Cinema Journal* 45 (2): 7–42.

4

VIDEO ACTIVISM ON THE SOCIAL WEB

Chris Tedjasukmana and Jens Eder

Introduction

Many forms and practices of video activism and radical film have changed profoundly with the emergence of the Social Web. Video can be shot cheaply, easily and inconspicuously; it can be spread anonymously, instantaneously, internationally and sometimes virally; and it facilitates networking and interaction. On the other hand, online video is also subject to ubiquitous surveillance and depends on the logics of 'platform capitalism' (Srnicek 2017) and its competitive attention economy. Activists have adapted to this new media environment and make use of various Internet services in order to document, initiate or comment on political action. Online video activism deals with the whole range of political problems, be they global like social inequality and climate change; or be they more local like state oppression against indigenous communities. Activist videos on the Internet make such problems and injustices visible. They translate complex issues into moving images and affecting stories, mobilise for rallies and campaigns, initiate public debates and give rise to protest movements. Some activist videos reach millions of viewers in large parts of the world. Witness videos, for instance, contributed to the formation of the #BlackLivesMatter movement by documenting racially motivated police violence against African American citizens (Jackson and Foucault Welles 2016). The Chinese environmental documentary *Under the Dome* (2015) was clicked 200 million times in the first few days after its release and sparked heated debates in China before the government attempted to block the video (Yang 2016). In addition to such attempts to raise public awareness, video activists also address individual decision-makers, oppressed communities or supporters. The NGO Witness, for instance, provides lawyers with eyewitness videos and proposes legal measures (Gregory 2012). Radical groups like the German collective Leftvision gather local social movements around specific political causes. And 'artivists' such as the Peng! Collective spread videos of their activist pranks to their media-savvy urban followers and the press (Kara 2015).

These are only a few examples of the diverse geopolitical, ideological and aesthetic spectrum of video activism emerging on the Social Web. The concept of webvideo activism refers to the production and distribution of political online videos by individual citizens, grassroots movements and NGOs who act largely independently of state authorities, corporations or professional mass media. With its roots in the New Social Movements and political documentaries of the 1960s and 1970s, video activism has also been labelled 'radical' (Askanius 2014, 453). However, it only partly overlaps with the diverse radical film cultures (as characterised in this volume): although all video activism is politically engaged and is predominantly committed to progressive politics and struggles for social justice, it often is not 'radical' in the sense of striving for revolutionary or fundamental political changes. And while activist videos take a considerable variety of forms, few of them seem aesthetically radical.

Video activism can also be described as a specific kind of online activism or 'cyberactivism' (McCaughey 2014) in order to highlight the novelty of digital media environments. Online video production is characterised by low costs, easy use and new possibilities of co-creation and remediation. Distribution is networked, algorithmic, potentially less restricted, globally and permanently accessible, but also involves new forms of dataveillance and control. Reception is characterised by generally small, mobile screens, frequent distraction, but mainly by new possibilities for interaction: Videos are re-edited and spread across various platforms, often entering legacy media. As part of current 'hybrid media systems' (Chadwick 2013), video activism is interlinked with traditional ways of making and watching films, on the one hand, and with professional journalism and entertainment in the mass media, on the other. For instance, one and the same video may first be shown at radical film festivals, then circulate through various Internet platforms, and finally be featured in television programmes or cinemas, as in the case of the Greek documentary *Debtocracy* (2011).

The body of research on video activism is rapidly growing in several disciplines like media and visual culture studies, sociology, communication science or political science. The first publications were how-to manuals that guided video makers in producing and distributing advocacy videos offline rather than online (Harding 2001; Gregory et al. 2005). Other authors started to describe online video activism in the context of the anti-globalisation movement (Edwards 2004). Today, one may turn to general surveys of the field (Askanius 2014; Eder, Hartmann and Tedjasukmana 2020); historical accounts (Robé 2016); systematic video typologies (Askanius 2012; Mateos and Gaona 2015; Notley, Lowenthal and Gregory 2015); studies of particularly influential videos like *Kony2012* (Torchin 2016); papers dealing with specific countries like the UK (Presence 2015); or work on specific kinds of videos like those by eyewitnesses (Andén-Papadopoulos 2014; Ristovska 2016) or nonfictional forms that are part of 'new documentary ecologies' (Nash, Hight and Summerhayes 2014). One can turn to quantitative studies about specific platforms (Thorson et al. 2013) or to qualitative work on video aesthetics (Chanan 2012). There are research projects examining, for instance, witness videos in the

MENA region (led by Kari Andén-Papadopoulos 2015–2018), journals that regularly publish relevant papers (e.g., *The Journal of Alternative and Community Media*), and online sources like the Radical Film Network or our own project website videoactivism.net. Activists themselves continuously reflect on their own practice, they share reports, tutorials and guidebooks both online and offline (Gregory 2012; witness.org; v4c.org) and also initiate their own studies on questions regarding, for instance, ethical responsibility or social impact (Notley, Lowenthal and Gregory 2015).

Nevertheless, there are still considerable research gaps due to the scope of and rapid changes in the field. This chapter therefore attempts to integrate interdisciplinary research and provide a concise overview of, first, the historical roots of activist video; second, its dominant forms of organisation and practice; third, its challenges in forming counterpublics on the Social Web; and, finally, its dominant types, aesthetic forms and affective strategies. Due to the biographical background of its authors, the geographical focus lies predominantly on the Global Northwest.

The emergence of video activism

Contemporary video activism has its historical roots in political documentary film, video and television as well as in news journalism, art and public relations. One of its main influences is the tradition of 'committed documentaries' (Waugh 1984) that attempts to give voice to marginalised groups or propagate social justice. Predecessors of video activism date back to the Soviet agit trains of the 1920s (Hogenkamp 2013) as well as the 1960s countercultural film movements such as the French cinéma militant, the anticolonial Third Cinema as well as feminist and queer documentaries. The introduction of the Sony 'portapak' in 1967 marks the technical birth of video activism. Comparably cheap and easy to handle, this mobile production system was enthusiastically explored for artistic and political purposes. Numerous activist media workshops or 'guerrilla television' groups such as videofreex emerged and sought to develop new forms of radical filmmaking (Boyle 1997; Nigg 2017; Stein 2001). During the 'camcorder revolution' and the early AIDS epidemic of the 1980s, video activists participated in groups like ACT UP, documented rallies and successfully produced and disseminated 'safer sex' education videos (Juhasz 1995). One of the most consequential cases of camcorder activism was the witness video of the Rodney King beating incident in 1991, which sparked antiracist uprisings and led to the foundation of the NGO Witness (Schwartz 2009; Gregory 2012). In the context of the anti-WTO protests in 1999, activists founded the global non-profit online activist network Indymedia, which also allowed video uploads and provided video streaming applications in 2004. But recurring security issues, the waning of the alter-globalisation movement and the rise of corporate Social Media led to the successive decline of the platform (Giraud 2014).

With the proclamation of web 2.0, Social Media platforms have – despite ubiquitous state and corporate dataveillance – become highly relevant infrastructures for a new generation of activists and organisers. The spread of wireless broadband Internet access, the common use of smartphones with integrated Internet access, video cameras, live streaming apps and editing software have enabled a new kind of video activism. Initially, citizen activists used only their own static homepages. Around 2005, they established channels on commercial video-sharing platforms like YouTube and set up profiles on Social Networking Sites such as Facebook or microblogging services like Twitter. All this has resulted not only in a greater independence from mass media gatekeepers and a more visible flow of interlinked videos, but also in a larger dependency on commercial platforms and an intensified struggle for attention.

In the age of 'mass self-communication' some activist videos nevertheless take part in the construction of 'networks of outrage and hope' (Castells 2012), organise 'connective action' (Bennett and Segerberg 2012) and have a demonstrably strong impact. Videos, for instance, played crucial roles in mobilising and documenting the uprisings in Iran in 2009 (Malkowski 2017) and in the MENA region around 2011 (Westmoreland 2016), as well as in anti-capitalist protests movements like Occupy or the Indignados (Thorson et al. 2013; Robé 2016).

Contemporary video activism

Today, there is an enormous variety of video activism in many parts of the world (see the links on videoactivism.net and radicalfilmnetwork.com), but their work has only rarely been examined (with notable exceptions such as Presence 2015). Provisionally, we can distinguish between three different types of video activism:

1. *Temporary networks and informal 'hashtag activisms'* produce and circulate their videos in a comparably spontaneous manner, without being based on stable organisational structures. Activist networks such as #BlackLivesMatter may start from a few witness videos that virally spread across platforms and media. Most of their participants are only loosely connected via Facebook groups or Twitter hashtags. In many cases, however, seminal videos can also be traced back to well-organised actors or 'influencers' or to counter-movements trying to sabotage the thread.

2. *Media collectives* are small activist groups that specialise in certain topics, strategies or types of videos. For instance, they may focus on human rights violations (Witness), regional war zones (like the Syrian documentary project Abounadarra Films or the Syrian Archive), repressive regimes (The Mosireen Collective in Egypt or Sendika.org in Turkey), anti-capitalism (Global Uprisings, Labournet, Leftvision, subMedia.TV), migration (Cross-point, Let's Stay) or Internet policy (Tactical Technology Collective). They also concentrate on a variety of strategies and generic forms. Audiovisual citizen or counter-journalists such as Democracy Now! produce political news otherwise neglected in mass media, while 'artivists' like The Peng! Collective invent satirical video campaigns in order to raise awareness for serious political problems.

3. *Established NGOs* such as Greenpeace or Amnesty International have grown into influential, financially potent global players with a professional organisation, often including video or Social Media departments. Since their work is financed through donations and membership fees, they are particularly dependent on public attention, which determines the amount of donations and their success. Videos play a key role in their cross-media campaigns and are increasingly produced and distributed in collaboration with the advertising, consulting and technology industries. Due to their collaboration practices and internal structures, NGOs are often not considered activist by radical or grassroots organisations as well as many researchers. Nevertheless, NGOs ought to be included in a critical examination of activism, because they usually share its prototypical aims, practices and problems.

Most activists aim at achieving 'social impact' and social change (Finneran 2014; Nichols 2016), for instance by directly addressing powerful decision-makers, by mobilising local protesters or by fostering internal group connection or empowerment. However, many forms of social impact can only be achieved by addressing larger publics in the context of the 'attention economy' (Lanham 2006) of the Social Web, where 'a wealth of information creates a poverty of attention' (Simon 1971).

In this environment, a diverse range of strategies and tactics develops in three fields of practice: (1) *Manufacturing strategies* aim at effective practices of production, financing, organisation and cooperation with other actors. For instance, one can observe the formation of heterogeneous 'production alliances', when established NGOs cooperate with professional film production companies or advertising agencies. (2) *Design strategies* focus on the rhetorical, aesthetic and affective form of the videos, their potential for persuasion and impact, their technological fascination (e.g., 360° videos) and their suitability for specific web environments. And (3) *dissemination strategies* attempt to optimise the reach of videos through network distribution, including the utilisation of Social Media dynamics.

Distribution, platforms and publics

Distribution strategies have become ever more important because Social Media have changed the modalities in which videos circulate and political discourses develop. Social video distribution is characterised by its potential for interaction and participation: individual videos may be collected in channels and playlists, sorted into categories, tagged, recommended, linked to other videos, searched, selected, aggregated, liked, commented on, re-edited, shared and spread across platforms. In this way, videos become meaningful elements of networked interaction and co-creation, of their viewers' public self-expression, their identity formation and social struggles (Sundar 2015).

Moreover, online video distribution depends less on previous forms of editorial gatekeeping and more on 'gatewatching' (Bruns 2018). Internet platforms function as 'online intermediaries' (Schmidt et al. 2017), as novel filters and amplifiers, their secret algorithms serve as influential sorting tools of 'calculated' or 'automated' publics (Gillespie 2018; Pasquale 2017). Facebook's newsfeed, YouTube's video recommendations and Google's search results are calculated from a multitude of personalised facts and individually adjusted to user interests. But whereas previous gatekeepers such as mass media or government agencies have often ignored or distorted activists' messages, the new gatewatchers encourage and even depend on constant user participation and data production.

This encouragement of participation makes these platforms useful for minority communities and video activists who use them as tools to quickly disseminate their messages (Jackson and Foucault Welles 2016). But while those platforms seem indispensable for activists, they are at the same time far from being neutral spaces. As corporate 'advertising platforms' (Srnicek 2017, 49ff), their primary aim is to collect user data and sell it to advertisers. In order to stimulate use and receive more data, they provide various incentives such as clickbaits or autoplay functions. Their algorithms favour sensationalist and feedback-provoking content as well as messages that reinforce preexisting opinions.

Accordingly, the public sphere is also undergoing a pivotal transformation (Schäfer 2015) and hardly corresponds to the democratic ideal of rational deliberation (Habermas 1989 [1962]). Networked technologies, algorithms and volatile affective dynamics (boyd 2010; Papacharissi 2015) are increasingly shaping contemporary publics as well as 'subaltern counterpublics' (Fraser 1990). Publics are intertwined with corporate platform infrastructures, thereby creating hybrid spaces with ambivalent effects. Their algorithms may have homogenising effects contributing to the formation of 'echo chambers' (Sunstein 2001) or 'filter bubbles' (Pariser 2011) that often involve hate directed at outsiders and minority positions. Amplified by the 'online disinhibition effect' (Suler 2004), a result of being 'privately public' on Social Media sites (Lange 2007), this hatred may lead to furious 'cybercascades' (Sunstein 2017). Another negative aspect is the proliferation of hate videos, 'fake news', jihadism and right-wing extremism (Ekman 2014).

Moreover, any citizen profile, channel and content can be controlled and deleted, while state actors can gain access to personal user data. Facebook's introduction of their 'real name' policy, for example, led to the deletion of many activist profiles and to the exposure and imprisonment of dissidents (Tufekci 2017, 139ff). Autocratic regimes are now generally using Social Media to their advantage by way of censorship and decentralised diversion tactics: Armies of trolls spread lies, discredit dissidents and drop 'rumor bombs' (Tufekci 2017, 132ff) in an attempt to confuse and paralyse the public discourse. And even when critical videos, e.g., WikiLeaks' *Collateral Murder* (2010) about a war crime committed by the US army in Iraq, attract an unusual amount of attention online, they may be ignored by the mainstream media (Christensen 2017) and often trigger widely divergent responses in different audiences (Eder 2018).

Activist webvideos: types, forms and strategies

Despite the problematic effects of platforms, such media environments remain indispensable for activists who react with specific distribution, production and design strategies. As activist videos compete for attention in their oversaturated media ecologies, their specific genres and forms become crucial. After all, they are the means by which videos arouse attention, interest, concern and motivation for action. Compared with cinema or television, the reception of online videos is characterised by usually smaller, often mobile screens, and by a higher degree of viewer distraction. Accordingly, video activism favours 'small media' (Chanan 2012): short, fragmented, spontaneous forms. But the common focus on short witness videos or 'social spots' does not suffice. Political online videos may take on any forms and genres; they may be short or long, fictional or nonfictional, live-action or animated. Their structure may be narrative (telling a story), rhetorical (developing an argument [Hesling 1989]), descriptive, categorical or associative. The variety of their audiovisual forms and experiential qualities is even broader.

In attempts at an overview, several authors have distinguished between general kinds or genres of activist videos (Askanius 2012, 2014; Mateos and Gaona 2015). Such forms are connected to typical uses, for instance as visual evidence, 'as a direct form of address to decision-makers', 'in community-mobilizing campaigns', but also as 'viral marketing', 'political entertainment', 'community-building and community-branding' or for individual expression (Askanius 2014). Considering different discourse strategies, goals, actors and forms of communication, five dominant video types can be identified: (1) witness videos, (2) webdocs, (3) vlogs, (4) mobilisation and campaign videos and (5) communication guerrilla videos.

Witness videos (e.g., in the context of #BlackLivesMatter), exposure videos (Wiki-Leaks' *Collateral Murder*) and legal evidence videos (as collected by the NGO Witness) are based on digital camera recordings of acts of injustice and human rights abuses. They address the public from the 'inside' of those events or at close range. They are uploaded directly, live-streamed or handed over to journalists. Due to the massive spread of networked cameras and increasing citizen awareness, the number of witness videos has risen sharply. In order to gain public attention, activist witness videos have to be long enough to count as a document but at the same time short enough to be effective in the struggle for attention. After crossing a certain publicity threshold in Social Media, classical news media serve as multipliers, before the videos flow back into the archives of the Social Web (particularly YouTube). As a consequence of this hybrid media flow, it is often difficult to locate the original footage. Verification problems, pseudo-forensic counter-analysis, allegations of manipulation and conspiracy theories accompany many witness videos. As a result, they often turn out to be politically consequential, but contested as legal evidence, as the 1992 Rodney King beating trial and other cases demonstrate (Schwartz 2009).

Web documentaries such as *Under the Dome* make use of the conventions of film and television documentaries in order to inform their audience about current public affairs. The producers may be independent citizen journalists, NGOs or grassroots movements. They often combine the presentation of facts and evidence with rhetorical argumentation and storytelling. In some cases, they include found footage and archival material or they apply web-specific formats such as 360° video or interactive and augmented reality elements.

Videoblogs or vlogs are a form of audiovisual political commentary. They function similarly to newspaper op-eds; in addition, however, vloggers address their viewers directly and personally through their webcam. Along with explicitly political channels, many vloggers only engage in occasional activism. YouTubers and Social Media influencers from the entertainment sector sometimes participate in coordinated forms of action such as the German anti-hate campaign #*Ichbinhier* ('I am here'). Vlogs can be quickly produced and are highly opinionated, and are therefore particularly suitable for directly influencing the viewers.

Mobilisation and campaign videos such as *Kony2012* are produced strategically and are usually embedded in broader online and offline campaigns. They are predominantly commissioned by NGOs and in some cases apply viral marketing strategies. Whether it is reformist or radical, activism usually requires some kind of 'public relations' efforts. As political advertisements, these videos try to maximise their 'spreadability' (Jenkins, Ford and Green 2013) and aim to make viewers act – sign petitions, donate money or take part in an event. In order to achieve that, mobilisation videos are usually short and involve emotional rhetoric or dramatic storytelling. Often, they rely on pathos formulas, community feelings or other positive emotions.

Communication guerrilla videos include *artivist, mash-up and memetic videos*, for example found footage remixes like Cassetteboy's *Cameron's Conference Rap* (2014). They aim to address the public in particularly innovative and entertaining ways. They often use parody and satire to subvert and appropriate hegemonic representations, irritate conventional views and reinterpret cultural signs (Lasn 1999). As small, quick-witted and media-savvy units, these video activists rely on the David-versus-Goliath principle. They often parody advertising clips by powerful corporations or state propaganda or they document their own site-specific offline action.

In addition to these main types of activist videos there are further ones such as tutorial videos. All these different types make use of various design strategies in order to evoke the viewers' political emotions (Eder 2017). (1) The most basic form consists in *presenting visible evidence* of violence, suffering or protest, as in countless witness videos. Viewers are invited to share an eyewitness' perspective and emotional reaction to a striking event, often captured in rough images and sounds signalling authenticity. (2) *Storytelling* is often used in mobilisation videos: a cast of heroes, villains, victims and helpers interacts in a dramatic conflict, framed from a certain perspective. The viewers are invited to take part in the fight for a positive resolution. Charged with moral values and corresponding emotions of sympathy, antipathy and empathy, video narratives take part in political 'story wars' (Sachs 2012). (3) Activist webdocs or citizen journalist news make frequent use of *rhetorical argumentation*: they put forward political claims and attempt to support them with arguments and evidence, aiming to convince their viewers (Hesling 1989). Such rhetorical structure is also charged with intense emotions ('pathos' being a crucial strategy of classic rhetoric). Presenting evidence, storytelling and rhetorical argumentation may be the most widespread forms of activist videos, but there are many others, some of which are specific to the Social Web.

Conclusion

Today's hybrid media environments are contested and complicated terrains for video activism and radical filmmaking. They offer new potentials for forming counterpublics and proliferating alternative views, but at the same time enable surveillance, propaganda, doxing and trolling. On commercial platforms, video activists struggle for attention and, without becoming manipulative, they invent new design, production and distribution strategies.

References

Andén-Papadopoulos, Kari. 2014. 'Citizen Camera-Witnessing: Embodied Political Dissent in the Age of "Mediated Mass Self-Communication"'. *New Media & Society* 16 (5): 753–769.

Askanius, Tina. 2012. *Radical Online Video: YouTube, Video Activism and Social Movement Media Practices*. Lund: Lund University.

Askanius, Tina. 2014. 'Video for Change'. In *The Handbook of Development Communication and Social Change*, edited by Karin Gwinn Wilkins, Rafael Obregon and Thomas Tufte, 453–470. New Jersey: John Wiley.

Bennett, W. Lance and Alexandra Segerberg. 2012. 'The Logic of Connective Action'. *Information, Communication & Society* 15 (5): 739–768.

boyd, danah. 2010. 'Social Network Sites as Networked Publics: Affordances, Dynamics, and Implications'. In *Networked Self: Identity, Community, and Culture on Social Network Sites*, edited by Zizi Papacharissi, 39–58. New York: Routledge.

Boyle, Deidre. 1997. *Subject to Change: Guerrilla Television Revisited*. Oxford: Oxford University Press.

Bruns, Axel. 2018. *Gatewatching and News Curation: Journalism, Social Media, and the Public Sphere*. New York: Peter Lang.

Castells, Manuel. 2012. *Networks of Outrage and Hope: Social Movements in the Internet Age*. Cambridge: Polity.

Chadwick, Andrew. 2013. *The Hybrid Media System: Politics and Power*. Oxford: Oxford University Press.

Chanan, Michael. 2012. 'Video, Activism and the Art of Small Media'. *Transnational Cinemas* 2 (2): 217–226.

Christensen, Christian. 2017. 'Images That Last? Iraq Videos from YouTube to WikiLeaks'. In *Image Operations: Visual Media and Political Conflict*, edited by Jens Eder and Charlotte Klonk, 118–127. Manchester: Manchester University Press.

Eder, Jens. 2017. 'Affective Image Operations'. In *Image Operations: Visual Media and Political Conflict*, edited by Jens Eder and Charlotte Klonk, 63–78. Manchester: Manchester University Press.

Eder, Jens. 2018. 'Collateral Emotions: Political Web Videos and Divergent Audience Responses'. In *Cognitive Theory and Documentary Film*, edited by Catalin Brylla and Mette Kramer, 183–204. London: Palgrave Macmillan.

Eder, Jens, Britta Hartmann and Chris Tedjasukmana. 2020. *Bewegungsbilder: Politische Videos in Sozialen Medien*. Berlin: Bertz + Fischer.

Edwards, Richard L. 2004. 'Torrents of Resistance'. *Film International* 2 (4): 38–47.

Ekman, Matthias. 2014. 'The Dark Side of Online Activism: Swedish Right-Wing Extremist Video Activism on YouTube'. *MedienKultur* 30 (56): 79–99.

Finneran, Patricia. 2014. *Documentary Impact. Social Change through Storytelling*. Toronto: Hotdocs. Outspoken Understanding.

Fraser, Nancy. 1990. 'Rethinking the Public Sphere: A Contribution to the Critique of Actually Existing Democracy'. *Social Text* 25/26: 56–80.

Gillespie, Tarleton. 2018. *Custodians of the Internet: Platforms, Content Moderation, and the Hidden Decisions That Shape Social Media*. New Haven: Yale University Press.

Giraud, Eva. 2014. 'Has Radical Participatory Online Media Really "Failed"? Indymedia and its Legacies'. *Convergence: The International Journal of Research into New Media Technologies* 20 (4): 419–437.

Gregory, Sam. 2012. 'The Participatory Panopticon and Human Rights: WITNESS's Experience Supporting Video Advocacy and Future Possibilities'. In *Sensible Politics: The Visual Culture of Nongovernmental Activism*, edited by Meg McLagan and Yates McKee, 517–549. New York: Zone Books.

Gregory, Sam, Gillian Caldwell, Ronit Avni and Thomas Harding. 2005. *Video for Change: A Guide for Advocacy and Activism*. London: Pluto Press.

Habermas, Jürgen. 1989 [1962]. *The Structural Transformation of the Public Sphere: An Inquiry into a Category of Bourgeois Society*. Cambridge: MIT Press.

Harding, Thomas. 2001. *The Video Activist Handbook*. 2nd ed. London: Pluto Press.

Hesling, Willem. 1989. 'Documentary Film and Rhetorical Analysis'. In *Image-Reality-Spectator*, edited by Willem de Greef and Willem Hesling, 101–131. Leuven: Acco.

Hogenkamp, A. P. 2013. 'The Radical Tradition in Documentary Film-making, 1920–50s'. In *The Documentary Film Book*, edited by Brian Winston, 173–179. Basingstoke: Palgrave Macmillan.

Jackson, Sarah J. and Brooke Foucault Welles. 2016. '#Ferguson is Everywhere: Initiators in Emerging Counterpublic Networks'. *Information, Communication and Society* 19 (3): 397–418.

Jenkins, Henry, Sam Ford and Joshua Green. 2013. *Spreadable Media: Creating Meaning and Value in a Networked Culture*. New York: New York University Press.

Juhasz, Alexandra. 1995. *AIDS TV: Identity, Community, and Alternative Video*, Durham, London: Duke University Press.

Kara, Selmin. 2015. 'Rebels without Regret: Documentary Artivism in the Digital Age'. *Studies in Documentary Film* 9 (1): 42–54.

Lange, Patricia G. 2007. 'Publicly Private and Privately Public: Social Networking on YouTube'. *Journal of Computer-Mediated Communication* 13 (1): 361–380.

Lanham, Richard. 2006. *The Economics of Attention: Style and Substance in the Age of Information*. Chicago, London: The University of Chicago Press.

Lasn, Kalle. 1999. *Culture Jam*. New York: Eagle Brook.

Malkowski, Jennifer. 2017. *Dying in Full Detail: Mortality and Digital Documentary*. Durham, London: Duke UP.

Mateos, Concha, and Carmen Gaona. 2015. 'Video Activism: A Descriptive Typology'. In *Global Media Journal: Use of Social Media and Media Coverage*. http://www.globalmedia journal.com/open-access/video-activism-a-descriptive-typology.php?aid=62532 (accessed August 2019).

McCaughey, Martha. 2014. *Cyberactivism on the Participatory Web*. London, New York: Routledge.

Nash, Kate, Craig Hight and Catherine Summerhayes, eds. 2014. *New Documentary Ecologies: Emerging Platforms, Practices and Discourses*. Basingstoke: Palgrave MacMillan.

Nichols, Bill. 2016. *Speaking Truth with Film: Evidence, Ethics, Politics in Documentary*. Oakland, CA: University of California Press.

Nigg, Heinz. 2017. *Rebel Video: The Video Movement of the 1970s and 1980s*. Zürich: Verlag Scheidegger & Spiess.

Notley, Tanya, Andrew Lowenthal, and Sam Gregory. 2015. '*Video for Change: Creating and Measuring Social Impact*'. https://video4change.org/wp-content/uploads/2015/07/video4 change-impact-working-paper-2015_final.pdf (accessed August 2019).

Papacharissi, Zizzi. 2015. *Affective Publics: Sentiment, Technology, and Politics*. Oxford, New York: Oxford University Press.

Pariser, Eli. 2011. *The Filter Bubble: What the Internet Is Hiding from You*. London, New York: Penguin.

Pasquale, Frank   (2018): The Automated Public Sphere. In: *The Politics and Policies of Big Data: Big Data, Big Brother?*, edited by Ann Rudinow Sætnan, Ingrid Schneider and Nicola Green, 110–128. London, New York: Routledge.

Presence, Steve. 2015. 'The Contemporary Landscape of Video-Activism in Britain'. In *Marxism and Film Activism: Screen Alternative Worlds*, edited by Ewa Mazierska and Lars Kristensen, 186–212. London: Berghahn Books.

Ristovska, Sandra. 2016. 'Strategic Witnessing in an Age of Video Activism'. *Media, Culture & Society* 38 (7): 1034–1047.

Robé, Chris. 2016. 'Criminalizing Dissent: Western State Repression, Video Activism, and Counter-Summit Protests'. *Framework: The Journal of Cinema and Media* 57 (2): 161–188.

Sachs, Jonah. 2012. *Winning the Story Wars: Why Those Who Tell and Live the Best Stories Will Rule the Future*. Boston, MA: Harvard Business Review Press.

Schäfer, Mike. 2015. 'Digital Public Sphere'. In *The International Encyclopedia of Political Communication*, edited by Mazzoleni Gianpietro. New York: Wiley.

Schmidt, Jan-Hinrik, Lisa Merten, Uwe Hasebrink, Isabelle Petrich and Amelie Rolfs. 2017. *Zur Relevanz von Online-Intermediären für die Meinungsbildung*. Hamburg: Verlag Hans-Bredow-Institut.

Schwartz, Louis-Georges. 2009. *Mechanical Witness: A History of Motion Picture Evidence in U. S. Courts*. Oxford: Oxford University Press.

Simon, Herbert. 1971. 'Designing Organizations for an Information-Rich World'. In *Computers, Communications and the Public Interest*, edited by Martin Greenberger, 37–72. Baltimore: Johns Hopkins University Press.

Srnicek, Nick. 2017. *Platform Capitalism*. Cambridge: Polity Press.

Stein, Laura. 2001. 'Access Television and Grassroots Political Communication in the United States', In *Radical Media: Rebellious Communication and Social Movements*, edited by John Downing, 299–324. Thousand Oaks: Sage.

Suler, John. 2004. 'The Online Disinhibition Effect'. *CyberPsychology and Behavior* 7 (3): 321–326.

Sundar, Shyam. 2015. 'Toward a Theory of Interactive Media Effects (TIME)'. In *The Handbook of the Psychology of Communication Technology*, edited by Shyam Sundar, 47–86. Hoboken: Wiley-Blackwell.

Sunstein, Cass R. 2001. *Echo Chambers: Bush vs. Gore, Impeachment, and Beyond*. Princeton, Oxford: Princeton University Press.

Sunstein, Cass R. 2017. *#Republic: Divided Democracy in the Age of Social Media*. Princeton: Princeton University Press.

Thorson, Kjerstin, Kevin Driscoll, Brian Ekdale, Stephanie Edgerly, Liana Gamber Thomson, Andrew Schrock, Lana Swartz, Emily K.Vraga and Chris Wells. 2013. 'YouTube, Twitter and the Occupy Movement'. *Information, Communication & Society* 16 (3): 421–451.

Torchin, Leshu. 2016. '*KONY* 2012: Anatomy of a Campaign Video and a Video Campaign'. In *The Routledge Companion to Cinema and Politics*, edited by Yannis Tzioumakis and Clair Molloy, 123–134. New York: Routledge.

Tufekci, Zeynep. 2017. *Twitter and Tear Gas: The Power and Fragility of Networked Protest*. New Haven, London: Yale University Press.

Waugh, Thomas. 1984. *Show Us Life: Towards a History and Aesthetics of the Committed Documentary*. Metuchen: Scarecrow Press.

Westmoreland, Mark R. 2016. 'Street Scenes: The Politics of Revolutionary Video in Egypt'. *Visual Anthropology* 29: 243–262.

Yang, Fan. 2016. 'Under the Dome: "Chinese" Smog as a Viral Media Event'. *Critical Studies in Media Communication* 33 (3): 232–244.

5

TV INTERVENTIONS

Artists, activists and alternative media

Ieuan Franklin

Introduction: artists as theorists and activists

Taking as its credo the title of the late Chuck Kleinhans' chapter within this collection (see Chapter 2), I want to examine some of the intellectual arguments and creative solutions devised and deployed by video artists and activists to subvert, reform or reshape television, in order to consider how this might inform and conceptualise radical media and/or media history. Partly intended as a modest contribution to the development of (critical) theory in the study of alternative media (see Sandoval and Fuchs 2010; Fuchs 2010; Andersson 2012; Mowbray 2015), this chapter will cite specific examples of media activism for their intrinsic significance but also to highlight the pitfalls and shortcomings of any rigid or limited ideological framework to map the diverse range of practices which fall under the rubric of 'alternative media'.[1] I would like to suggest that closer attention could be paid to the ideas and arguments of artists in the development of theory around alternative media, and this will be illustrated by a discussion about how video artists have quite naturally and readily assumed roles as theorists and/or activists, in developing arguments about the role that television could and should play in society. I will also emphasise the need to contextualise alternative media examples, by investigating the institutional and regulatory structure and frameworks which can shape and determine media practice on a number of levels. Finally, the chapter will tackle the thorny and controversial question of whether participatory processes inhibit the accessibility, reach and popularity of alternative media.

Enter or subvert

Whilst it is beyond the scope of this chapter to give any sort of detailed account of the rich history of artist interventions on TV – from commissioned programmes on mainstream television to experiments that have positioned themselves in opposition to the medium – it is important to look both at the 'big picture' and the nature of the very distinction I have just referred to. Introducing their 2008 exhibition 'Broadcast Yourself', which took place as part of the AV Festival in Newcastle in February of that year, curators Kathy Rae Hoffman and Sarah Cook noted: 'In the 1970s and 1980s, artists approached television from two different perspectives: some wanted their video works broadcast, while others wanted to control how broadcasting functioned' (reprinted in Cook and Huffman 2012, 3).

There has always been a continuum between these two 'poles' (of *enter* or *subvert*), with some video artists criticising the way in which the medium operates, and others content to play with or critique its conventions or forms. In a recent interview with the present author, the video artist and media scholar David Garcia explained how the Amsterdam cable TV pirates of the 1980s, such as Rabotnik, had inspired him to consider the 'communicative possibilities' of television, rather than just seeing it as a possible outlet for video art (as video artists in the UK tended to regard the early Channel 4) (Garcia 2018). At its most overtly political, early video art did question 'what it meant for "the people" to be construed as an audience that received images and sounds via one-way broadcasts that delivered them into the hands of advertisers and disenfranchised the public sphere' (Kaizen 2016, 2).

As Kaizen notes, this was the exact subject of *Television Delivers People* by Richard Serra and Carlotta Faye Schoolman. First shown late at night on a commercial television station in Amarillo, Texas, in 1973, it undoubtedly came as quite a shock to the average viewer. The video is unsparing in its attack on the medium while remaining within it, evoking nicely the concept of 'working against the established institutions, whilst working in them' (Marcuse 1972, 55). Incorporating excerpts from academic texts critiquing commercial television, the style and form of the video exemplifies the seduction of TV advertising which facilitates this 'delivery of people', with easy listening Muzak accompanying the scrolling white sentences.

> Commercial television delivers 20 million people a minute.
> In commercial broadcasting the viewer pays for the privilege of having himself sold.
> It is the consumer who is consumed.
> You are the product of t.v.
> You are delivered to the advertiser who is the customer.
> He consumes you.
> The viewer is not responsible for programming——
> You are the end product.
>
> *(Serra and Schoolman 1973)*

In a sense much early video art was not just reminiscent of the media critique of the Frankfurt School, but was instead a material embodiment of the ideas of Bertolt Brecht and Walter Benjamin. It pointed to the way in which filmmaking could challenge the fundamental assumptions of bourgeois culture which located work as productive and relegated art to leisure and consumption (Johnston 1976). Another key influence was Hans Magnus Enzensberger's essay 'Constituents of a Theory of the Media', which critiqued the unidirectional flow and the undemocratic, unaccountable structure(s) of the media industries (Enzensberger 1970). In some ways these 'TV interventions' anticipated the future work of tactical media practitioners like Critical Art Ensemble, who developed participatory events to 'demonstrate [the] critique through an experiential process' (quoted in Kluitenberg 2011, 37).

David Hall's *This is a Television Receiver*, one of the few pieces of video art created to be broadcast on British TV around this time (in 1976) had another Brechtian aim or effect – to break the imaginary relationship between the performer/text/screen and the viewer. Whereas the majority of video artists considered television to be an entirely inadequate medium for the transmission of video art, some were keen to work with and within the medium. It can be emphasised that Hall's work should be considered as 'television' – what is experienced in an auditorium or gallery today is a video record of a work originally beamed unannounced into people's homes. Furthermore, the piece was designed specifically to shatter the illusion of television as a window onto the world, through the visual feedback and image loss involved in filming off the screen. As Mark Wilcox (1984) observed,

> In *This is a Television Receiver* the well known TV newsreader, Richard Baker, delivers a didactic text which exposes the illusion that a human being is talking to us. We learn from him, for instance, that his voice is emitting not from his lips but from a loudspeaker in the TV set. This address is repeated and each time the image and sound are re-recorded and degenerated his face and voice become more grotesquely distorted. This figure of authority is reduced to what, in essence, he is – a series of pulsating patterns of light on the surface of a glass screen ... The illusion of transparency is shattered. This is deconstruction in its primary, irreducible form; only by remembering these important lessons have artists subsequently been able to venture out of the enclosure of self-reflexivity and into the perilous world of representation and narrative.

Such TV interventions by artists like David Hall and Tamara Krikorian – which were designed to interrupt, dematerialise or demystify the flow of television programming – were nevertheless commissioned by, or developed in close cooperation with, broadcasters. As Mike Stubbs has noted, they were

> perhaps historically the most radical in terms of disruption to audience expectation and viewing patterns ... This was a time when a few creative broadcasters had not got totally consumed by revenue targets and artists wanted to experiment with the medium.
>
> *(Stubbs 1999, 70–71)*

Although early video artists have occasionally been characterised as having a 'radical political agenda' (Dowling n.d.), historical examples of overtly oppositional work like *Television Delivers People* are nevertheless fairly rare. A recent account has argued that:

The change brought about by the artists who developed early video art was undertaken less as an act of iconoclasm than as one of radical revision and is best characterised as a 'soft revolution'. Rather than destroy either commercial television or the art gallery, these artists set out to recast institutions related to both in a different mould.

(Kaizen 2016, 2)

Whilst Kaizen's focus is on early video art as it developed in the United States – which benefitted from the support of public television stations WGBH, WNET and KQED – it is interesting to consider whether the same is true of early video art in the UK, in terms of seeking and pursuing a radical revision/reform of television. It would be a mistake to think that television in the UK – both public service and commercial – was completely unaffected by the ideas and work of video artists. It would also be a mistake to overlook the fact that political sympathies were common to video artists and activists (Cubitt 2012: 163), and that there were significant transnational influences or exchanges. Interviewed in 2013, the late John 'Hoppy' Hopkins, a video pioneer as well as a prime mover within the British counterculture of the 1960s, spoke about how his trips to the United States to research a book entitled *Video and Community Development* inspired him to conduct experiments with radical television.

> I was very interested in what was happening in California, in particular in San Francisco. There was a place called the National Centre for Experiments in Television, or NCET, which was run by a man and woman called Bryce and Rita Howard. And he was into getting people, mainly from cable TV companies, to come and experiment in an open-ended way … I was completely overwhelmed by seeing what they could do with video … I felt really inspired by Bryce Howard, and when we came back to England, in 1970 I think it was, through my contacts we made some sort of liaison with some people running a studio at the BBC. And they said to us why don't you come and make some experimental programming.[2]

This led to *Videospace* (1970), an experimental happening that took place in a small BBC TV studio, combining different formats of film (Super 8 and 16 mm), black and white (2 inch) video, and live studio action (including a light show, dancer, musicians and spoken dialogue). This was mixed in real-time and involved around ten to fifteen people connected to Hoppy's experimental television workshop TVX (see Dickson 2012, 129). Whilst it was not ultimately broadcast, it did lead to the commissioning of two short 'promos' (long predating the invention of the term/form), which used similar techniques (see also Webb-Ingall 2015).

Hoppy and his close collaborator Sue Hall (who together founded the video editing facility Fantasy Factory in 1973) were amongst those working in independent film and video invited to a 'Consultation with Independent Producers' about the future fourth UK TV channel (to eventually be established in 1982 as Channel

4) at the headquarters of the Independent Broadcasting Authority (the IBA, the regulator for commercial radio and television), in Brompton Road, London, on September 26, 1979. Such invitations were in recognition of the tireless campaigning on the part of these filmmakers and producers, under the aegis of the London-based Independent Filmmakers Association (IFA) and various lobby groups (such as The Channel Four Group), for a fourth television channel that would be genuinely independent and which would provide a platform for new voices, experimental work and minority interests. At this IBA consultation, the film and video artist Malcolm Le Grice expressed their collective commitment to new forms of television:

> This group of [independent] film and video makers, people who are concerned with the possibility of a new Channel, are not simply concerned with the concept of producing material which fits into a slot or into a preconceived notion of a television presentation, but they are concerned with whole methods of production within television and film and, in particular, with the relationship between the production and the audience. I think we are breaking down some of the alienation between the producer and the consumer … I want to suggest that we have money set aside by the IBA for a foundation, which is in a sense like a research and development sector of television broadcasting.[3]

Following this consultation, a letter was sent from the IFA to the IBA, proposing that a foundation should be established to provide Research and Development funds for new programmes and broadcasting modes and concepts rather than commercial 'seed money' for small entrepreneurs.[4] This would 'set up a series of experimental workshops in every region'.[5] Although the IBA were wary of the IFA's radicalism, one or two senior executives were sympathetic and receptive to some of its arguments. Reporting on the 'Public Meeting on TV4', held at the ICA shortly afterwards (on December 17, 1979, organised by *Time Out* and The Channel Four Group), an unnamed senior executive noted:

> The point put by [Simon] Hartog [a filmmaker who, with Le Grice, had co-founded the London Film-makers' Co-op in the 1960s] was echoed several times: that whilst British TV is the best in the world in an overall way, it is certainly not the best in encouraging experimental material: and as it would be impossible to expect a Controller to be good at choosing all types of programmes, there must be a small part of the Channel set aside (money and people) which is committed to helping this type of programming. It is my impression that the gap between the majority of talented, independently-minded producers and ourselves is not as large as either they or some of us here would imagine. For political reasons, I think we should continue to meet them – both at Chairman level and at staff level.[6]

On April 24, 1980 Philip Whitehead MP put forward an amendment to the 1980 Broadcasting Bill proposed by the IFA, which pressed for a foundation 'to be set up by the channel, but at arm's length from it, which would facilitate the making of innovative and experimental films' (Darlow 2004, 250). Whilst it was ultimately rejected, the amendment received significant cross-party support, and was acknowledged by Leon Brittan as 'a serious obligation imposed by Parliament with bipartisan support' (quoted in Darlow 2004, 250).

Whilst Channel 4's first Chief Executive Jeremy Isaacs also came to reject the IFA's foundation proposal, he 'agreed to a minimum of 2 hours a week of [innovatory and experimental] material and that all three areas outlined in the foundation document should be funded, i.e. regional production units, "one-off" funding, and production facility centres'.[7] Channel 4's Independent Film and Video Department was duly established (in 1981) as the 'small part of the Channel' with the greatest responsibility to uphold Channel 4's remit to innovate and experiment, and this was achieved largely by its funding of a network of film and video workshops throughout the country.

Recent scholarly work has illuminated the role of the IFA – which in some ways was the voice of the workshop movement – as an agent of change between filmmakers and state, in terms of national film and broadcasting policy (Perry 2016; Presence 2019). However, what is far less well known is that Isaacs' interest in radical television had been piqued by an article in *Broadcast* written by the British film producer Keith Griffiths about the US public broadcaster WNET/13, which had set up an experimental television lab in New York in 1972 (see Buchan 2011, 24) to support artists in the creation of video art. Isaacs wondered if the nascent Channel 4 could do a similar thing.

Participation, impact and sustainability

Having demonstrated the way in which artists have both successfully critiqued the closed and unreceptive structures of television, and achieved some traction in pressing for an opening up of the medium to new ideas and approaches through interventions in media policy, the remainder of the chapter will look at the potential and actual challenges and problems that can be involved when artists or projects seek to engage with institutional or commercial structures of distribution and exhibition. In doing so I will briefly summarise some recent trends in the debate around the definition and evaluation of alternative media. In particular I would like to critique what I regard to be a polemical and usefully synoptic but nonetheless problematic and dogmatic contribution to this debate – Sandoval and Fuchs' (2010) article 'Towards a Critical Theory of Alternative Media'.

One simple way of summarising the thrust of the article is that the authors appear to wish to develop a theory of alternative media which essentially 'dethrones' participation as its *sine qua non*. John Downing has observed that radical media (his preferred cognate term) need not necessarily be participatory (media) (cited in Sandoval and Fuchs 2010, 147). Seemingly taking this to also mean that participatory media are therefore not typically radical, Sandoval and Fuchs drive a wedge through this gap, explicitly prioritising communicative potential (establishing an alternative micro-public sphere) and critical content (e.g. reporting about oppression) over the realisation of participatory production processes. This is in stark contrast to the position traditionally taken by community video activists, for example, who have typically tended to prioritise process over product, dialogue over rhetoric, and participation over professionalism. This debate – essentially about whether participation is a good in itself (Atton 2010, 217) – has echoed through the history of radical film and video culture.

Participatory media approaches can give voice and representation to those who need it most, but to the extent that they reject professional organisation they 'often suffer from a lack of resources, which makes it difficult to gain public visibility' (Sandoval and Fuchs 2010, 143). Alternative or community media projects have sometimes been criticised for a lack of professionalism, particularly a neglect of distribution, marketing and promotion, which has sometimes meant remaining in an 'alternative ghetto' (Landry et al. 1985, 95, 101). Other issues cohere around the issue of amateurism and sustainability – scholars often claim that the horizontal organisation and short-term nature of 'tactical media', for example, limit their impact and reach. But Sandoval and Fuchs go so far as to state the following about small-scale alternative media projects:

> In many cases, they will remain an expression of lifestyle politics that please and console their producers or even become ideologies that forestall collective political struggles because these producers find no time for political activism and consider their individual product as a sufficient statement. But a statement that does not reach the masses is not a significant statement at all, only an individual outcry that remains unheard and hence ineffective.
>
> *(Sandoval and Fuchs 2010, 143)*

The issue here (aside from the dismissal of lifestyle politics as not constituting *real* political activism) is that Sandoval and Fuchs are so concerned with critiquing these producers for the pleasures that they take in their projects, that they entirely ignore the importance of the social conditions and relations of production and reception, resulting in an ahistorical notion of converting 'the masses' to the cause. In some ways this is symptomatic of a broader trend within the field of alternative media studies – what Uzelman (2011) has termed a 'determinism of technique', whereby 'particular techniques are assumed to have effects (generally positive) independent of the social relations in which they are embedded or the purposes to which they are directed' (29).

Another issue with Sandoval and Fuchs' rather programmatic approach to defining and evaluating alternative media (as 'critical media') is their apparent faith in the ability of media projects to readily gain access to, and utilise, professional and institutional structures (e.g. of ownership, production, exhibition etc.) without impediment. Whilst they briefly acknowledge that resorting to commercial or institutional mechanisms of financing might involve compromise, they do not consider issues of artistic control, editorial freedom, censorship and regulation.[8]

Sandoval and Fuchs are, however, right to suggest that independence from commercial mechanisms is desirable but not always feasible, and to highlight the difficulties in funding and sustaining effective counter-institutions. This can be illustrated through reference to filmmaker Miranda July's *Joanie 4 Jackie* project (1995–2000). In 1995 July was an American film school dropout inspired by the Riot Grrrl DIY punk movement who felt that aspirant female filmmakers were not achieving anything like the exposure that musicians were. To redress this, July solicited videos from female filmmakers which she then compiled into video mixtapes or chain letters. This 'video as fanzine' or 'xerox television' approach built up a community of likeminded video makers through the development of an alternative circuit of distribution and exhibition ostensibly not reliant on extant structures and commercial operators. Yet cultural production never occurs in a vacuum, and even non-broadcast projects cannot be completely autonomous or impervious to the commercial sector. As Mary Celeste Kearney notes, Miranda July is one of the few participants in the punk feminist media community who has drawn attention to her connections to the capitalist sector of cultural production, and the deals and compromises that she has made in order to raise awareness of *Joanie 4 Jackie*.

> Though July originally reproduced the chain letters herself on used video cassettes purchased at second-hand stores, she now relies on commercial video duplication services to mass-produce copies of the tapes, which has sometimes resulted in attempted censorship of the films she distributes.
>
> *(Kearney 2006, 81)*

Fuchs (2010) also believes that alternative media organisations that are lacking in resources will inevitably be hamstrung by self-exploitation and precarious labour (178). But with the rise of casualisation and the so-called gig economy, the experience of precarity is a fact of life even for media professionals. There is also a plausible counter-argument that a degree of financial precarity obligates alternative media outfits to develop effective strategies for grassroots funding, for cross-subsidising work, and for attracting volunteers. In an interview with the present author, Tony Dowmunt (2013) reflected:

> I think there was a way in which Channel 4, although it was enormously beneficial in lots of ways, also actually acclimatised a lot of us to being funded properly. I always find it interesting to contrast it with the States, where organizations like Deep Dish and Paper Tiger TV have kept going for decades, but [have] never been properly funded, so they sort of develop that technique of being able to survive on zero funding by just using voluntary labour ... we lost the knack of that, because of being funded by the GLC [Greater London Council] and Channel 4, and all that.

Given the heavy emphasis that Sandoval and Fuchs place on the need for alternative media to reach broad audiences, it is also worth highlighting two things. First, the scarcity of research into the audiences and reception of alternative media output should be noted (see Mowbray 2015, 26), which surely makes it difficult to argue in any empirical fashion that participatory methods limit audience reach. Second, there are plenty of historical examples of alternative media projects which utilised participatory methods and which did reach wide audiences, such as *Framed Youth: Revenge of the Teenage Perverts* (Lesbian and Gay Youth Video Project, 1983) (see Franklin 2014; 2019). Another prime example from the same period is the *Miners' Campaign Tapes* (1984), a series of short videos made by collectives and workshops such as Platform Films, Chapter Film Workshop and Birmingham Film and Video Workshop, and widely distributed through the National Union of Mineworkers and the network of support groups developed to raise funds and generate support for the strike. It has been estimated that 4,000 copies of the *Miners' Campaign Tapes* circulated in Britain on VHS at the time (Kelliher 2017: 604), and this does not account for pirated copies that were subsequently made and shown domestically, e.g. in the South Wales Valleys.

Moreover, there are also potential issues and problems with a privileging of *reach* over other considerations such as participation, impact, quality or diversity of content. Garcia and van Oldenborgh (2011) have commented, for example, about the tendency of Amsterdam cable initiatives (like Park4DTV) to 'expand laterally, bringing more programmes to more people in more places, and in other media … rather than to focus more resources on the core activity and achieve growth in "depth" and quality', arguing 'that this could be seen as a failure to develop the main idea into something more durable' (100).

Historical or contemporary case studies that assess the relative success and impact of collaboratively made videos – more broadly, 'the counterhistory within documentary in which subjects have taken on forms of agency and editorial control in the process' (Rose 2014, 203) – are equally (and especially) useful for both media producers and media historians. For example, they give an opportunity to explore the question of whether the concept of DIY is problematic for documentary. A British community video experiment like the aforementioned *Framed Youth* bears the unmistakeable imprint of post-punk DIY aesthetics and energy, but DIY is typically associated with *individual* agency and creativity, which is less relevant to the kind of group or participatory production processes that were emblematic and constitutive of *Framed Youth* (see Franklin 2014; Franklin 2019). As Rose (2014) has observed, an awareness that a DIY approach to documentary making is not universally available 'prompts a questioning of the valorisation of the concept of DIY in the context of complex media production' (203). Rose has instead proposed the concept of DIWO (Do-It-With-Others) as better suited to capturing the dynamics and aims of collaboratively made projects.

However, in adopting DIWO we should not lose sight of the importance of the role of artist as facilitator (or author as producer), acting as 'the safe conduit through which the rabble can be admitted to the broadcast media space' (Iles and Berry Slater 2008, 38). The role of artist and facilitator is crucial even with work which is not broadcast. As Ted Purves has observed:

[A] key factor of the *Joanie 4 Jackie* project is the way in which its structure and potential for success hinge on the presence of July as creative director/author of the overall concept. Her involvement and frequent presence as one of the filmmakers on the compilation tapes acts as a leveraging agent for the enterprise, ensuring that her own success and notoriety within the film and art world are, in a very real sense, redistributed to the more unknown or aspiring artists whose works are given a new level of consideration via association.

(Purves 2005, 134)

As the *Joanie 4 Jackie* archive has recently been acquired by the Getty Research Institute, the individual works may now have a greater 'critical mass' in terms of cultural prestige. Researchers will now be better placed to assess the extent to which these feminist films *are* 'an expression of lifestyle politics', and the extent to which this expression may actually be used as a tool of dissent or radical activism within this context. This would serve to counter or complement Fuchs' polemical warning about the tendency for small-scale, local alternative projects to 'develop into psychological self-help initiatives without political relevance that are more bourgeois individualist self-expressions than political change projects' (Fuchs 2010, 189).

Conclusion

There are, of course, valid reasons to interrogate and debate (the relative importance of) participation – for example, the widespread use of the term in the era of Web 2.0 participatory media has tended to mean it has lost a precise, meaningful definition. Can participatory media be truly alternative given the 'participatory turn' in mainstream media (i.e. the rise of convergence culture and the 'prosumer'), whereby many of the characteristics once ascribed to alternative media now have become part of everyday mainstream media consumption (Andersson 2012, 760)?[9] In the context of the 'communicative abundance' of digital culture, it is even more crucial to differentiate between superficial and intensive modes of participation (Mowbray 2015, 24; Carpentier 2011, *inter alia*). But in this context can we really regard participatory production processes as ensuring marginality and inefficiency, obstructing the clear communication of 'critical content' to a wide audience? Granted, radical media need not necessarily be participatory, but is participatory media always marginal? And what about projects which have moved from the margins to the mainstream?

Whilst this chapter has highlighted the importance of working *within and against* the dominant institutions (in terms of media organisations and regulators), there is a need to counter the tendency towards what Hamilton (2008, 252) has called a 'mediacentric' understanding of social change, which refers to the idea that what is needed to transform social relations are simply better texts (i.e. counter-information). Such positions 'not only assume that the answers to political problems have already been found and thus need only to be transmitted, they also underemphasize the importance of more democratic forms of education, research and experimentation' (Uzelman 2011, 27, citing Hamilton). Whiteman's 'coalition model' of film production and distribution, for example, advocates taking a broad but detailed view of the political impact of film and video work, by considering factors such as the impact on activist groups and social movements that might contribute to or use the work. As Whiteman remarks, many political documentaries never achieved widespread distribution and do not enter mainstream public discourse, 'but still have an impact in certain subcultures, mobilizing activists working to create social change' (Whiteman 2002, n.p.). As we have seen with the example of the IFA's influence on UK broadcasting regulation (the IBA) and government policy, media producers, artists and filmmakers themselves have often played a campaigning role in influencing and shifting media policy. This chapter will hopefully have demonstrated that there is much we can learn from the tactics and interventions of artists who have pursued a radical revision of television in an increasingly commercial media ecology.

Notes

1 For reasons of limited scope, I will not devote attention to the question of whether 'alternative media' is a problematic term, especially as that has been discussed widely in recent years (see, for example, the work cited above).
2 John 'Hoppy' Hopkins, interviewed by Heinz Nigg and Andy Porter, June 2013. Transcribed by the present author. Video and transcript available at http://www.the-lcva.co. uk/interviews/58db835cf6aab40c5cfa3748 (accessed June 14, 2018).
3 IBA File 3201/1 Vol. 2, 'ITV 2 Consultation – Independent Producers'. IBA/ITA Archive, Bournemouth University.
4 Letter to Colin Shaw from Peter Wollen, October 3, 1979. From IBA File 3201/1 Vol. 2, 'ITV 2 Consultation – Independent Producers'. IBA/ITA Archive, Bournemouth University.
5 The proposal was made at the time in the aftermath of much discussion about the possibility of a fourth channel not regulated by the IBA but by an Open Broadcasting Authority (OBA), an independent 'Foundation' which would operate as a publishing outlet for programme supplied by independent producers, individual ITV companies, and the Open University.
6 'Time Out/Channel Four Group Meeting, Monday 17 Dec', sent from STSO to DT. In IBA File 3200, Vol. 16, 'Second ITV Service'. ITA/IBA Archive, held at Bournemouth University.
7 IFA National Executive Minutes January 10, 1981. Independent Film, Video & Photography Association Archive, Sheffield Hallam University.
8 We can note, for example, that one of the aforementioned promos made by Hopkins and TVX for the BBC, *Tell Me You Love Me*, garnered a complaint from Mary Whitehouse due to its use of White Panther Party (a far-left anti-racist collective) imagery, which resulted in the Corporation terminating their contract with TVX (Dickson 2012, 129).
9 Furthermore, what happens when the kind of subcultural shock tactics and tactical media disruption that were once hallmarks of the New Left are utilised by the Alt-Right (Nagle 2017)?

References

Andersson, Linus. 2012. 'There Is No Alternative: The Critical Potential of Alternative Media in the Face of Neoliberalism'. *TripleC: Communication, Capitalism & Critique. Open Access Journal for a Global Sustainable Information Society* 10 (2): 752–764. doi:10.31269/triplec.v10i2.357
Atton, Chris. 2010. 'Alternative Media and Journalism Practice'. In *Digital Media and Democracy: Tactics in Hard Times*, edited by Megan Boler, 213–227. Cambridge, MA: MIT Press.

Buchan, Suzanne. 2011. *The Quay Brothers: Into a Metaphysical Playroom.* Minneapolis: University of Minnesota Press.

Carpentier, Nico. 2011. *Media and Participation: A Site of Ideological-Democratic Struggle.* Bristol: Intellect Books.

Cook, Sarah, and Kathy Rae Huffman. 2012. 'Introduction'. In *TV Like Us*, edited by Hanna Harris, Suvi Kukkonen, Olli-Matti Nykänen, and Jenni Tuovinen, 3–5. The Finnish Institute in London: Reaktio.

Cubitt, Sean. 2012. 'On the Reinvention of Video in the 1980s'. In *Rewind: British Artists' Video in the 1970s & 1980s*, edited by Stephen Partridge and Sean Cubitt, 160–177. New Barnet: John Libbey Publishing.

Darlow, Michael. 2004. *Independents Struggle: The Programme Makers who took on the TV Establishment.* London: Quartet Books.

Dickson, Malcolm. 2012. 'Vide Verso: Video's Critical Corpus'. In *REWIND: British Artists' Video in the 1970s & 1980s*, edited by Sean Cubitt and Stephen Partridge. New Barnet: John Libbey Publishing.

Dowling, Hazel. n.d. '"Television Delivers People"'. *Review* 31. http://review31.co.uk/article/view/257/television-delivers-people (accessed June 6, 2018).

Dowmunt, Tony. 2013. Telephone interview with Ieuan Franklin, January 21, 2013.

Enzensberger, Hans Magnus. 1970. 'Constituents of a Theory of the Media'. *New Left Review*, 1 (64): 13–36. https://newleftreview.org/I/64/hans-magnus-enzensberger-constituents-of-a-theory-of-the-media

Franklin, I., 2019. 'Precursor of Pride: The Pleasures and Aesthetics of Framed Youth'. *Open Library of Humanities* 5(1): 34. doi:10.16995/olh.326

Franklin, Ieuan. 2014. 'Talking Liberties: Framed Youth, Community Video and Channel 4's Remit in Action'. In *Queer Youth and Media Cultures*, edited by Christopher Pullen. London: Palgrave Macmillan.

Fuchs, Christian. 2010. 'Alternative Media as Critical Media'. *European Journal of Social Theory* 13 (2): 173–192. doi:10.1177/1368431010362294

Garcia, David. 2018. Interview with Ieuan Franklin, Bournemouth, March 28, 2018.

Garcia, David, and Lennaart van Oldenborgh. 2011. 'Alternative Visions of Television'. In *The Alternative Media Handbook*, edited by Kate Coyer, Tony Dowmunt, and Alan Fountain. Abingdon: Routledge.

Hamilton, James Frederick. 2008. *Democratic Communications: Formations, Projects, Possibilities.* Lanham, MD: Lexington Books.

Iles, Anthony, and Josephine Berry Slater. 2008. 'Citizens Banned'. *Mute Magazine* 2 (9), July. www.metamute.org/editorial/articles/citizens-banned

Johnston, Claire. 1976. '*Notes on the Idea of an "Independent Cinema"*. British Artists' Film and Video Study Collection.

Kaizen, William. 2016. *Against Immediacy: Video Art and Media Populism.* New Hampshire: Dartmouth College Press.

Kearney, Mary Celeste. 2006. *Girls Make Media.* Abingdon: Taylor & Francis.

Kelliher, Diarmaid. 2017. 'Contested Spaces: London and the 1984–5 Miners' Strike'. *Twentieth Century British History* 28 (4): 595–617. doi:10.1093/tcbh/hwx029

Kluitenberg, Eric. 2011. *Legacies of Tactical Media.* Amsterdam: Institute of Network Cultures.

Landry, Charles, David Morley, Russell Southwood, and Patrick Wright. 1985. *What a Way to Run a Railroad: An Analysis of Radical Failure.* London: Comedia Publishing.

Marcuse, Herbert. 1972. *Counterrevolution and Revolt.* Boston: Beacon Press.

Mowbray, Mike. 2015. 'Alternative Logics? Parsing the Literature on Alternative Media'. In *The Routledge Companion to Alternative and Community Media*, edited by Chris Atton. Abingdon: Routledge Handbooks Online.

Nagle, Angela. 2017. *Kill All Normies: Online Culture Wars From 4Chan And Tumblr To Trump And The Alt-Right.* Alresford: John Hunt Publishing.

Perry, Colin. 2016. '*Into the Mainstream: Independent Film and Video Counterpublics and Television in Britain, 1974–1990*'. PhD diss., University of the Arts London.

Presence, Steve. 2019. 'Organising Counter-cultures: Challenges of Structure, Organisation and Sustainability in the Independent Filmmakers Association and the Radical Film Network'. *Screen* 60 (3): 428–448.

Purves, Ted. 2005. *What We Want Is Free: Generosity and Exchange in Recent Art.* Albany, NY: SUNY Press.

Rose, Mandy. 2014. 'Making Publics: Documentary as Do-It-with-Others Citizenship'. In *DIY Citizenship: Critical Making and Social Media*, edited by Matt Ratto and Megan Boler, 201–212. Cambridge, MA: MIT Press.

Sandoval, Marisol, and Christian Fuchs. 2010. 'Towards a Critical Theory of Alternative Media'. *Telematics and Informatics* 27 (2): 141–150. https://doi.org/10.1016/j.tele.2009.06.011

Serra, Richard, and Carlotta Faye Schoolman. 1973. '*Television Delivers People*'. Museum of Modern Art. https://youtube/LvZYwaQlJsg (accessed December 27, 2018).

Stubbs, Mike. 1999. 'Beyond Public Service Broadcasting'. In *New Media Culture in Europe*, 69–71. Amsterdam: De Balie.

Uzelman, Scott. 2011. 'Dangerous Practices: "Determinism of Technique" in Alternative Media and Their Literature'. *International Journal of Media & Cultural Politics* 7 (1): 21–35. doi:10.1386/mcp.7.1.21_1

Webb-Ingall, Ed. 2015. '*Community Video/Community TV*'. LUX. June 25, 2015. https://lux.org.uk/writing/community-video-community-tv-ed-webb-ingall

Whiteman, D. 2002. 'Impact of "The Uprising of '34'": A Coalition Model of Production and Distribution'. *Jump-Cut: A Review of Contemporary Media*, 45 (Fall). www.ejumpcut.org/archive/jc45.2002/whiteman/index.html#2 (accessed December 15, 2018).

Wilcox, Mark. 1984. *Deconstruct: Subverting Television (Catalogue).* Arts Council of Great Britain. British Artists' Film and Video Study Collection.

PART II

Interventions in practice and politics

6

SPACES OF THE POSSIBLE

Developing the Radical Film Network in Scotland

David Archibald

When Henry Kissinger suggests that 'History is the memory of states', he highlights how nation states are central to the construction of official historical narratives. Participants in radical film cultures, on the other hand, often seem more pre-occupied with the tasks of the present – organising the next crucial campaign, the next big festival, the next important screening – than documenting their own activities for posterity. In his work on early Lesbian and Gay Film Festivals in Canada, Ger Zielinski (2016) notes that film festival scholars often rely on ephemeral materials, on occasion little more than scraps of paper in the archive, as they attempt to construct the histories of marginal and oppositional political movements in film culture. This lack of attention to documenting activity is not simply a question for the past. As Kissinger's wry quote suggests, the past is fundamental in how the future is brought into being. As such, it is important for radical film activists, makers and scholars to look after it.

With this perspective in mind, this chapter reflects on some key events in the development of the Radical Film Network (RFN) in Scotland between 2015 and 2019.[1] The particular focus of the chapter is on the 2016 Radical Film Network Festival and Unconference, which took place in Glasgow. I was a participant in these events and this chapter provides a report of these activities which draws on my own experience; however, in keeping with the collective ethos of the RFN, the chapter draws heavily on the perspective offered up in interviews with fifteen of the event's key participants. These are as follows: film programmers Laura Ager and Maria Suarez; Film Studies PhD students Chelsea Birks and Kathi Kamleitner; trade union activist Tommy Breslin; Scottish Queer International Film Festival activist Marc David; artist Ken Davidson; filmmaker and programmer Fran Higson; Glasgow Short Film Festival Artistic Director Matt Lloyd, filmmakers Basharat Khan and Carla Novi, film worker Angela Ross; Film Studies scholar Maria Vélez-Serna, and film producer and programmer Richard Warden.[2] As such, the chapter draws on active participation in the research activity, interviews with key individuals, and autoethnography – a methodology best summarised and widely quoted as 'an approach to research and writing that seeks to describe and systematically analyze (*graphy*) personal experience (*auto*) in order to understand cultural experience (*ethno*)' (Ellis, Adams and Bochner, 2010).

The inaugural Radical Film Network (RFN) conference took place at the University of Birmingham in February 2015. I was unable to attend the event, but prior to the conference I had a number of telephone conversations with RFN founder, Steve Presence, during which I offered to host the follow-up conference at the University of Glasgow. There were four main reasons why I thought Glasgow was a particularly suitable host location. First, Glasgow has a strong tradition of radical political and cultural activity; second, in recent years, the city has developed a vibrant grassroots film culture, spanning various film festivals and activities; third, in the wake of the 2014 Scottish Independence Referendum, I had detected a significant increase in grassroots political activity, often manifesting itself in radical cultural activity, and, finally, Film and Television Studies at the University of Glasgow has a well-established history and, as a member of staff there, I knew I would be able to draw on its reputation and its not inconsiderable resources. As I saw it, hosting the RFN conference at Glasgow represented an opportunity to contribute to the development of a nascent organisation, to contribute to the development of radical film cultures in the city, and to intervene in positioning radical cultural activity as a factor in how the city of Glasgow understands itself.[3]

In the immediate aftermath of the Birmingham conference, I and a number of the Glasgow-based attendees had considerable informal discussion about whether the established academic format which had been utilised there – 20-minute papers and keynote addresses delivered in an academic register – was the best form for attempting to build a network of academics, filmmakers and activists. Richard Warden recalls: 'When I was at Birmingham it was a bit dry, a bit academic. What was clearly lacking – and I wasn't the only person who thought this – was screening events.' Fran Higson, commenting on her experience of the conference, echoes this perspective: 'You had people delivering papers one after the other, and it was quite dense. So we thought, "fuck that." We wanted to have films, more open discussions and be a bit more radical really.' Eager to develop a more level playing field for all RFN participants, during a series of monthly organising meetings at the University of Glasgow between April 2015 and April 2016, we explored options to break with the traditional conventions of the academic conference. After extensive discussion, we decided to adopt two measures. First, we would host an 'Unconference', an attempt to move to a less hierarchical organisational form. Second, we would also host a small parallel film festival. The desire was that both events would create opportunities for the event participants to break out of their normal space and create a greater level of dialogue for all involved. We hoped to deterritorialise the conventional learning space of the University and develop what we might term 'spaces of the possible'; that is, spaces in the city which would be transformed, even if only temporally, into radical spaces for the purposes of screening films, and, crucially, which would foster new dialogues with disparate groups and communities with a view to opening up new ways of thinking and being. This was also an attempt to move beyond critique into praxis; to bring new worlds, however small or temporary, into being through our own actions. Sonia Tascón (2017) suggests that 'the activist festival as a space of disruption and irruption, enhance proximity between spectator and film subject, mostly by enabling complexity to emerge, a necessary condition of fostering solidarity and a stronger commitment to social change' (23). We were undoubtedly attempting to foster a sense of solidarity, although not simply between spectator and subject; we were also seeking to build solidarity between the various constituent parts of the festival. The upshot, then, was the 2016 Radical Film Network Festival and Unconference, which took place in Glasgow over the 2016 May Day bank holiday weekend.[4] Around 100 participants from across Scotland, the UK and beyond attended the Unconference and there were 1,825 admissions at the festival. The latter included 99 film screenings (including shorts) at 46 separate events in 27 venues across the city.[5]

The festival

Although the festival became quite a major event, our initial thinking had been to organise a small festival involving perhaps up to ten events. Very quickly, however, attendance at the monthly organising meetings mushroomed to twenty to thirty people at every meeting with new attendees arriving continually, bringing new ideas and fresh proposals. Rather than viewing the festival as a centrally pro-grammed event, we took the view that the organising committee was not a pro-gramming body. Although the central body took strategic decisions in terms of scheduling, fundraising, marketing and the organisation of some central events, the festival screenings and events were organised by its constituent parts.[6] In *The Origins of Collective Decision Making* (2016), Andy Blunden suggests that the mode of decision-making utilised by groups in the present is connected to the type of world that they want to bring into being. We utilised a consensus model of decision-making, or at least we had that as an ideal. In practice, many day-to-day decisions were made by those appointed to coordinating positions; Fran Higson as Festival Coordinator, Maria Vélez-Serna as Unconference Coordinator and myself as the event's Overall Coordinator. The aim, however, was to act as a communal body rather than as an organisation led by the Artistic Director-type figure so common on the film festival circuit. As Marc David puts it, 'it seemed like the RFN and festival was very much about provocation and about trying to do things in a very different fashion from festivals of its kind'. This openness appealed to many of the participants. For instance, Basharat Khan recalls that 'non-curatorship of it was a big part, that the festival was allowing people to put together events, films that they were passionate about and didn't need to control that. So, I thought that was quite a liberating thing'. As the Unconference attempted to destabilise academic hier-archies, the festival followed suit in developing an approach to programming, which developed from the grassroots as opposed to the top-down approach so prevalent in cultural activity. As Kenneth Davidson reflects, 'I think a lot of culture tends to be sprung on people and so the extent of involvement and the diversity of events was very strong'.

The de-centred programming strategy led to a festival comprising events in many disparate parts of the city, only one of which took place in a conventional cinema. Events ranged from a Documentary Human Rights Film Festival bicycle ride along the River Clyde, bookended with talks on the history of socialist cycling clubs in Scotland, and politics, bikes and activism; a series of screenings under the banner of Radical Home Cinemas, Feminist Filmmaking, Feminist Histories at Glasgow Women's Library which explored women's documentary and archiving practices, and a Love Music Hate Racism concert hosted at the University of Glasgow's Queen Margaret Union. Being in receipt of funding from state bodies Creative Scotland and Film Hub Scotland ensured that all events bar the traditional cinema screening were free, thereby liberating the festival from the market basis of commercial cinema, enabling the event to function to some degree as a temporary crack in the system, à la John Holloway's notion outlined in *Crack Capitalism* (2010).

The politics of the festival was also reflected in its spaces of activity. First, the hosting of the Unconference at the University of Glasgow positioned the university sector as an important actor in developing radical film cultures. Dina Iordanova (2012, 14–15) has noted that public intellectuals and academics have played a role in activist film festivals and a number of the academics involved were keen to stress the ongoing importance of academia in supporting and promoting radical film culture. Second, the centrality of the Scottish Trades Union Congress headquarters as a hub venue positioned the labour movement as an important contributor and foregrounded class politics as a central concern. To draw on the work of Oscar Negt and Alexander Kluge, in *Public Sphere and Experience: Analysis of the Bourgeois and Proletarian Public Sphere* (Negt and Kluge 2016), a proletarian public sphere or a proletarian cultural sphere was created as we transformed the STUC headquarters into a pop-up cinema and a social space for social and cultural activities. In this space we screened activist films about blacklisting, a documentary about a Scottish anarchist who became the English-language voice of anarchist radio during the Spanish Civil War, *An Anarchist's Story: The Life of Ethel MacDonald* (BBC Scotland, 2006), a series of trades union education films, a retrospective on the short films of Jean Gabriel Périot, and a campaigning film by trade union campaigners Better Than Zero about zero-hours contracts that was shot and edited earlier that day. The venue was also the site for the launch of an edition of *The Drouth: Scotland's Literary Quarterly* dedicated to the theme 'Radical', and for Fail Better, an experimental cabaret evening hosted over two nights with a line-up which included performance poets, bands and live cinema events, indicating that pleasure and play was an important part of our practice. Tommy Breslin notes, 'it was uplifting to see so many young people with real social understandings and socio-political understandings who were perhaps not engaged with the more traditional organisers you see through the different trade unions and activism we're involved in'. Breslin also notes that the specificities of space were important in attracting new audiences:

[W]e were all quite taken aback by the diversity of the audience. For example, there were some young people from the Basque country and they would see the International Brigades memorial that's on the wall, so there was a sense of being part of the building as well, which is kind of a strange thing to really contextualise, but people felt the venue was really important because it was absolutely part and parcel of the aims and objectives and ideas that were circulating around the table for the RFN.

Khan, who organised a series of screenings in a local non-conventional space also notes the importance of space in terms of programming: 'you've got to be much more localised at times to engage people into cinema and film and stories, by utilising their neighbourhoods, their areas, their spaces'. Rather than the ideas being consigned to discussions in the Unconference, Richard Warden led a series of events organised by the Scottish Mental Health Arts Festival at their venue, Flourish House. He comments,

I was really proud of having offered a platform for people who were coming to the Unconference – that it wasn't all going to be academic papers to present. So there were filmmakers there, heck, filmmakers are academics, some are not, but hey here's a space that you can put your film on, but not all the work that was put on was from academics and unconference attendees, it was an open call for people who'd heard about the RFN so it did feel quite democratic and a nice mix of material and people.

What is the 'radical' in the RFN has been the focus of ongoing and intense discussion and debate since the formation of the organisation. Although this was an ongoing topic for discussion, we did not to attempt to arrive at a steadfast definition. Although we discussed utilising discourses around safe space to deal with any racist or far-right 'radicalism' that might have attempted to intervene, we decided that it was not up to a central group to determine what was, or was not, radical. As Matt Lloyd recalls, 'in the meetings, no one was forcing a definition of what was radical on any of us – if you identified as radical, you were radical. That seemed to be the approach'. As Lloyd adds, 'I think that it was quite a brave project to take on, to kind of actively resist any kind of top-down control or coordination as such, and just to let all these different groups pick their own definition of radical'. Indeed, the concept of 'radical' was continually developing through the development of the event itself. As community film worker Angela Ross observes: 'We'd never really considered what we're doing as being radical as such, but being part of the festival makes you redefine the word as well; it's about doing things differently.' Certainly a key aspect of the event's radicality lay simply in its open structure. Reflecting back, Warden notes:

One thing that really struck me was that decentralisation can work – coming from a film producer background I can be – control freak sounds negative [laughs], but someone who likes things to be organised and likes to know what's going on and what everyone's doing, and there did seem to be just the right level for that event of gathering to keep each other informed but at the same time letting people get on with it and letting people get on with gathering the audiences that they knew best so that was a real lesson for me.

The radicality also lay in the juxtaposition of its component parts, with blacklisted building workers, queer performance poets, community filmmakers working on local concerns encountering films dealing with the complexities of struggles, contemporary and historical, domestic and international, from Partick to Palestine and Bridgeton to the Basque Country. This cinematic representation of a confluence of struggles sought to seek alliances and build solidarity amongst what might seem to be disparate components.

The Unconference[7]

A departure from mainstream academic convention, the Unconference sought to actively engage with a non-academic audience beyond traditional academic terrain. In doing so, it also sought to enrich the experience of the academics in attendance through discussion and debate with active participants in radical film culture. Maria Vélez-Serna, who proposed the idea, recalls that this represented an opportunity to experiment with new organisational forms, or, as she puts it, 'an opportunity to maybe try something out'. The website established for the Unconference highlights the definition offered by Aidan Budd et al. (2015):

> [A]n unconference is a participant-oriented meeting where the attendees decide on the agenda, discussion topics, workshops, and, often, even the time and venues. The informal and flexible program allows participants to suggest topics of their own interest and choose sessions accordingly. The format provides an excellent opportunity for researchers from diverse disciplines to work collaboratively on topics of common interest. The overarching goal for most unconferences is to prioritize conversation over presentation. In other words, the content for a session does not come from a select number of individuals at the front of the room, but is generated by all the attendees within the room, and, as such, every participant has an important role.

With this as a guide, over two days, academics, filmmakers and film activists assembled for a series of discussions. The Unconference dispensed with keynote addresses, formal 20-minute papers and a set agenda. Participants had been given the chance to submit proposals for short talks – but the weekend's content was largely shaped by plenary sessions which took place each morning and which drew up the agenda for the day. The debate and discussion mostly consisted of smaller sessions in which attendees discussed what had been selected for discussion in the plenary sessions. An Unconference requires much more commitment from academics than simply turning up at an event for their own individual presentation; as such it can encourage more developed dialogue than the conventional conference format. The response of participants was overwhelmingly positive; Laura Ager reflects that: 'It felt like the [Un]conference in Glasgow was really trying to address that [the perceived imbalance between academic and non-academic participants] in quite a practical way. I hadn't encountered anything quite like that before – it definitely worked.' Maria Suarez indicates something of how the event worked in practice when she recalls:

> [I]t allows some people who may not be that vocal and who may not feel confident speaking in front of everyone, [to] maybe have their say and maybe even think of things they may not think before. The Unconference approach really changed my way of seeing things.

Kathi Kamleitner notes that the conference also broke down the hierarchies amongst different layers of academics. She says:

> Academic conferences are quite hierarchical and structured, so when you're a PhD student you might not feel like you've the right level of knowledge or degree yet to participate as equal to a professor of whatever. It can feel like quite an anxious place, like you're just not supposed to participate in the same capacity. Whereas at the Unconference everyone's contribution was equally valuable and it was encouraged for people to speak who weren't necessarily the loudest voices in the room.

The general feeling amongst the attendees and the interviewees was that the Unconference was successful in breaking down the barriers between academics and film activists. Carla Novi, for instance, presented a talk on directing *Rana Plaza* (2014) about the Bangladeshi factory workers killed when their workplace collapsed, and *Desaparecidos* (2015) which deals with the 43 'disappeared' students from Guerrero, Mexico, reflecting on working on difficult and traumatic subject matter. She notes:

> it's so hard when you're working with these subjects, it's very difficult and can be overwhelming and you kind of lose the perspective of things sometimes. The problems are so massive today that they're totally overwhelming. But when you go to an event like this and see so many people coming together and you just try to show that we all care and that we can all make a difference, make a change, it makes a big difference for everything – for my practice, especially on the hard days when you feel like it's not possible, but it is, you come together and it's possible to make a bigger impact.

As Novi's words illustrate, the Unconference created a space in which participants in radical film culture felt able to discuss their practice and gain a sense of solidarity in the process, hopefully enriching the experience across the activist/filmmaker/academic divide.

The Unconference represented an attempt to move in a non-hierarchical direction, although a number of interviewees noted that in practice the event was not free of hierarchies. This was something that the organisers were conscious of in advance. Vélez-Serna recalls: 'there's nothing that's completely non-hierarchical but it's kind of the ethos of it rather than the actual implementation, because it's only non-hierarchical to an extent and that's a work in progress'. It is also fair to say that the interviewees did not have a uniform opinion of the event. For instance, Chelsea Birks comments favourably about the event and notes that 'the Unconference taught me a great deal of flexibility', but adds 'I still prefer the old-fashioned way of planning/ attending an academic conference.' There were also other factors that arose in discussions over the weekend which reflect the downside of this type of event. For example, it can be more difficult for academics to secure funding for an event that might be viewed as less likely to lead to publication. Perhaps the event would have been larger if it had followed a conventional (and less radical) format. On balance, however, the organisers and interviewees regarded the experiment as a significant success, with the notion of a completely hierarchy-free event perhaps held on to as an ideal rather a practical possibility.

'68 and its afterlives

In organising these activities we took the view that we were developing a specific event, keen to hand the baton onto the organisers of the 2017 RFN conference and uncertain as to how, if at all, the RFN in Scotland would be organised. Rather than fetishise the continuity of one organisation, we were alive to the possibility that the event might well be a one off and that its effectiveness would lie in the connections that were established between the different groups regardless of what organisational framework these continued under. That said, RFN Scotland was involved heavily in the 2018 event that celebrated the fiftieth anniversary of 1968. At the 2016 Unconference, Ager had raised the prospect of organising a widespread festival celebrating the anniversary year and, as she puts it, 'used it as a chance to test the plan'. This event proceeded to be rolled out across the UK, and in Scotland we attempted to build on the links established in 2016 and programmed two weekends of activities, mostly at Glasgow's Centre for Contemporary Arts and the STUC headquarters but with other events across the country. In total, we utilised nine screening locations and had twenty-seven separate screening events with forty-two films screened and a total of 1,321 admissions.[8] This activity was overseen by a Core Committee drawn from various aspects of radical film culture: Brian Beadie (journalist), Tommy Breslin, Amparo Fortuny, Ian Gasse (trade unionist), Fran Higson, Eirene Houston (Glasgow Havana Film Festival), Richard Warden and myself. We were unsuccessful in our funding bid to Creative Scotland and changes at Film Hub Scotland meant that we could not access funds from that source. But we did receive a small amount of funding from Film Hub Midlands's 'Uprising! Spirit of '68' programme, which was allocating money on behalf of the BFI Audience Network.[9] In addition, we received in-kind support from the STUC and additional support was provided from branches of various unions including the National Union of Journalists, Communication Workers Union, GMB and the Broadcasting, Entertainment, Communications and Theatre Union, further developing the links with trades unions.[10] The connection between radical film cultures and the conditions facing festival workers was addressed directly in 'Labour of Love – Festivals Speak Out on Working Conditions', an event organised by Films Studies PhD student, Alexandra Colta, and sponsored by the STUC. The event brought together trades union activists with festival workers in a fruitful exchange that explored the need to champion the working conditions of festival workers, whilst cognisant of the precarious nature of the organisations themselves. Of course, the RFN in Scotland has been a prime example of an activist-led festival, which has juggled the practicalities, and ethics, of organising activities on less than a shoe-string budget and addressed the line between what might be classified as low- or un-paid labour and what might be classified as activism. A small fee had been paid to several of the non-academic core festival organisers for the 2016 event but with the lack of funding for the 2018 event this was severely reduced and highlighted the sustainability, or lack thereof, of the model, an ongoing problem for radical film culture participants (Presence 2017).

At the time of writing (July 2019), the RFN in Scotland has no planned public activities although plans are in place to organise a report back from the 2019 conference with a view to appraise how we might take things forward. The connections established in 2016, however, continue to reverberate. As Tommy Breslin recalls:

> When we got to May Day last year [2017] through contacts at the RFN we were able to speak to Paul Laverty and he actually came along and was our key speaker at Glasgow's May Day rally. I don't think that would have happened if it hadn't been for the engagement with RFN. Interestingly, we also had Ken Loach speaking at our STUC congress last year. These things can be a wee bit coincidental, but I think it's part of a wider picture.

In reflecting on these events, I do not offer the Glasgow model as one that should necessarily be emulated elsewhere. As subsequent RFN conferences in New York City and Tolpuddle (2017), Dublin (2018) and Nottingham (2019) have demonstrated, there are particularities of politics and of place that have ensured a rich diversity of experience on a variety of scales at the various events. I would, nevertheless, contend that the spirit driving the strategies that were put in place in Glasgow, to marry the efforts of all participants in radical film culture, with all their strengths and weaknesses, and striving to ensure that it was a space in which all felt comfortable contributing, are worth examining for those interested in developing radical film cultures both in and beyond the academy.

Notes

1 Information about RFN Scotland is available at https://rfnscotland.com (accessed April 15, 2019).
2 Interviews were conducted by Rebecca Bartlett.
3 The 2016 event received some significant press coverage, from tabloids, broadsheets and online blogs; see for instance, 'Radical Film Festival Glasgow 2016: Life beyond the multiplex' in *Daily Record*, March 22, 2016: https://www.dailyrecord.co.uk/whats-on/film-news/radical-film-festival-glasgow-2016-7605928; 'Radical Film Festival to provide alternative to the mainstream'. *The Herald*, January 18, 2016: https://www.heraldscotland.com/news/14210791.radical-film-festival-in-glasgow-to-provide-alternative-to-mainstream/; 'Activists unite for city's Radical Film Network Festival', *The National*, April 28, 2016: https://www.

thenational.scot/news/14865011.activists-unite-for-citys-radical-film-network-festival/ (accessed 15 April 15, 2019).

4 A short film, *Glasgow: RFN 16* (McIlwraith/McGoff, 2016), provides a valuable audio-visual record of the event. The film is published in an edition of *Screenworks* devoted to radical film. Available at: http://screenworks.org.uk/arhive/volume-7-3/glasgow-rfn-16 (accessed May 18, 2018)

5 Attendance figures from reports to Creative Scotland and Film Hub Scotland.

6 The event received funding from Creative Scotland (£10,000) and Film Hub Scotland (£5,000) and several smaller donations from trades union branches, mostly to support the Love Music Hate Racism concert at the University of Glasgow's Queen Margaret Union. The event also received significant in-kind support from the STUC, the University of Glasgow and the Queen Margaret Union.

7 Further information about the Unconference is available at http://rfnglasgow.info (accessed April 13, 2019).

8 Attendance figures from report to Film Hub Midlands.

9 See https://filmhubmidlands.org/major-programmes/uprising-spirit-of-68/ for more information (accessed July 11, 2019).

10 The 2018 festival was centred in Glasgow; however, a small number of events were organised in other parts of Scotland.

Acknowledgement

This chapter is dedicated to the memory of the performance maker, artist and Glasgow RFN stalwart, Kenneth Davidson, who died in November 2018.

References

Archibald, D. (Ed.) 2016. 'Radical' *The Drouth: Scotland's Literary Quarterly* 55.

Blunden, A. 2016. *The Origins of Collective Decision Making*. Leiden: Brill.

Budd, A., Dinkel, H., Corpas, M., Fuller, J.C., Rubinat, L., Devos, D. P.*et al*.2015. 'Ten Simple Rules for Organizing an Unconference'. *PLoS Comput Biol* 11 (1): e1003905. http://journals.plos.org/ploscompbiol/article?id=10.1371/journal.pcbi.1003905 (accessed April 15, 2019).

Ellis, C., Adams, T. E. and Bochner, A. P. 2010. 'Autoethnography: An Overview'. *Forum Qualitative Sozialforschung/Forum: Qualitative Social Research*, 12 (1). Available online: www.qualitative-research.net/index.php/fqs/article/view/1589/3095

Holloway, J. 2010. *Crack Capitalism*. London: Pluto Press.

Iordinova, D. 2012. 'Film Festivals and Dissent: Can Film Change the World?'. In D. Iordanova, and L. Torchin (Eds.), *Film Festivals and Activism* (Film Festival Yearbook; Vol. 2). St. Andrews: St. Andrews Film Studies.

Negt, O. and Kluge, A. 2016. *Public Sphere and Experience: Analysis of the Bourgeois and Proletarian Public Sphere*. London and New York: Verso.

Presence. S. 2017. 'One Screening Away From Disaster: Precarity and Commitment in the Radical Film Network's Community Exhibition Sector'. In C. Chapain, R. Comunian and S. Malik (Eds.), *Community Filmmaking: Diversity, Practices and Places*, 210–226. New York: Routledge.

Tascón. S. 2017. 'Watching Others' Troubles: Revisiting "The Film Act" and Spectatorship in Activist Film Festivals'. In S. Tascón and T. Wils (Eds.), *Activist Film Festivals: Towards a Political Subject*. Bristol: Intellect.

Zielinski, G. 2016. 'On Studying Film Festival Ephemera: The Case of Queer Film Festivals and Archives of Feelings'. In Marijke de Valck, Brendan Kredell, and Skadi Loist (Eds.), *Film Festivals: History, Theory, Method, Practice*, 138–158. London, New York: Routledge.

7

CIUTAT MORTA/DEAD CITY

Agency, ICTs and critical urban documentary in the Spanish context

Ana Rodríguez Granell

In recent years, urban issues have been shaping many of the counter-discourses in audio-visual production linked to social movements, in the knowledge that these struggles, situated in everyday life, are establishing a dialogue with a global model of capitalist restructuring and with neoliberal market logics. Considering the Catalan and Barcelona context (Balibrea 2001) and, on a larger scale, some of the sequence of events in the Spanish history, the links between the establishment of production models and urban transformations provide a landscape of drastic changes in which social action and the use of media have often played a significant role. It is possible to trace a long history of entrenched social and cultural militancies within these urban boundaries, in which agents are today offering radical forms of democratic participation that are reshaping the political agenda and institutions (Pickvance 2003). This chapter aims to highlight the relationship between these economic, cultural, urban and ICT (Information and Communication Technology) processes in order to determine the nature of the tensions they generate and the political agency achieved by some organisational models at the margins of cultural industry.

In doing so, we will analyse the case of the documentary *Ciutat Morta* (Dead City) (Xavier Artigas and Xapo Ortega 2015) produced by the audio-visual platform Metromuster. This documentary recounts the dismantling of the 4-F case: the events that took place in Barcelona on February 4, 2006, when an officer of the city's Guardia Urbana police force was seriously injured after receiving a blow to the head during the eviction of squatters from a theatre. Several people were arrested and tortured, and four received prison sentences despite repeatedly proclaiming their innocence. One of them, Patricia Heras, who was not even at the scene of the crime, committed suicide on April 26, 2011, while on leave from prison. *Ciutat Morta* is presented as a paradigmatic case since it includes various aspects that we will analyse here: the reshaping of the alternative media's political agenda by global economic dynamics and the model of the city brand, and the practice and transformational capacity of the militant documentary in the digital age.

Some minimal consideration must be given to the long history which aids in the understanding of the current context of the emergence of film practices. As a result, I will establish a history of relations between the production model, urban transformations and militant cinema in Spain, and subsequently highlight the current framework using Barcelona as a paradigm of the city brand. On the one hand, this context engages in a dialogue with a specific historical legacy and, on the other, it provides an understanding of the meanings within current politicised cultural practice.

This context will help us to think if militant film creators should no longer be considered as prototypical outsiders working on activist culture. As practices embedded in the cultural sphere, the flows of the digital economy run through militant audio-visual practices and they are even central to it in their flexible working conditions, involving voluntary and unstable work (Terranova 2000), while we argue that activism has also been prone to generating transforming economies. What are cultural labour's new political concerns today, and what organisational models do these activist agents offer? What relations are created with established cultural institutions? What level of self-reflection do alternative audio-visual production platforms engage in, and how are these practices related to the rise of protests that we have seen since May 2011? These are some of the questions that I will answer, or at least outline in the context of a country that is heavily committed to free culture, like Spain. In the Catalan context, it is significant to note that since the so-called creative documentary in the early twenty-first century, two of its leading lights, José Luis Guerín and Joaquim Jordà, with *En construcción* (*Work in Progress*, 2002) and *De nens* (2003), portrayed the processes of transformation in Barcelona that were rendered invisible by the institutional promotional narratives found in blockbusters such as *Todo sobre mi madre* (*All About My Mother*, Pedro Almodóvar 1999). The promotional strategies culminated in the famous government-funded example of cinematic branding, *Vicky Cristina Barcelona* (Woody Allen 2008). In fact, the links between film and the city have always been very close. As an agent involved in the construction of imaginaries that affirm identities, Balibrea (2005) pointed out how cinema was also involved in the inception of the Barcelona brand.

The structural consequences of an industrial model: the militant documentary against Spanish capitalism

The link between audio-visual production and social movements has a long history in the Spanish context, and has been an active response to urban problems arising from the implementation of specific economic models. There have been a number of filmmakers and collectives working in the country's largest cities since the early 1960s. They have taken advantage of technological developments and legal loopholes to use film as a political tool, in collaboration with the struggles of self-organised neighbourhood movements, in factories' worker representation committees or, on a broader basis, in the waves of anti-Franco dissent. Much of the output of the militant Spanish cinema that emerged in the second half of the

Franco dictatorship was organised around problems arising from the industrial boom that affected both the morphology of the working class and the urban morphology of the country's major cities. Consequently, the contemporary cases mentioned here are modern responses to the dismantling of the industrialist model, and the implementation of economic strategies rooted in post-Fordism.

The origins of the Spanish economic model, which collapsed after the burst of the housing bubble in 2008, are rooted in the modernisation programmes undertaken by the technocrats of the Franco dictatorship during the late 1950s (Stabilisation Plans and Development Plans), when the regime finally decided to embrace the development of mass tourism, due to the consequent inflow of foreign exchange that would nourish the country's infrastructure. The transformation brought about by the development of tourism led to an economy based on the tertiary sector and the promotion of ownership of land, as well as the proliferation of restaurant businesses and industries related to the hospitality sector, which in turn stimulated the other engine of the Spanish economy: construction. As well as the emergence of tourism, the period between 1960 and 1970 saw constant waves of migration from the countryside to the cities. The massive growth of cities where the industrial areas were concentrated – such as Madrid, Barcelona and Bilbao – led to an aggressive development of the real estate industry, which was in turn dependent on the financial resources of the banking oligopoly. The shortcomings of the Franco regime's management of urban and housing policies and the lack of metropolitan plans led to a rapid sprawl in the form of slums or shanty towns on the outskirts of cities, forcing their inhabitants to organise themselves with no governmental support in order to resolve the problems which they suffered from. Networks of relationships such as Catholic workers' organisations, neighbourhood associations, social workers, regional associations, etc., were used to recreate a forum for social and political activism (Domènech 2003).

The conquest of the public space also took the form of the organisation of film-viewing sessions in parish churches and cultural associations, in discussions at neighbourhood associations, and in debates on cinema and urban planning convened by militant groups of architects and engineers as such as Equipo Urbano (Borja 2003). As a result, the film projects presented a challenge to the regime's mechanisms of censorship and its syndicated structures. Thanks to the sale of Super 8 film – not subject to censorship – and of lightweight cameras, these networks were given increased mobility and capacity for action when producing and disseminating counter-hegemonic audio-visual content. We can mention here documentary films such as Llorenç Soler's films *52 domingos* (1966) and *Será tu tierra* (1966), and *Largo viaje hacia la ira* (1969); those by the Cine de Clase collective (Helena Lumbreras and Mariano Lisa), and *La ciudad es nuestra* (1975) by Tino Calabuig.

After what had been the most extensive mobilisation in the twentieth century, in the early years of democracy, taking in the first right wing UCD government and the first Socialist government (1982–1996), the legacy of the Spanish capitalist model continued, based on agreements between the reformers of the Franco regime and the political left (López and Rodríguez 2010). This Transition on the basis of the negotiations at the top – the Moncloa Pacts of 1977 – together with Spain's deindustrialisation, defused the social conflict, and with it the opportunities for participatory democracy that had been created in factories and neighbourhoods during the dictatorship (López and Rodríguez 2010). The Spanish economic model, which remained unchanged and was ultimately based on a strategy of accumulation centred on income from finances and real estate, together with the development of cognitive capitalism, had its counterpart in the urban development discussed below.

Towards the city-brand model: urban problems of the Barcelona brand and the new political economy of culture

Turning now to the specific case of post-industrial cities, such as the contemporary Barcelona, we should focus on how, during the 1990s, urban policies began to adopt new measures and strategies for urban revitalisation and regeneration, based on the creation of cultural and educational facilities. This was due to the introduction of new management models, and increasing competitive pressure to position post-industrialised cities on the international map. This leads us to paradigmatic examples such as post-Olympic Barcelona (1992–1999), in which the transformations in the city created a style of planning and management policies that came to be known as the Barcelona Model (Marshall 2000, 299–319). These dynamics involve economic growth based heavily on the real estate business and on the creative economy. Although culture is not a sector with a high percentage of workers or a very large direct impact on the city's economy, the creative economy generates large positive externalities (Harvey 2005) from which sectors such as real estate and tourism can benefit.

And so we come to a phase in 1999–2007 characterised by a discourse based on the promotion of the creative economy and urban planning policies defined by this concept of a brand. In a decentralised state, local government bodies such as the City Council play a role in facilitating the various interests of private investors, in which market-driven development priorities determine decision-making processes (Borja 2010). Groups of cultural workers, who are now employed by cultural management companies, temporary employment agencies or large multi-service groups, have been affected by the loss of public control over issues relating to management and recruitment, so that minimum working conditions are not always guaranteed, and sometimes irregular or illegal situations arise.

Numerous critical texts analyse how cultural workers, artists, hackers, designers and those linked to the creative and knowledge industry, and the implementation of labour relations based on the regulation, end up creating vulnerability and *instability* (Lazzarato 1996; Terranova 2000; Lorey 2008).

The relationship between urbanism and culture in the new operating framework of public policy and private intervention thus places us before a state of elements that constitute modern ways of living and working that go far beyond those of Florida's (2002) *creative class*, forming a new majority social class marked by vulnerability, the *precariat*. This is a heterogeneous group made of growing immigration, overqualified or under qualified workers, single mothers, and young people from deprived areas and the long-term unemployed (Standing 2011).

The story of a *Dead City*: the political agency of culture in the digital age

In addition to the deterioration in living conditions of the *precariat* and even of the middle class after the crisis of 2008, all these processes of public dispossession led to the areas of action and the political challenges that make up the agenda of the broad range of protests of the last twenty years, which eventually converged in the 15-M movement. In the Catalan context, the conflict arising from the Forum of Cultures 2004[1] can be considered a turning point, and an example of one of the milestones in the renewed visibility and reorganisation of the critical movements. A well-known militant and low-cost mockumentary such as *El taxista ful* (Jo Sol 2005) (Rodríguez Granell 2015) emerged from the atmosphere that was created after the anti-Forum mobilisations.

Metromuster, the production company of *Ciutat Morta*, was established precisely as a critical response to the modern framework of urban policies and the model of local creative industries. In 2009, the director and the staff involved decided to establish themselves as a limited company, with the consequent entry in the Catalan Register of Companies, in order to produce *No Res. Vida y mort d'un espai en tres actes* (Xavier Artigas 2012), a documentary financed collectively and collaboratively that portrayed the eviction and demolition of one of the last workers' colonies in Barcelona to be replaced by housing blocks.[2]

What emerged from this experience was a number of achievements at the level of political agency: the production of a documentary with a high aesthetic level that would be broadcast beyond militant circles, moving beyond the idea of low cost, which adopted crowdsourcing and crowdfunding formulas and used social networks, while respecting two key ethical points: the use of free licences and the rejection of forms of precarious employment (voluntary work). *No Res* received the National Award for the Best Feature Film at the 9th edition of the well-known Documenta festival in Madrid in 2012, enabling a freely licensed film to compete for the first time. In its relationships with public institutions, Metromuster succeeded in gaining TV3's participation with a co-production contract and a première respecting the Creative Commons licence.

After the emergence of the 15-M movement in 2011, the protests in the streets changed the course of events. Metromuster assumed another dimension after the collapse of the project, with Artigas' full personal involvement with the anti-austerity movement. However, the audio-visual project was subsequently reinforced by the cooperative spirit that was created as a result of the work in the streets, and which later fuelled the Metromuster project after *No Res* had ceased to be viable. While it was possible to produce *No Res* thanks to the creation of a community of kindred spirits and followers involved in the 15-M movement, Metromuster became diluted within it and specialised in providing audio-visual services free of charge, while acting as a documentary filmmaker of all the events that took place over three years in its role as a member of the 15-M Audio-visual Committee. An entire network of collaboration that would give new significance to the production company was thereby created. Working with the new recruit Xapo Ortega, Xavier Artigas began working voluntarily on the filming and documenting of a movement that, among other work, strengthened the existing network of activists at local and national levels (Rodríguez Granell 2015).

This already existing community and the digital environment gave a strong boost to the media profile of what would become *Ciutat Morta*. [3] The film is a documentary about police and institutional corruption in Barcelona, arising from the need for restoration and gentrification of the city's old quarter. *Ciutat Morta* is a paradigmatic case in this study since it involves various levels: agency; institutional corruption with police abuse and repression and political complicity; the influence of public mobilisation after the 15-M protests; the role of government bodies in the city's process of marketing and gentrification; the problems of cultural labour and the use of ICTs and collaborative work in militant documentary films.

In late 2011 the opportunity to focus on the events of the 4-F case arose, due to a news story published by *La Directa* and contact with a stable community: individuals close to the case and relatives of the accused. A collaborative network for the project was established including the lawyers working on the case, journalists from *La Directa*, the 4-F support platform (www.desmontaje4f.org), journalists in charge of research and designers responsible for creating promotional material.

The possibility of access to a co-production with the Catalan public television company (TV3) with a more personal project focusing on the figure of Patricia Heras as a poet was initially considered. In Catalonia, TV3 acts as a guarantor of legitimacy in access to grants for television documentaries (ICEC and ICUB grants if a prior co-production agreement is obtained). This is a requirement imposed by the European MEDIA programme. Grants from the ICEC for innovative documentaries were refused, and TV3's refusal led to some exhaustion.

The creative process continued voluntarily. In short, the high level of commitment led to a project with a high human cost becoming unsustainable, since it emerged as a result of a context involving unpaid collaborative work, which reduced the personnel to two people (Xavi Artigas and Xapo Ortega), which on a largely unplanned basis initially raised 5,000 euros (only 5 per cent of the project's total cost) through a Verkami crowdfunding initiative. It is only thanks to the film's many awards and presentations – fourteen to date – that the investments in production are retroactively making a profit. The use of Twitter and informal WhatsApp and Facebook groups acted as improvised platforms for appeals like those for access to equipment, subtitling in English and Blue-ray editing, which were based on the militant networks of trust in the 15-M movement and a community that was committed to the project. That community, the political interest in the case and the unconditional nature of the audio-visual work on 15-M by Metromuster made it possible to produce *Ciutat Morta*, which premièred on June

8, 2013, and led to a commitment to release the film on February 4, 2015. With this release, TV3 had an excuse to not show it on television, and the film thereby lost the high profile that a broadcast on a public channel would have provided.

The media and social impact strategies for *Ciutat Morta* began at that point. The première (under the title *4F: Ni oblit ni perdó*) took place during the squatting of a movie theatre in central Barcelona, in which 800 participated. The authors refer to that time as the materialisation of the 15-M protests, when the strategy of squatting helped and created plural collectives that would probably not have come together under other circumstances. *Ciutat Morta* was thereby an actor which thus made the multifaceted nature of 15-M possible, e.g., among anti-capitalist left-wing groups, the lack of identification with any political group, the pro-independence Catalan left, anarchist groups, the Podemos movement, artists, etc. The news channel covered it that night. The film began to be shown at alternative venues and in civic centres, as well as on both Catalan and Spanish mainstream film platforms. According to Artigas (personal communication), '[with] this documentary we wanted to shatter the Barcelona brand, and we are very excited about presenting it at the cultural centre CCCB because it is a way to begin to destroy it from within'. *Ciutat Morta* began to be seen and to win awards at major festivals in Spain, including the prize for the best documentary at the Málaga Festival, with the consequent press impact.

The strategy, based on this visibility in the mainstream media, was to send a public tweet to TV3 asking about the possibility of showing what was now an award-winning film, free of charge. At this point the MP David Fernández interceded in the Parliament of Catalonia when, during the proceedings of the supervisory committee of the Catalan Audio-visual Media Corporation (CCMA), he asked about whether the documentary would be shown, leading to the consequent social pressure and media attention. Finally, the documentary was shown on TV3's secondary channel Canal 33, with a few seconds censored by court order, and which Artigas and Ortega strategically lengthened to five minutes. This created a Streisand effect,[4] and the extensive public excitement that was generated led to a record audience for the channel, with 569,000 viewers and a 19 per cent share (*El País* 2015). According to the directors, 'the media blockade ended at that point' (Artigas and Ortega, personal communication).

Soon after, Barcelona City Council asked the Office of the Prosecutor to include the documentary as possible new evidence. The Parliament of Catalonia unanimously approved an institutional statement calling on the Office of the Prosecutor to reopen the case and on the Ombudsman to compile all the reports by the authorities involved in the case of 4-F, although the Office of the Prosecutor has made it clear that it has no intention of reopening the investigation. Nonetheless, *Ciutat Morta* has succeeded in creating a discourse in which the casuistry of the facts is transcended and structural issues are considered. The documentary has been effective in highlighting what the city brand needs to conceal giving its narrative credibility. In this regard, urban marketing also involves sanitation. According to its directors (Artigas and Ortega, personal communication), *Ciutat Morta* is yet another story of police impunity, accompanied by a heavy dose of racism, class prejudice and the violation of basic rights, all protected by a judicial system that is a legacy of the Franco regime and politicians obsessed with the real estate business provided by the Barcelona brand at the expense of the citizens.

Finally, *Ciutat Morta* received the Ciutat de Barcelona prize from the ICUB, in another media landmark that included a refusal to collect the award from the mayor.

In terms of an organisational model, the *Ciutat Morta* experience has reshaped the significance of Metromuster, making it into a production company that provides audio-visual communication projects focusing on political corporate video. To some extent, the production company has maintained its original philosophy based on the three cornerstones of its political project: aesthetic quality, free licences and a work ethic, by taking advantage of a market niche including foundations, NGOs and associations, with communication needs and political objectives that Metromuster is able to meet with professionalism, and making the production company a sustainable business as well as formalising the initial cooperative model thanks to its contact with the collaborative network that emerged in the wake of the 15-M movement. This community generates an ecosystem that defines the limits of the production company – such as by refusing to work with some clients that do not share its aims.

As a result, by aiming to end 'the vice of believing that everything is free in movements' and doing 'pedagogy of creative work' (a rejection of self-exploitation), Metromuster is reshaping its production model while maintaining its own political agenda.

The commercial Creative Commons licence will allow it to engage in trade while restricting exclusivity, so that conventional distributors can provide more widespread showings and the benefit does not merely remain in the company. For example, bookshops and publishers with politically related aims have arranged a contract of 30 per cent of DVD sales without exclusivity arrangements (as is the case with conventional distributors). As for the cultural industries, their openness to new paradigms is becoming apparent. For example, the platform VOD Filmin has included the documentary in its catalogue despite its release on the Internet, while respecting its non-exclusive licence.

Conclusions

We have seen how, in terms of their agenda, the documentaries analysed still focus on urban issues as their central subject matter, highlighting the processes that determine the reorganisation and configuration of the city. Today these are processes linked to global capitalism, which cut across the national policies inherited from the Franco system. We have been able to trace an entire cinematic tradition dedicated to highlighting the problems for urban planning and life arising from certain economic models. In the 1960s and 1970s, the political emphasis fell on the organisational models of film production itself, and on the creation of participatory communities that challenged the hierarchical models of the mainstream industry.

However, it is necessary to wait for a development and stabilisation of the Free Culture and the use of ICTs and an increased capacity for agency on the part of social movements. While free culture depends to a large extent on the development of digital tools, it is also true that demands including the equitable distribution of profits, participatory creation, greater control by creators over their works and an understanding of culture as a common good are crucial factors in social and economic transformation that transcend the purely technological sphere. In the early 2000s, collaborative and non-hierarchical work and self-financing were obviously inseparable from activist media, but if we consider political agency, it is possible to appreciate a wider scope since the rise of Free Culture, and greater self-awareness of their status as cultural workers on the part of activists.

In this case, Metromuster resolves this dual contradiction that once was known as outsider cinema. As agents involved in social movements and as cultural agents, the members of Metromuster have reflexively developed their role in the coordinates of the new economy, so that as a political and cultural project it consciously includes the challenge of precarious conditions and transforming economic models. The use of digital tools has driven processes that were already under way, and which without the existence of a community would not have been subject to conditions of emergency and impact. Metromuster's capacity for agency operates on several levels ranging from legal protocols, such as the use of free licences, to the sustainability of the project through cooperative models, and therefore the rejection of voluntary forms of work. According to its members (as said by Xavier Artigas during an interview with the author), the capacity for agency is working for social movements 'without having to work at McDonalds'. The political significance of Metromuster once again involves the design of its production model, but, perhaps most acutely, it is its transcending of the cycle of activism through its inclusion in conventional media.

In the absence of public resources, the ICTs have fostered decentralised initiatives that facilitate audio-visual production, and social networks and the free circulation of content have created an unprecedented social impact. However, by maintaining its ethical lines, Metromuster also includes this social cross-cooperation in the need to create fissures in a public sphere dominated by traditional media such as public television and the daily newspapers, and platforms for cultural legitimacy such as art centres and established festivals. Without these media, the issue of police impunity in cases of torture would not have formed part of the local political agenda. By understanding the need to negotiate with public and private institutions, and focusing on a model for a transformational economy, outsiders thus become a central agent in the processes of social action.

Notes

1 The 2004 Forum, a large-scale event designed to mobilise public and private resources for a major urban regeneration project and based on 'Multiculturalism and Human Rights', which was paradoxically sponsored by multinational corporations repeatedly condemned for attacks on the environment and indigenous peoples by consumers and workers, which were committed to the war economy and neo-imperialism (Delgado 2004).

2   The Colonia Castells was built in 1920 and condemned to demolition in 2003 to make way for the construction of apartment blocks on the site, dismantling the residents' community network in central Barcelona. In its wake, the demolition left tenants who had a rental or ownership agreement going beyond 2001, who had no right to re-housing or compensation (for more information see Rodríguez Granell 2015)

3   The film can be seen on various online platforms, e.g., at https://vimeo.com/118697248

4   As one can read on Wikipedia: 'The Streisand effect is a phenomenon whereby an attempt to hide, remove, or censor a piece of information has the unintended consequence of publicizing the information more widely, usually facilitated by the internet' https://en.wikipedia.org/wiki/Streisand_effect

References

Balibrea, Mari Paz. 2001. 'Urbanism, Culture and The Post-Industrial City: Challenging the "Barcelona Model"'. *Journal of Spanish Cultural Studies* 2 (2): 187–210.

Balibrea, Mari Paz. 2005. 'Barcelona: Del Modelo a la Marca'. In *Desacuerdos 3. Sobre Arte, Políticas y Esfera Pública en el Estado Español* edited by Jesús Carrillo and Ignacio Estella Noriega, 263–267. Barcelona: Arteleku-MACBA-Universidad Internacional de Andalucía.

Borja, Jordi. 2003. *La ciudad conquistada*. Madrid: Alianza Editorial.

Borja, Jordi. 2010. *Luces y sombras del urbanismo de Barcelona*. Barcelona: Editorial UOC.

Delgado, Manuel. 2004. *La otra cara del Fòrum de les cultures S. A.* Barcelona: Edicions Bellaterra.

Domènech, Xavier. 2003. 'La otra cara del milagro español. Clase obrera y movimiento obrero en los años del desarrollismo'. *Historia contemporánea* 26: 91–112.

Florida, Richard. 2002. *The Rise of the Creative Class: And How It's Transforming Work, Leisure, Community and Everyday Life.* New York: Basic Books.

Harvey, David. 2005. *Capital financiero, propiedad inmobiliaria y cultura.* Barcelona: MACBA-Universitat Autónoma de Barcelona.

Lazzarato, Maurizio. 1996. 'Immaterial Labor'. In *Radical Thought in Italy: A Potential Politics* edited by Paolo Virno and Michael Hardt, 133–147. Minneapolis and London: University of Minnesota Press.

López, Ignacio, and Emmanuel Rodríguez. 2010. *Fin de ciclo. Financiarización, territorio y sociedad de propietarios en la onda larga del capitalismo hispano (1959–2010).* Madrid: Traficantes de sueños.

Lorey, Isabel. 2008. 'Gubernamentalidad y precarización de sí. Sobre la normalización de los productores y las productoras culturales'. In *Producción cultural y prácticas instituyentes. Líneas de ruptura en la crítica institucional* edited by Boris Budenet al.57–78. Madrid: Traficantes de Sueños.

Marshall, Tim. 2000. 'Urban Planning and Governance: Is there a Barcelona Model?' *International Planning Studies* 5 (3): 299–319.

Pickvance, Chris. 2003. 'From Urban Social Movements to Urban Movements: A Review and Introduction to a Symposium on Urban Movements'. *International Journal of Urban and Regional Research* 27 (1): 102–109.

Rodríguez Granell, Ana. 2015. 'De agencias y dispositivos. El vídeo militante actual: de *El taxista ful* a *No Res* en el contexto histórico de los movimientos sociales'. In *Videoactivismo y movimientos sociales. Teoría y praxis de las multitudes conectadas* edited by Francisco Sierra and David Montero, 257–279. Barcelona: Gedisa.

Standing, Guy. 2011. *The Precariat: The New Dangerous Class.* London: Bloomsbury.

Terranova, Tiziana. 2000. 'Free Labor: Producing Culture for the Digital Economy'. *Social Text*, 18 (2): 33–58.

8

THE PRACTICE AND POLITICS OF RADICAL DOCUMENTARY CIRCULATION

A case-study of tactical media in India

Shweta Kishore

Introduction

The circulation of documentary film speaks to practices of differentiation and classification which regulate the prominence and perception of documentary in the public domain. Independent Indian filmmakers such as Anand Patwardhan, Deepa Dhanraj, Nakul Singh Sawhney, Amudhan R. P., K. P. Sasi and others take a political view of 'circulation' – the dissemination of films through informal practices in contrast to state-sanctioned distribution – and have reiterated their commitment to an expanded documentary public by going beyond the critical and aesthetic limitations of bourgeois film festivals and cultural institutions. In Anand Patwardhan's (2010) words:

> I would like my films to make a difference in the real world. I'm not content to make a film and let it sit idle or let it go only to some film festival or museum and be appreciated by a tiny fraction of well-to-do people. I want the films to be in the mainstream and do as much as I can to get into that mainstream, so that they have an impact in the real world.

This approach to circulation is part of an interventionist agenda that seeks to traverse new social and geographical territories to those reached by state-sanctioned and commercial distribution circuits, but has concomitant implications for the films' reception and impact. By focusing upon practices of circulation and the wider sociological arrangements of infrastructure, labour, public policy, institutions and technology, I am concerned with how circulation may be repositioned as 'mediator': a form of intervention that determines not only access to documentary cinema but contains the possibilities for the transformation of social relations of media production and consumption and of the public perception of documentary itself (Latour 2005, 39).

My focus is on the practices developed by independent Indian documentarists to counter historical regulatory forces that limit the circulation of documentary and thus its ability to 'alter the world' (Nichols 1991, 3). In India, the circulation of 'dangerous' cultural forms such as documentary are governed by two regulatory regimes: official state censorship and, more recently, an aggressive form of unofficial censorship enforced by pressure groups. The effects of these regimes range from official state bans and demands for cuts in films to more violent vigilante forms of suppression. A third, less overt but equally significant form of regulation relates to the use of documentary by non-governmental organisations (NGOs). Since the 1980s, NGOs have used documentary as a form of social communication with an emphasis on objectives such as documentation and knowledge transmission (Wolf 2013, 929). However, this framing effectively permits approved documentaries to occupy public space, and therefore also inhibits the circulation of independent documentaries.

In this chapter, I will analyse these modes of regulation and their impact upon texts, circulation and perception of documentary in India. I will argue that by deploying new media technologies, citizen participation and historical practices of organising, filmmakers not only construct innovative structures and modes of circulation but theorise and mobilise new forms of resistance against a regulated public domain. What emerges is a politically formulated circulation praxis organised around the operation of 'tactical media' practices that contest the subordination of cultural production to market and institutional 'utility' (Garcia and Lovink 1997). Of wider significance is how these circulation practices constitute a direct challenge to social authority, albeit via an array of minor practices through which filmmakers and citizens transform the reified categories of and relations between producer and viewer. Inviting more material and corporeal modes of participation, 'tactical circulation' functions to create participant-publics or publics formed not only through the negotiation of textual meaning but through the concrete acts of intervention in creation of culture. For documentary, these practices hark towards alternative knowledge and effects beyond the site of spectatorship and its affective transactions.

Regulatory forces

(i) Censorship and vigilante groups

Jean-François Lyotard (1984) argues that the modern public domain privileges certain classes of statements (and ways of saying them) while restricting others. As discourse, censorship enshrines the state as the primary actor in the staging of public interest. It operates by constructing and modifying rules and evolving boundaries of debate, and not only restricts the flow of material that threatens the state but manages the terminologies through which ideas and concepts are defined. The state censor – the Central Bureau of Film Certification (CBFC) – censors films in one of three ways: 1) grant an Adult-only (A) certificate; 2) demand cuts to render a film eligible for Unrestricted (U) public exhibition, a necessary condition for television broadcast; or 3) issue an outright ban based upon perceptions of threat to the public order. Using these methods, the CBFC significantly restricts the flow of cultural meanings, counter information and alternative semiotic orders, and its censorship thus fragments the public domain as a strategy of containment.

Artworks are categorised and regulated using state-nominated value-based concepts – often grounded in values derived from Western industrial modernity – like 'anti-scientific', 'anti-national' and 'obscurantist', amongst others (CBFC, 2017). To the extent that terminology reflects symbolic judgements, the interpretation of these categories by state-appointed functionaries is, in practice, selective and targeted. The treatment of Rakesh Sharma's *Final Solution* (2004) illustrates this process. The film is an investigative account of state complicity in the sectarian violence against the Muslim community of Ahmedabad, Gujarat in 2002 that left many thousands dead. In 2004, the CBFC refused to grant a censor clearance certificate to the film. Denying the opportunity for public exhibition, the Board noted that the film 'attacks the basic concept of our Republic i.e. National Integrity and Unity' with the additional fear of endangering 'public order' (K. Sharma 2004). While the film won the Wolfgang Staudte award at the Berlin International Film Festival and the Humanitarian Award for Outstanding Documentary at the Hong Kong International Film Festival, domestically it was consigned to private circulation. This action follows several earlier instances in which particular films were prevented from entering the public domain.[1] With eight of his films subjected to the CBFC's demand for cuts, Anand Patwardhan is the most visible and vocal opponent of censorship of independent documentary, alongside others including Shubradeep Chakravarty and Meera Chaudhry, Pankaj Butalia, Tapan Bose and Suhasini Mulay. These filmmakers choose to explicitly challenge such censorship in the courts, and in several cases have secured significant victories through the Film Certification Appellate Tribunal and the higher courts.[2] However, while this demonstrates that state censorship can be contested and defeated in the courts, it is a time- and resource-consuming process that is far from guaranteed. Moreover, this is no defence against the second regulatory regime: vigilantism.

In the 1990s, vigilante groups sought to censor images of women's sexuality and sexual freedom as 'inimical to Indian culture', claims which later extended to representations of religion, caste, language and other cultural symbols (Seshu 2016, 251). In their analysis of this threat to free expression paradoxically wielded by citizens themselves, Kaur and Mazzarella (2009) argue it is a consequence of the fragmentation of postcolonial notions of a national identity contiguous with the rise of consumerist desire and regional chauvinism. Propelled by the cultural effects of economic liberalisation, these shifts have fundamentally displaced the grand nation-building schemes of the Nehru years. Seen as 'coming from below' instead of the 'commanding heights of the [Nehruvian] Planning Commission', the fragmented assertions of identity-based citizenship have attained a new image of authenticity in the post-reform phase (Kaur and Mazzarella 2009, 19). Ideologically distinct from the framework of nationhood that underpins state censorship, the claims and counter-claims of the vigilantes are focused on issues of regional linguistic-, religious- and caste-based local self-interest. This is demonstrated by their flagrant circumvention of constitutional channels to prevent the circulation of alternative narratives, with certain religious groups, in particular, increasingly using physical and political intimidation to restrict the circulation of oppositional cultural narratives. As the film-maker Rakesh Sharma declared on the independent media site, Scroll.in, 'such extra-legal censorship is the bane of our lives' (Johari 2014).[3]

(ii) NGOs and the criteria of organisational utility

The frontline role of NGOs in the circulation and exhibition of documentary film in India has escaped substantive cultural analysis. With the gradual retreat of the Indian state from the function of social welfare, NGOs have assumed a partnership with the state for the delivery of social policy and development initiatives. Documentary is deployed by social sector NGOs for a variety of internal and external communication purposes including training, advocacy, institutional publicity, public awareness-building and knowledge-sharing connected to specific programmes and campaigns. At a fundamental level, the possession of knowledge by NGOs in a social context marked by uneven access to instruments and institutions of knowledge production produces negative social consequences. Access to a powerful cultural tool like documentary film reinforces the hierarchy of class relations that allow NGOs to maintain their status as 'developer' in relation to the subordinate position of the public as the subject of development (Jakimow 2012, 35).

The relation between cultural circulation and the production of meanings deserves greater examination particularly as NGO sponsorship translates into specific rules and criteria that intervene in public discourse and act to re-shape the function of public culture. In addition to the compromising effect of sponsorship on editorial independence in sponsored media production, circulation operates as the other side of the same coin by acting to control meanings at the point of reception. In India, involvement with documentary circulation may occur at the micro level where NGOs undertake to exhibit one-off films amongst their constituencies or at a macro scale through the sponsorship of public events such as film festivals, cultural festivals, educational seminars and workshops.

In his analysis of the production of neoliberal public culture, Jim McGuigan (2016) argues that the philanthropic and corporate sponsorship which has come to occupy the gap in public cultural funding has blurred the boundary between culture and commerce. While sponsorship is promoted merely as the disinterested patronage of good causes, sponsoring organisations are quite clear that it is not just a tool for communication but that it purposefully aims at the 'seduction of public opinion' (McGuigan 2016, 192). Arundhati Roy's criticisms of mining companies in India clearly identify such a function:

> Of late, the main mining conglomerates have embraced the arts – film, art installations and the rush of literary festivals that have replaced the 1990s obsession with beauty contests. Vedanta, currently mining the heart out of the homelands of the ancient Dongria Kond tribe for bauxite, is sponsoring a 'Creating Happiness' film competition for young film students who they have commissioned to make films on sustainable development.
>
> (Roy 2012)

With the blurring between documentary and corporate media communication, the questions at stake pertain to documentary's very capacity to summon dynamic publics and perform a meaningful social function. In the post-reform period, media cultures are marked by the unequal distribution of media and communication technology and the application of 'property rights' to cultural artefacts. In this context, the key question is how do independent documentary filmmakers mobilise circulation to produce counter-narratives and destabilise reified social relations?

Tactical circulation

Can circulation practices produce an alternative relation between culture and subject? Can documentary step beyond state-sanctioned distribution to perform an organising function? Elsewhere (Kishore 2018), I have explored how independent filmmakers have sought to consolidate the organising function of their work in relation to both their work practices and aesthetics. These include the development of self-funded, self-managed and cooperative modes of production, collaborative decision-making with film participants, sharing resources, and active position taking in relation to issues represented. However, here I will focus on how a political, non-market view of circulation and exhibition opens up alternative relations between artist and audience. I am concerned with the agents, systems and practices that re-organise social relations and media functions. Chief among these – in a context in which documentary circulation is proscribed, culturally marginalised and institutionally regulated – is the development of 'tactical circulation'. Distributed across a virtual and historical terrain, this form of circulation adapts and re-defines norms including those of 'copyright' and 'piracy' to mobilise not merely 'informed' publics but 'participant' publics (Atton 2002, 25).

Historically, independent documentary circulation in India is grounded in a culture of small-scale, one-off screenings across metropolitan and non-metropolitan circuits based in cooperative networks of people, institutions and venues. Against the near absence of organised distribution, alternative logics such as exchange, participation, community-building and solidarity produce a historical culture of free-to-attend screenings, hand-to-hand circulation of films and, increasingly, web streaming. Extending Michel de Certeau's (1984) 'tactics of practice', tactical circulation subverts the regulatory logic of gatekeeping by drawing ordinary people into significant relationships with documentary film cultures. Consistent with David Garcia and Geert Lovink's 'typical heroes', filmmakers and concerned citizens take advantage of available resources and technologies to construct the context-specific response of tactical circulation (Garcia and Lovink 1997). Seeking to address the 'crisis' of the dominant system, for Garcia and Lovink 'tactical media' is a distinctly political response by groups and individuals who 'feel aggrieved by or excluded' from the mainstream culture. Tactical circulation rests upon a related political reconceptualisation of intellectual property rights that authorises filmmakers to use cultural production and technologies for functions other than consumption and profit generation. The construction of 'participant publics' becomes possible in the structural as well as symbolic reorganisation of circulation methods and infrastructures across metropolitan cities and regional towns in Northern and Southern India.

An undoing of copyright

The tactical re-conceptualisation of circulation rests upon disputing the 'creative economy' view of cultural production, the economic logic of which confers status upon the cultural producer as entrepreneur or 'wealth creator' (McGuigan 2016, 22). Copyright is the legal foundation of this economic logic. By criminalising unauthorised exchange or piracy, copyright laws claim to 'create social and economic conditions conducive to creative intellectual activity' and the promotion of cultural enterprise in modern economies (Fisher 2001, 171). However, copyright, patents and trademarks also reinforce an entrepreneurial self-formation insofar as culture is no longer primarily about a mode of self-expression or disinterested social contribution but tied to notions of investment, career and self-maximisation (McGuigan 2016, 22). In contrast, following the CBFC ban of the release of *The Final Solution* in 2004, Rakesh Sharma adopted an approach to circulation that pushed economic value to the periphery of his concerns. Sharma commenced a 'Pirate-and-Circulate Campaign' wherein he distributed for free video CDs to members of the public on the proviso that they circulate forward at least five copies of the film.[4] By February 2007, the *Hindustan Times* estimated that 14,000 video CDs and 4,000 DVDs were in circulation. By April 2018, the film had been uploaded to YouTube by several users with one upload attracting nearly 100,000 views.

Participant publics

Northern India

Independent filmmakers have shown that they view the audience as evaluative, selective subjects, and circulation as a site of meaningful exchange and dialogue leading to embodied publics. De-centering the profit motive from film production and circulation paves the way for democratic collaborations between filmmakers and concerned citizens, in contrast to hierarchies of knowledge produced through censorship and institutional distribution. These modes of circulation give rise to expanded networks that address not only the digital divide in India but the ideological organisation of people – vis-à-vis categories of urban–regional, educated–illiterate, centre–periphery – which underpins that divide. Jan Sanskriti Manch (JSM) exemplifies this approach to circulation. Founded in 1985 by progressive artists and social activists, JSM's flagship activity is *Cinema of Resistance* (COR): a series of free-to-attend film festivals that deploy innovative technological and organisational solutions to address historical cultural inequalities and enable individuals from a range of socio-economic and geographical locations to 'participate' in events 'rather than report them' (Garcia and Lovink 1997). JSM organises seven to ten COR festivals a year in regional districts, towns and villages across Northern and Eastern Indian states. Each festival is undergirded by principles of site specificity, decapitalisation and participatory production. For instance, festival publicity is tailored to the available infrastructure and combines social media and local small-media (newspapers, radio, public hoardings) with rickshaw-mounted PA systems, handbills and word-of-mouth methods. The low-cost, decentralised mode of screening also mobilises on-site technologies: DVDs are donated by filmmakers, laptops are used to play them, generators power equipment and high school halls or factory buildings are repurposed into screening spaces (Kishore 2017).

Via this ingenuously simple organisational model, JSM's place-based methods contest the dominance of the White Cube museum interior, a hegemonic practice which effaces histories and struggles and transforms functional objects into objects of 'aesthetic appreciation' (Grunenberg 1999, 31). It also militates against essentialist discourses of nationhood and contrasts with the individualist, self-focused subjectivities produced by neoliberal media institutions and viewing cultures. Instead, JSM's active consideration of specific cultural histories, infrastructures and forms of social organisation emphasises locality in the relation between culture and people and involves greater investment in collective-building. This new form of place-based participatory circulation has encouraged active collaboration from other geographically and socially marginalised groups – such as Udaipur Film Society and Peoples Film Collective (Kolkata) – hitherto viewed in terms of market categories by the commercial film industry (Ganti 2004).[5]

Southern India

Founded in 1994 by filmmaker Amudhan R. P., media activism group Marupakkam (The Other Side) has organised over 200 micro-screenings and large film festivals in association with workers' groups, trade unions, student groups, university departments, film societies and activist organisations on common-issue platforms across Southern Indian states (Tamil Nadu, Kerala, Karnataka). As this suggests, Amudhan's commitment to documentary as a filmmaker also extends to building documentary viewing cultures, and in 1998, through Marupakkam, Amudhan founded the Madurai International Documentary and Short Film Festival and the Chennai International Documentary and Short Film Festival in 2013. I will illustrate how, via these events, Marupakkam challenges the neoliberal cultural logics of individualisation and interrogates the forms of inclusion and exclusion produced by neoliberal media cultures, and in the process creates opportunities to build new collectivities.

One of the most striking aspects of this process is Marupakkam's refusal to establish an institutional identity or anything that might suggest it, including 'branding and logos, individual personalities or formulaic institutional activities' says Amudhan (conversation with the author on January 23, 2018). According to Banet-Weiser (2012, 140), branding – the attaching of social or cultural meaning to commodities – does more than establish a commercial identity: it connects ideas, objects and emotions with individuals privileged enough to associate with the exclusionary brand. Branding thus depends upon exclusion and is inevitably incompatible with collective meaning-making.

Marupakkam therefore rejects branding entirely. Apart from its name, Marupakkam possesses no promotional or representational presence such as a logo, website, office or institutional registration. Instead, it exists as a set of ideas, symbolic associations and cultural functions. Marupakkam's refusal to adopt a concrete or defined identity in favour of an ambivalence and openness enables it to work with a diverse array of partners and to fulfil a variety of needs across each of its events. Rather than engaging in single-issue advocacy, Marupakkam's approach creates fertile ground for mounting concept-based collaborations which result in diversely themed film festivals and screening programmes.[6] For example, in 2017 Marupakkam and the Periyar Self Respect Media Department, a social service organisation founded on the modern rationalist thought of Tamil philosopher E. V. Periyar, collaborated to produce a six-day screening schedule of nineteen films under the banner *Documentary Series from/on Tamil Nadu.* [7] Exploring historical and contemporary meanings of place and identity, the films addressed intensely local issues of urban development in Tamil Nadu (*Chennai, The Split City*; Chakravarthy 2006) and expanded into broader national and transnational concerns around nuclear energy policy (*Nuclear Hallucinations*; Nizaruddin 2016) and gendered social norms (*SheWrite*; Jayasankar and Monteiro 2005) to encourage conceptual re-evaluation. By rejecting 'property ownership' principles over ideas, institutions and culture, Marupakkam has instead enabled collaborators to inhabit its entity and re-appropriate its structures and meanings for the dissemination of ideas, imaginations and actions.

Marupakkam therefore operates as an umbrella platform that enables marginalised issues and perspectives to occupy space and create new publics. Furthermore, its mode of organisation enables Marupakkam to respond rapidly to current events, explicitly addressing narratives submerged in mainstream discourse, and to work with its partners to carefully expand the documentary audience. For example, Marupakkam's core focus is on the programming of the films and on-site discussions. This reduces the lead-up time to prepare the event and maximises its ability to respond quickly to current events. Marupakkam also mobilises activist and civil society networks to maximise its audience and move the films and the issues with which they engage beyond peripheral activist circuits into mainstream space and consciousness – as evidenced by Marupakkam's collaboration with the Department of Humanities and Social Sciences of the elite state-funded Indian Institute of Technology in Madras, to host the 2011 *International Documentary & Short Film Festival On Development, Culture and Human Rights*.

The expansion of the documentary audience is a complex manoeuvre requiring intimate knowledge of venues, institutions and localised cultural politics, and this is also reflected in Marupakkam's practices; these are carefully calibrated at each location to consider political sensitivities and to ensure that screenings are not disrupted and that curation maintains political integrity. Particular attention is paid to the sequencing of the programme such that controversial films, instead of being presented as headline or centrepiece items, are embedded alongside non-controversial films in order to deflect official scrutiny. Similarly, screening literature and promotional materials amplify not only the films but conceptualise themes that deserve public attention. For example, *Aadhar and Politics of Surveillance 2018* focused on the issue of surveillance as much as the films that engaged with that topic.

Conclusion

The public circulation of independent films in India must contend with the official and unwritten institutional and political rationalities that regulate the gathering of documentary publics. Central amongst these are censorship and the gatekeeping functions of NGO sponsors, who privilege instrumental applications of documentary communication while also effectively partitioning the social collective into normative audience groupings. Through the examination of a variety of contemporary documentary circulation practices, I have illustrated the development of context-specific, adaptable and reflexive solutions whose radical function exceeds beyond exhibition to produce political subjectivities and ways of being in the world. Garcia and Lovink's (1997) conceptualisation of a politics of tactical media is grounded in a pragmatics of repurposing non-specific resources to construct temporary, targeted and low-cost media interventions. While the permanence and longevity of these initiatives is not guaranteed, measures of success must consider the radical potential of the small scale and participatory as a tactical response to the exploitative precarity of contemporary cultural economies. In contrast to the rigidity of top down institutions, by resisting the reproduction of hierarchy, Cinema of Resistance and Marupakkam are not only examples of tactical circulation; their collaborative public interventions present new agendas for the consideration of place and coalition-building. In terms of radical potential, the cooperative model of circulation and exhibition materialise a historically grounded space and practice where resistant meanings, counter narratives, alliances and subjects can emerge from within the cultural-economic logics of neoliberalism.

Notes

1 Other films to face the CBFC's disapproval in this phase include *A Time to Rise* (Anand Patwardhan 1981), *Bombay Our City* (Patwardhan 1985) and *Bhopal: Beyond Genocide* (Mulay, Bose and Shaikh 1986).
2 A selection of films that have successfully challenged the CBFC include *Textures of Loss* (Pankaj Butalia 2013), in whose favour the Delhi High Court recommended the grant of a 'U' certificate, *En Dino Muzaffarnagar* (Chakravorty and Chaudhary 2014), which was recommended an A certificate in January 2015 by a judicial order of the Delhi High Court, and *An Insignificant Man* (2017), which was cleared by the Film Certification Appellate Tribunal after the filmmakers successfully challenged the CBFC direction to seek 'No Objection Certificates' from the politicians featured in the film.
3 Right-wing vigilante groups disrupted the screening of *Ocean of Tears* at the VIBGYOR Film Festival in Thrissur Kerala on February 14, 2014. On the same day they also vandalised the offices of the festival-organising committee. For more information, see Aarefa Johari's (2014) report on the attacks and Ezra Winton's Chapter 15 in this volume. Ten months later, right-wing Rashtriya Swayam Sevak (RSS) vigilantes publicly burnt copies of Perumal Murugan's book, *Madhorubagan* (2010) in Tamil Nadu, prompting the writer to give up writing. See Soutik Biswas' (2015) BBC online report on the factors leading up to Murugan's decision.
4 Video compact disc followed the VHS as a popular home video format in Asia until DVD became affordable in the late 2000s.

5 Other radical cultural groups in non-metropolitan towns, such as the Hirawal (Patna), Azamgarh Film Society and Sankalp (Ballia), belong to what the commercial Hindi film industry pejoratively refers to as the 'interiors', symbolising unsophisticated, under-developed cinematic taste cultures. These groups now collaborate with the Cinema of Resistance on festival organisation and the curation of political and arthouse cinema, with many launching smaller regional offshoots.

6 Marupakkam has organised numerous issue-specific festivals including the 2018 Women's Film Festival in Chennai, the 2018 Social Justice Film Festival in Chennai, Bangalore and Patna, and the 2011 Open Sesame: International Documentary & Short Film Festival On Development, Culture and Human Rights in Chennai, amongst many others.

7 The Self-Respect Movement was launched by E. V. Ramasamy, 'Periyar' after he broke ranks with the Indian National Congress in November 1925 to pursue his resolutions seeking 'communal reservations' (that is, caste-based reservations in favour of the non-Brahmins). He declared his political agenda to be 'no god, no religion, no Congress, and no Brahmins'. For accounts of the Self-Respect Movement, see Pandian (1993).

References

Atton, Chris. 2002. *Alternative Media*. London: Sage Publications.

Banet-Weiser, Sarah. 2012. *AuthenticTM: The Politics of Ambivalence in a Brand Culture*. New York: NYU Press.

Biswas, Soutik. 2015. 'Why Indian Author Perumal Murugan Quit Writing'. BBC, January 15, 2015. https://www.bbc.co.uk/news/world-asia-india-30808747

Butalia, Pankaj. 2013. *The Textures of Loss*. DVD. New Delhi: Magic Lantern Movies.

Central Board of Film Certification. CBFC. 2017. 'What Guides the CBFC in its Decisions'. Ministry of Information and Broadcasting. Government of India: New Delhi. https://www.cbfcindia.gov.in/main/certification.html

Chakravarthy, Venkatesh. *2006. Chennai: The Split City*. DVD.

Chakravorty, Shubhradeep and Meera Chaudhary. 2014. *En Dino Muzaffarnagar/These Days in Muzaffarnagar*. DVD. Produced by Shubhradeep Chakravorty and Meera Chaudhary.

De Certeau, Michel. 1984. *The Practice of Everyday Life*. Berkeley: University of California Press.

Fisher, William. 2001. 'Theories of Intellectual Property'. In *New Essays in the Legal and Political Theory of Property*, edited by Stephen Munzer, 168–199. Cambridge: Cambridge University Press.

Ganti, Tejaswini. 2004. *Bollywood: A Guidebook to Popular Hindi Cinema*. London: Routledge.

Garcia, David and Geert Lovink. 1997. 'The ABC of Tactical Media – Tactical Media Files'. http://www.nettime.org/Lists-Archives/nettime-l-9705/msg00096.html

Grunenberg, Christoph. 1999. 'The Modern Art Museum'. In *Contemporary Cultures of Display*, edited by Emma Barker, 26–49. New Haven: Yale University Press.

Jakimow, Tanya. 2012. *Peddlers of Information: Indian Non-Government Organisations in the Information Age*. Virginia: Kumarian Press.

Jayasankar. K. P. and Anjali Monteiro. 2005. *SheWrite*. DVD. New Delhi: Magic Lantern Movies.

Johari, Aarefa. 2014. 'Attack on Film Festival in Kerala's Cultural Capital Shows Rising Hindutva Presence in Liberal State'. *Scroll.in*, March 1, 2012. https://scroll.in/article/657425/attack-on-film-festival-in-keralas-cultural-capital-shows-rising-hindutva-presence-in-liberal-state

Kaur, Raminder, and William Mazzarella. 2009. *Censorship in South Asia: Cultural Regulation from Sedition to Seduction*. Bloomington: Indiana University Press.

Kishore, Shweta. 2017. 'Reframing the Margin: Regional Film Festivals in India, a Case Study of the Cinema of Resistance'. In *Activist Film Festivals: Towards a Political Subject*, edited by Tyson Wils and Sonia Tascón, 159–179. UK: Intellect.

Kishore, Shweta. 2018. *Indian Documentary Film and Filmmakers: Independence in Practice*. Edinburgh: Edinburgh University Press.

Latour, Bruno. 2005. *Reassembling the Social: An Introduction to Actor-Network-Theory* (1st edition). Oxford: Oxford University Press.

Lyotard, Jean-François. 1984. *The Postmodern Condition: A Report on Knowledge*. Minneapolis: University of Minnesota Press.

McGuigan, Jim. 2016. *Neoliberal Culture*. London: Palgrave Macmillan.

Mulay, Suhasini, Tapan Bose, and Salim Shaikh. 1985. *Bhopal: Beyond Genocide*. Videocassette. New Delhi: Cinemart Foundation.

Nichols, Bill. 1991. *Representing Reality: Issues and Concepts in Documentary*. Bloomington: Indiana University Press.

Nizaruddin, Fathima. 2016. *Nuclear Hallucinations*. DVD. Produced by Professor Joram Ten Brink.

Pandian, M. S. S. 1993. '"Denationalising" the Past: "Nation" in E. V. Ramasamy's Political Discourse'. *Economic and Political Weekly* 28(42), 2282–2287.

Patwardhan, Anand. 1981. *A Time to Rise*. DVD. Co-produced by Anand Patwardhan and John Monro. India: http://patwardhan.com.

Patwardhan, Anand. 1985. *Bombay, Our City*. DVD. Produced by Anand Patwardhan. India: http://patwardhan.com

Patwardhan, Anand. 2010. Interview with Vikhar Sayeed. *Frontline*, 27 (25), 64–68.

Roy, Arundhati. 2012. 'There's No Escape from the Corporations that Run India'. *Guardian*, March 19, 2012. https://www.theguardian.com/commentisfree/2012/mar/19/corporations-india-arundhati-roy

Seshu, Geeta. 2016. 'Women and the Internet in India: Denial of Access and the Censorship of Abuse'. In *India Connected: Mapping the Impact of New Media*, edited by Sunetra Sen Narayan and Shalini Narayanan, 237–260. New Delhi: Sage.

Sharma, Kalpana. 2004. 'Censor Board Bans Film on Gujarat Violence'. *The Hindu*, 6 August 2004. https://www.thehindu.com/2004/08/06/stories/2004080604471200.htm

Sharma, Rakesh. 2004. *Final Solution*. DVD. Produced by Rakesh Sharma.

Wolf, Nicole. 2013. 'Foundations, Movements and Dissonant Images: Documentary Film and Its Ambivalent Relations to the Nation State'. In *Routledge Handbook of Indian Cinemas*, edited by K. Moti Gokulsing and Wimal Dissanayake, 910–948. Abingdon: Routledge.

9

ACTIVIST FILMMAKING IN AFRICA, WITH A FOCUS ON CAMEROONIAN JEAN-MARIE TENO

Mette Hjort

Geographically, Africa is the second largest continent, although maps of the world almost invariably obscure this fact. Africa is also the second largest of the continents in terms of population size, with approximately 1,310,624,823 citizens in early 2019. Africa encompasses fifty-four countries, the original borders having been largely established without regard for the integrity of ethnic groups and as a means, among other things, of destroying traditional trading routes and preparing the ground for colonialism. The perpetrators of the varieties of violence in question were the European leaders who, in 1885, participated in the so-called Berlin Conference.[1]

Given the sheer scale of Africa, the diversity of the continent, and the complexities of its history since the late 1880s when filmmaking was invented, it would be foolhardy to proffer self-confident assertions about the nature of activist African filmmaking, across the many decades of its existence and in different parts of the continent. The very concept of African filmmaking has itself been questioned by African filmmakers, and thus any attempt to define *activist* African filmmaking must certainly involve a good deal of circumspection. Yet, if handled with care and given the necessary provisos, some generalisations, including about African cinema and activist African filmmaking, do have a legitimate role to play. Among other things, they make it possible to pinpoint certain tendencies, and to describe shared challenges, solutions and goals. They help to capture the nature of collective action and transnational collaboration across the continent of Africa, but also the roles and purposes of filmmaking in African societies. What is more, claims of a more general nature offer a basis for comparative reflections, for example about the differences between European and African contexts, as they relate to activist filmmaking.

In what follows I approach the phenomenon of activist filmmaking on the African continent through a series of brief evocations in support of my central contention, which is that much of the filmmaking by African filmmakers can legitimately be described as activist, in some sense of the term. Indeed, it is my view that a pervasive commitment to effecting change through moving images makes filmmaking by African filmmakers a considerable resource and source of public value, not only in Africa, but globally. In addition to fuelling creativity and giving shape to the works of specific filmmakers, activist commitments have had a decisive impact, in Africa, on film-related institution-building (film schools and festivals) and transnational discourses and alliances. Whether or not the envisaged changes have been effectively implemented, filmmakers' activist intentions, across the continent and throughout the post-colonial era, have produced something of great public value, namely, a conception of filmmaking that has the potential to offer much needed resistance to dominant models of film production that yield forgettable (or worse still, ideologically questionable) content at astronomical costs, all supported by production practices that are not only unsustainable but a factor in the perpetuation of a variety of types of injustice, including those related to race and gender. The idea that filmmaking can and should effect worthwhile change is surely one that is well-suited to a now global environment of formidable challenges. The probing and committed ways in which African filmmakers have long thought about film, with reference to critique, norms, hope and the articulation of different and better ways of organising human existence, deserve a much wider hearing than they have traditionally received.[2]

To make a convincing case for seeing activism as a pervasive rather than peripheral feature of African cinema, examples of activist intentions and undertakings in various areas are needed. Reference will thus be made to the commitments that shaped significant manifestos, declarations and resolutions (from 1973 to 1991) and to how some of Africa's most influential filmmakers have defined the purpose of filmmaking. Reference will also be made to the goals that inform one of the most effective attempts to develop the next generation of African filmmakers (the alternative film school, IMAGINE, in Ouagadougou, Burkina Faso), and to the role that a given film festival, the Zanzibar International Film Festival (ZIFF), plays in bringing human rights thinking to local communities for the purpose of effecting change. I will also discuss some of the external factors, originating in the development policies of the Global North, that create a problematic convergence in a particular form of activist filmmaking, namely social justice filmmaking. First-hand testimony from Judy Kibinge, a Kenyan human rights filmmaker, suggests that the activist tendency that is rightly associated with filmmaking on the African continent is multifaceted and complex. Social justice filmmaking arises, in part, we shall see, in response to a set of constraints imposed by development policies in the Global North, the result being limited possibilities for other types of filmmaking. Having created a context for considering the work of a specific activist filmmaker, I conclude with some remarks about Jean-Marie Teno; remarks, for example, about the telling decisions this filmmaker has had to make in order to pursue the interests of social justice, as it relates to colonial and postcolonial realities, but also indigenous African customs and practices.

Formal declarations by African filmmakers

Mbye B. Chan offers a characterisation of African cinema by evoking a Fulani saying about art in general: 'It is entertainment, it is educational and it is functional.' Mbye's point is that 'African cinema is integral to the wider social and collective effort on the part of Africans to bring about a better life for the majority of Africans' (Chan 1996, 4). Mbye's claims are made with reference, among other things, to five formal texts, all reproduced in *African Experiences of Cinema*, in a section entitled 'Manifestos, Declarations and Resolutions'. Inferences about the activist aspirations of African filmmakers are prompted by even the most cursory engagement with the relevant declarations, the first of which has a scope extending well beyond Africa: 'Resolutions of the Third World Film-Makers' Meeting, Algiers, Algeria, 1973' (Bakari and Chan 1996, 17–36).[3] Activist intentions are especially evident in 'The Algiers Charter on African Cinema, 1975', where it is a matter of rejecting Western concepts and practices (for example, 'the stereotyped image of the solitary and marginal creator') and of charting a very different path for Africa ('The issue is not to try to catch up with the developed capitalist societies, but rather to allow the masses to take control of the means of their own development, giving them back the cultural initiative by drawing on the resources of a fully liberated popular creativity'). The cinema is unambiguously charged with playing 'a vital part' on account of its potential to serve as a 'stimulus to creativity', but also as a 'means of education, information and consciousness raising' (Bakari and Chan 1996, 25). Inasmuch as those concerns require non-trivial forms of social and political change, filmmaking necessarily becomes an activist endeavour.

Selected African filmmakers on the purposes of filmmaking

For Teno, the core commitment to effecting change is fuelled by a profound desire to counteract the devastating impacts of colonialism, effects that continue to this day.

> We mustn't forget that during the colonial era, the colonial authorities used cinema as a way of influencing minds, of assigning people to 'their place', by formulating negative representations of them and their cultures, by valorizing the cultures they introduced and denigrating anything local.
>
> *(Thackway 2019, 91–2)*

For many African filmmakers, there is a compelling need to undo the psychological effects of colonialism as described, for example, by the psychiatrist Frantz Fanon in his now classic *Black Skin, White Masks*:

> My patient is suffering from an inferiority complex. His psychic structure is in danger of disintegration. What has to be done is to save him from this, and, little by little, to rid him of this unconscious desire .... If he is overwhelmed to such a degree by the wish to be white, it is because he lives in a society that makes his inferiority complex possible, in a society that derives its stability from the perpetuation of this complex, in a society that proclaims the superiority of one race ... the black man should no longer be confronted by the dilemma, *turn white or disappear,* but he should be able to take cognizance of a possibility of existence.
>
> *(Fanon [1952]1986, 100)*

It is Teno's contention that filmmaking by Africans has been shaped – from the very moment when pioneering filmmakers came together in the late 1960s to found the pan-African film festival, FESPACO, and the Carthage Film Festival – by a strongly critical, postcolonial desire to ensure that Africans are 'represented' on the screen, in stories that articulate issues of central concern to Africans (Thackway 2019, 91). Representation, in this case, has to do with agency and self-under-standings, with what Canadian philosopher Charles Taylor, referring to the writings of Fanon, describes as a 'politics of recognition' (Taylor 1992). Following Teno's line of reasoning, the activist core in African filmmaking has to do, quite fundamentally, with the rejection of demeaning representations of Africans,[4] in his case through a razor-sharp critique of how the machines of colonial and neo-colonial power (and not Africans' putative ontological deficiencies) produce the very conditions of poverty and various forms of societal dysfunction.

Speaking of filmmaking as a tool for education, and as a means of contesting the effects of an educational system that was 'not at the service of the people' but designed to 'keep them at a certain level' (Thackway 2019, 93), Teno refers to Ousmane Sembène. The reference is apposite, for Sembène's turn from literature to filmmaking was motivated by a desire, in a context of widespread illiteracy and strong oral traditions, to reach a much wider audience, and for the purpose of education and not merely entertainment. Acknowledging Sembène's recognition of the value of moving images, Shola Adenekan describes an epiphanic realisation on the part of the Senegalese filmmaker:

> Touring Africa [...] and sailing along the River Congo in the middle of the short-lived vitality of the socialist Patrice Lumumba government, Sembène said he had a vision: landscapes, people, movements and sounds to which no written document could do justice. He was not thinking of movies in the concept of Hollywood but cinema as 'école du soir' or night school.
>
> *(Adenekan 2007)*

Sembène, Adenekan continues, wanted 'to engage Africans in their own language, following the oral-tradition of the continent, where at night, people gather to hear stories told by the elders'. *Moolaadé* (2004), Sembène's last film before he died in 2007, was explicitly designed to effect social change on behalf of the rights of women and girls: 'Female circumcision is outdated. It is an attack on women's rights.' Sembène went on to describe the reality-based fiction film in question as a 'reference tool with which we can talk about the problems' (cited in Professor Samba Gadjigo's 'making of' film on the Artificial Eye DVD Extras).

Articulating Sembène's self-understandings as an African storyteller, Françoise Pfaff evokes the griot, a central figure in the oral traditions of Africa. Griots, she claims, 'are to be found either at the courts of chiefs or established on their own in towns and villages' where they act 'as story-tellers, clowns, heralds, genealogists, musicians, oral reporters, or paid flatterers or insulters' (Pfaff 1984, 29). In Sembène's Wolof society, a distinction is drawn between two types of griots: the gewel who acquires skills within the context of cast differences and a transgenerational process of transmission, and the lebkat who simply asserts a right to speak (30). In Sembène's *Moolaadé*, it is the female lebkat who, in defending the progressive heroine of the story against the conservative interventions of the gewel, becomes a vehicle for social change within the village community: 'My noble warrior has spoken. Admire my noble warrior. Collé Ardo Gally Sy has spoken. Collé from Niani has spoken. Djerissa women, fasten your belts. You are more valiant than men' (*Moolaadé*, 1:52 mins). In Sembène's self-styling as a modern-day griot we find the forging of connections to indigenous traditions as well as an action-oriented emphasis on critique and social change. The role of the griot has been more widely embraced by African filmmakers, and in similarly activist ways. Michael T. Martin's (2002) interview with Gaston Kaboré is, for example, tellingly entitled '"I Am A Storyteller, Drawing Water from the Well of my Culture": Gaston Kaboré, Griot of African Cinema'.

Making filmmakers: Gaston Kaboré's alternative film school, IMAGINE

Unlike many film schools in the United Kingdom and the United States (Miller 2013), some of the most significant sites of film training on the African continent reflect broadly activist intentions. A good example is Gaston Kaboré's IMAGINE, a unique environment for conferences, community building, visual arts exhibitions and musical performances, in addition to the core activity of training workshops aimed at developing the next generation of African talent. Kaboré established IMAGINE in 2003, with the support of his wife, the pharmacist and businesswoman, Edith Ouédraogo. Kaboré's vision throughout has been to engage aspiring young African filmmakers with the contributions of Africa to the world, an aim consistent with a politics of recognition that seeks to provide positive images of the continent. In 2013, for example, during FESPACO, IMAGINE featured an exhibition entitled *Africa's Gift to the World/Le don de l'Afrique au monde*. The exhibition offered young filmmakers participating in training workshops at IMAGINE, as well as visitors from around the world, an opportunity, among other things, to discover the thirteenth-century Charter of Mandé, a crucial human rights intervention that was 'kept intact and transmitted across the centuries' by griots (Stoneman 2019, 62). The significance of the exhibition in the context of a site devoted to the development of filmmakers is evident in Kaboré's account of how the curators sought to make a history of creative African agency vivid:

> [W]hen we decided to do this exhibition, the idea was to try to explain to Africans, particularly to the youth of Africa today, that it's not a terrible fate to have been born in Africa, meaning that they should not see themselves as being punished by destiny because they were born here … Africans have been able to create philosophy, to create myths and legends. They've been able to define visions of the world, to conceive different forms of artistic expression.
>
> *(Stoneman 2019, 61)*

Speaking to Rod Stoneman during FESPACO in 2019, in response to a question regarding the role of activist goals at IMAGINE, Kaboré affirmed their centrality. For example, he characterised the making of thirty-eight short films at IMAGINE, with Danish support, as an unambiguously activist intervention.[5] Made with the intent of contributing to political change, these films were designed to encourage voters in Burkina Faso to participate in the general elections of 2015. Kaboré further described many of the workshops offered by IMAGINE as part of a programme of change, the point oftentimes being to awaken a new generation to the possibility of provoking social change. IMAGINE, as Kaboré sees it, is guided by a two-fold commitment to art and social change, the latter having been clearly foregrounded, for example, in the 2014 workshop that was run in collaboration with Larry Sider, director of the School of Sound at the London Film School. That workshop was, quite simply, called 'Filmmaking for Advocacy and Activism'. At IMAGINE, audience-building is also a priority and here too the emphasis is on creating the conditions for effecting change. According to Kaboré, 'What are you doing to bring about change?' is the essentially activist question that consistently informs the full range of activities at IMAGINE, from audience-building to talent development.

Human rights thinking in the public sphere: the role of the Zanzibar International Film Festival

For anyone with an interest in African cinema, including African audiences, film festivals are of crucial importance, African screens having typically been controlled by non-African distributors who have favoured films from Hollywood and Asia as a standard business practice. Lindiwe Dovey (2015) offers an incisive account of the place of African cinema on the festival circuit, through a careful consideration of the policies of some of the oldest and most prestigious film festivals, but also the emergence of African film festivals in and outside Africa. Dovey describes the ZIFF, founded in 1998, as having initiated a 'flowering of new international film festivals' (2) in Africa. The brainchild of an American, a Dane and several Tanzanians, including Martin Mhando, ZIFF was established as a nonprofit organisation in 1998 (145–6), in the wake of the collapse of the cinema sector in Tanzania due to the International Monetary Fund's imposition of structural adjustments (145). ZIFF, claims Dovey, was marked from the outset by a '(dis)sensus communis' (146), a tension between the goals of business and social advocacy being 'evident across many aspects of the festival' (146). In the present context, it is ZIFF's role in supporting social advocacy that is of interest.

Writing about the significance of ZIFF in his capacity as the festival's founding director, Mhando tellingly chooses a title that makes social advocacy central not only to the intended mission of the festival but to its actual impact: 'The Zanzibar International Film Festival and Its Children Panorama: Using Films to Socialize Human Rights into the Educational Sector and a Wider Public Sphere' (Mhando 2019, 125–44). In Mhando's account of the design and implementation of the

Children Panorama – involving film screenings for children and young people in, for example, holiday camps, schools and open-air village settings – there is evidence to suggest that in the Zanzibari context the condition of possibility of successful social advocacy lies in a delicate mix of diplomacy, multicultural understanding and firm support for human rights:

> From a pedagogical perspective, ZIFF views human rights literacy as a matter of validating procedural activities that influence behavior without compromising current educational values. This way the program quietly contests positions that are held by those with strict religious or cultural views. Though a secular state, Zanzibar's value system is essentially based on Muslim and Bantu cultural values. Sometimes these value systems contradict each other, but in the discussions after watching the films, human rights values are brought forward to counter some cultural beliefs.
>
> *(127)*

Consistent with the term 'international' in its name, ZIFF features films from all around the world, with a clear emphasis, however, on East Africa and the Dhow countries. Films screened as part of the Children Panorama in 2016 included the Indian *Jaya* (2014, dir. Puja Maewal), which is about street children, and the South African film *Yesterday* (2004, dir. Darrell Roodt), which tells a story about HIV and AIDS. Offering a case study of the Tanzanian film *Faraja* (2014, dir. Nasir Mohamed Al Qassmi and Yusuf Kisokky), Mhando indicates that the film was programmed as a means of initiating reflection on a 'child's right to consensual marriage' (129). In the story, the 16-year-old Faraja travels to Zanzibar to visit her father, finding a suitor and arranged marriage awaiting her on arrival.

Citing feedback from some of the facilitators of the post-screening discussions that are an integral part of the Children Panorama, Mhando foregrounds the way in which a film like *Faraja* allows children, and especially girls to 'find their voices' (139). Social advocacy here is about creating safe spaces for self-reflection, the articulation of troubling experiences, and the thematisation of desires and beliefs that challenge rights-denying traditions and practices. Referring to the often less-than-convincing aesthetic qualities of the local films (due, for example, to a lack of training, equipment, funding and facilities), Mhando makes it clear that the works nonetheless have considerable value, due to their capacity to bring about desired changes relating to the realisation of human rights. In the context of activism, the properly public value of facilitating social change trumps aesthetic value, especially if the latter is a matter of appreciating formal properties in non-instrumental ways; that is, merely for their own sake.

That issues of justice and social transformation are a recurring feature of African films is strongly suggested by the twenty-eight Tanzanian submissions to ZIFF in 2019. In 2019, ZIFF received over 3,400 entries, including from Mainland China and Brazil.[6] Due to the new partnership between ZIFF and the Faculty of Arts at Hong Kong Baptist University, I was given the welcome opportunity to assist with the pre-jury selection process in 2019, opting to view the Tanzanian works in all categories (shorts, features and documentaries). The vast majority of the Tanzanian submissions qualify as activist, given the clear intent to use moving images to effect change. Among other things, the films draw attention to young girls' vulnerability to rape (*Tausi*, dir. Takura Maurayi), the persistence, despite laws prohibiting the practice, of female genital mutilation (*Supa Mama*, dir. Christina Pande), domestic violence (*Flower*, dir. Francis Waziri Mango), poverty (*Mizani*, dir. Mohammed Suleiman) and the impact of religious beliefs on environmental degradation (*Mazingira ni afya*, dir. Frank K. Bernard, Dominic P. Mushi, Imelder M. Munyaga and Nicholaus M. Agrey; and *Fahari Yetu*, dir. Richard Magumba).

The ambiguities of social justice filmmaking: development policies and their effects

Having suggested that activist-oriented social justice films are prevalent in the context of African filmmaking, it is important to draw attention to the complexity of the motivating factors. The filmmakers' desire to effect change is clearly often a significant element of the production process, but in some cases the relevant intentions emerge from a complex ecology where economic constraints are most easily counterbalanced by the pursuit of a specific *kind* of filmmaking opportunity. More specifically, African filmmakers working in Africa typically face a lack of funding and this recurring constraint can be overcome by developing projects that are consistent with the basic parameters of rights-based development policies originating in the Global North. For example, Judy Kibinge, who has a well-established reputation as an accomplished social justice filmmaker from Kenya,[7] is frank about her desire to be able to make a wide variety of films, including a 'romantic comedy' (cited in Hjort 2019, 111). Reflecting on her profile as a social justice filmmaker, Kibinge says: 'A lot of people in Kenya do a lot of these NGO films. And that's another reason why I've ended up doing so much of a certain kind of work, because that's actually how most people pay their rent' (cited in Hjort 2019, 116). Yet, as Kibinge points out, while the funding that is available for social justice films can be a magnet for the initially somewhat reluctant filmmaker, the actual experience of making these films can lead to changed self-understandings and new commitments:

> The thing is, the more you do NGO films – which have such a bad rep, because they're often made badly, or boringly – the more you see Kenya and the continent properly. Because you go to places where you'd never go; nothing would ever take you to these places. And so I really started valuing these experiences.
>
> *(cited in Hjort 2019, 116)*

Limitations of space make it impossible to explore the extent to which policies in the Global North facilitate and shape activist filmmaking on the African continent, or, for that matter, the ramifications of initiating and defining an activist agenda from outside.

Suffice it to say that it is important to understand that funding originating in the Global North tends to favour certain types of filmmaking, including social justice films. Inasmuch as activist intentions define the category in question, it is clear that the genealogy of directorial intentions underpinning activist filmmaking on the African continent is more complex than is often assumed.

The activist filmmaking of Jean-Marie Teno: on recurring targets of critique, stylistic choices, risk and residency outside Africa

Described by Melissa Thackway (2019, 89) as 'a tireless critic of social injustice, abuse of power, and the lingering effects of colonialism', Teno has mostly focused his efforts on documentary filmmaking. To date his filmography encompasses fifteen works, the earliest film being *Homage* (*Hommage*, 1985), and the most recent *Leaf in the Wind* (*Une feuille dans le vent*, 2013). Trained in audiovisual communication at the University of Valenciennes in France, Teno worked for French television as an editor from 1985 to 1997. He controls the production and distribution of his films himself, through his company, Les Films du Raphia, which is based in Paris (Thackway 2019, 89).

Teno's preferred conception of filmmaking encompasses a variety of elements, the clear emphasis being on the *efficacity* of moving images:

> I can't imagine myself speaking to say nothing, or speaking to just talk about the mood I'm in, to make a bourgeois poetic love story, or something like that. ... cinema is also entertainment, it's about emotions, but for me, it also has to lead to something, to serve a purpose.
>
> *(96)*

Injustices relating to (neo-)colonialism, post-colonial elites, and indigenous practices are all targeted in Teno's films, but so is 'stupidity' (97). Teno is explicit about the need to ensure that the scope of change-oriented critique includes African traditions:

> I have read books suggesting a kind of paradise in the precolonial period, but I do not buy that. Even in the villages some of the customs are oppressive ....
> The more I question how Africa is moving, the more I question our responsibility for its state. When you look over the past thirty years, there were many possibilities to reverse the course of things. Why did people in power not grab those opportunities? There is probably something within us, within our traditions, that we have to reconsider and question.
>
> *(Ukadike 2002, 309)*

Alex's Wedding (*Le mariage d'Alex*, 2002) offers an example of Teno's critical engagement with traditional practices; in this instance, polygamy.

The documentary poignantly captures the silence of the first wife, Elise, and the tears of the new wife, Josephine, foregrounding what Teno himself calls the 'unspoken pain' of the wedding celebration. *Chief!* (*Chef!*, 1999) similarly foregrounds the violence of

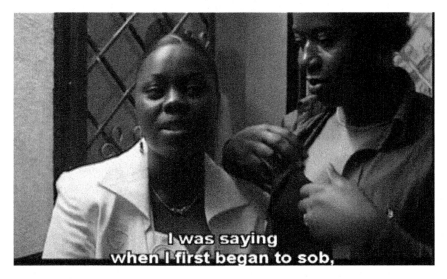

FIGURE 9.1 The bride and second wife, Josephine, reflects on her sombre mood in the documentary *Alex's Wedding* (*Le mariage d'Alex*, 2002), which concludes with Teno recalling his own miserable memories of a polygamous family.

traditional practices, with children subordinated to parents, women to men, villagers to chieftains, all in an interlocking system of hierarchy and subordination that creates the conditions of possibility for dictatorship.

Speaking of his recurrent approach, evident in certain stylistic continuities, Teno calls attention to the idea of 'shifting perspectives and looking at the world from the place of those who don't usually have a say' (Thackway 2019, 97). 'First-person narrative,' Teno claims, is not in his films a matter of 'using the first person as Teno speaking' but of using 'the first person as an African, or a Cameroonian, looking at a situation' marked by the

FIGURE 9.2 In *Chief!* (*Chef!*, 1999), Teno examines the impact of authoritarian thinking on women, as well as society more generally.

unholy alliance between the colonial era's 'official French discourse' and 'the official Cameroonian state discourse.' For Teno, an attack aimed at the Cameroonian state is also, inevitably, an attack aimed at 'the colonial master' (97–8). A good example is *Africa, I Will Fleece You (Afrique, je te plumerai*, 1992), a documentary that was prompted by the following questions: 'What is this culture? What's in the minds of the people running this country? What is it about the history of this country that means that we have rulers who do not even think of providing basic necessities to the people?' (95). As Teno sees it, the strategy of simultaneously 'attacking the state' and colonialism has been a challenging one, with the filmmaker inevitably ending up 'between a rock and a hard place' (98). Challenges that Teno has had to negotiate as a result of his choices as a filmmaker include the charge, typically articulated in France, that his 'cinema is not African' enough, due to the absence of 'idyllic, apolitical villages and landscapes' and the accusation, this time from Cameroonian officialdom, that he consistently creates 'a bad image of the country' (98).

For a filmmaker, the place between a rock and a hard place is one associated with economic risk, the funding for filmmaking being hard to come by if those controlling the purse strings are variously dissatisfied, even hostile.[8] But Teno's filmmaking does not merely evoke the spectre of economic risk, but also that of actual physical danger. In conversation with Teno, Nwachukwu Frank Ukadike (2002) recalls and interprets a remark by one of his students, following a viewing of *Africa, I Will Fleece You (Afrique, je te plumerai*, 1992): '"I don't think the filmmaker has been to Cameroon since he made this film", meaning that he did not think you would be allowed back in Cameroon after making such a revealing film' (308). Teno acknowledges that the secret service has taken an interest in his films, having visited him in Paris, with the clear purpose of intimidating him. Yet, he insists that any risks that he is taking pale in comparison with those taken by activists who continue their work from within Cameroon. Also, the risks, he insists, are perhaps not as great as those envisaged by Ukadike's student: 'I am not,' says Teno, 'part of a system which smuggles arms into the country to organize a coup. That is not my aim' (308).

Asked by Horst Rutsch (n.d.) to reflect on his status as someone who is 'passionate about the situation, the fact of Africa and of Cameroon' yet lives 'outside', in France, Teno acknowledges that he could have made the decision to return to Cameroon, following his education in France, and indicates that he rejected the possibility, because it would have meant becoming part of the system: 'I didn't want to end up like many of the people that I knew who had entered the system and become civil servants.' He agrees with Rutsch that he is 'in exile' but underscores that he is 'inside' while being 'outside' by virtue, for example, of his unfailing efforts to remain fully and properly informed about 'what is going on'. Teno's decisions regarding residency speak to some of the challenges of being an activist filmmaker. For example, he acknowledges that a degree of attachment and genuinely immersive involvement are necessary on a regular basis, citing a need to 'be part of the group', to 'be among the people I am making films about' (Rutsch n.d.). Yet, the distance, claims Teno, also facilitates a sharper critical perspective: 'Living in Paris made me more aware of what was going on in my country. Sometimes when you live in an environment, you don't have a critical mind about that place' (Ukadike 2002, 309).

Activist filmmaking in Africa is a complex phenomenon involving talent development, mobile screenings of issue-oriented films in remote villages, the forging of continuities with oral traditions, probing articulations of the effects of (neo-)colonial realities, and, in some cases, a quasi-exilic existence. At the heart of the activism of African filmmaking in all its guises we ultimately find a fundamental concern for basic human rights and the idea that motion pictures have a purpose far greater than that of mere entertainment: the power to effect positive change.

Notes

1 The now infamous gathering receives a good deal of attention in Cameroonian filmmaker Jean-Marie Teno's *The Colonial Misunderstanding* (*Le malentendu colonial*) a documentary from 2004 that, in the filmmaker's own words, 'looks at Christian evangelism as the forerunner of European colonialism in Africa, indeed, as the ideological model for the relations between North and South even today' (DVD jacket cover, Les Films du Raphia).

2 I am eager to contribute to the relevant process of expanding engagement with African cinema, and thus, in 2019, and in my capacity as Dean of Arts at Hong Kong Baptist University, I developed a partnership with the Zanzibar International Film Festival, for the purposes of developing a recurring summer programme that will see some twenty young students from Hong Kong embedded in various film-related milieus on Zanzibar. The point is to offer the students, most of whom have only been exposed to the norms of the commercial cinema (typically from Hollywood, Mainland China, Hong Kong and Korea), a life-changing experience of what it means to think of moving images as a powerful agent of change.

3 The other documents include 'The Algiers Charter on African Cinema, 1975', 'Naimey Manifesto of African Film-Makers, 1982', 'Final Communiqué of the First Frontline Film Festival and Workshop, Harare, Zimbabwe, 1990', and 'Statement of African Women Professionals of Cinema, Television and Video, Ouagadougou, Burkina Faso, 1991'.

4 See Françoise Pfaff (1984), on the prevalence of 'Tarzanistic images' (5) and the use of 'Africa merely as a background to the valiant deeds of European explorers winning over the African wilderness' (4).

5 Stoneman interviewed the filmmaker and other relevant persons staying at IMAGINE on my behalf, and for the purposes of the current chapter.

6 Personal communication with festival director Firdoze Bulbulia, March 3, 2019.

7 Relevant in this regard are the documentaries *Coming of Age: Democratic Evolution in Kenya* (2007), *Peace Wanted Alive: Kenya at the Crossroads* (2009) – about the post-election violence of 2007/2008 – and *Scarred* (2015) – a searing film about the previously neglected Wagalla Massacre in Northern Kenya in 1984.

8 See Hjort (2012) for discussions, from various perspectives, on film and its relation to different types of risk.

References

Adenekan, Shola. 2007. 'Writer and African Film Legend'. *The New Black Magazine*, July 4, 2007. http://www.thenewblackmagazine.com/view.aspx?index=884 (accessed April 14, 2019).

Bakari, Imruh, and Mbye B. Chan, eds. 1996. *African Experiences of Cinema*. London: British Film Institute.

Chan, Mbye B. 1996. 'Introduction'. In *African Experiences of Cinema*, edited by Bakari Imruh and Mbye B. Chan, 1–14. London: British Film Institute.

Dovey, Lindiwe. 2015. *Curating Africa in the Age of Film Festivals*. New York: Palgrave Macmillan.

Fanon, Frantz [1952]1986. *Black Skin, White Masks*. Translated by Charles Lam Markmann. London: Pluto Press.

Hjort, Mette. 2019. 'In Defense of Human Rights Filmmaking: A Response to the Sceptics, Based on Kenyan Examples'. In *African Cinema & Human Rights*, edited by Mette Hjort and Eva Jørholt, 103–124. Bloomington, IN: Indiana University Press.

Hjort, Mette, ed. 2012. *Film and Risk*. Detroit: Wayne State University Press.

Martin, Michael T. 2002. '"I Am a Storyteller, Drawing Water From the Well of My Culture": Gaston Kaboré, Griot of African Cinema'. *Research in African Literatures* 33 (4): 161–179.

Mhando, Martin. 2019. 'The Zanzibar International Film Festival and Its Children Panorama: Using Films to Socialize Human Rights into the Educational Sector and a Wider Public Sphere'. In *African Cinema and Human Rights*, edited by Mette Hjort and Eva Jørholt, 125–144. Bloomington, IN: Indiana University Press.

Miller, Toby. 2013. 'Good Bye to Film School: Please Close the Door on Your Way Out'. In *The Education of the Filmmaker in Africa, the Middle East and the Americas*, edited by Mette Hjort, 153–168. New York: Palgrave Macmillan.

Pfaff, Françoise. 1984. *The Cinema of Ousmane Sembène, A Pioneer of African Film*. Westport, CT: Greenwood Press.

Rutsch, Horst. n.d. 'Interview with Jean-Marie Teno'. African Film Festival; https://www.africanfilmny.org/2014/interview-with-jean-marie-teno-2/ (accessed April 14, 2019).

Stoneman, Rod. 2019. 'Africa's Gift to the World: An Interview with Gaston Kaboré'. In *African Cinema and Human Rights*, edited by Mette Hjort and Eva Jørholt, 60–69. Bloomington, IN: Indiana University Press.

Taylor, Charles. 1992. *Multiculturalism and 'The Politics of Recognition'*. Princeton: Princeton University Press.

Thackway, Melissa. 2019. 'Challenging Perspectives: An Interview with Jean-Marie Teno'. In *African Cinema and Human Rights*, edited by Mette Hjort and Eva Jørholt, 89–102. Bloomington, IN: Indiana University Press.

Ukadike, Nwachukwu Frank. 2002. *Questioning African Cinema: Conversations with Filmmakers*. Minneapolis: University of Minnesota Press.

10

RADICAL CINEMA IN ISRAEL AND PALESTINE AFTER OSLO

Unrealistic hopes and unwarranted expectations

Haim Bresheeth

Introduction: Oslo, a disaster perceived as a gate of hope

The period immediately following the signing of the Oslo Accords in 1993 was strange indeed; despite the clear perspective presented by Edward Said ([1995] 2007), the first to accurately evaluate and expose the lies and deep flaws embedded in the process, most radical activists, especially those living in Israel, managed to hang on to their totally unrealistic and unwarranted hopes for deep sea-change in the 'conflict'. Said's description of the Palestinian side of the negotiation table is strikingly redolent of the situation ever since, a searing judgement of the PLO (Palestine Liberation Organization) leadership:

> [I]n effect without maps of their own, without the requisite detailed knowl-
> edge of facts and figures possessed by the Israelis, without a firm commitment
> to principle and justice, the Palestinian negotiators – acting in all things under
> the instructions of Yasir Arafat – have yielded to Israeli and American pres-
> sures. What Palestinians have gotten is a series of municipal responsibilities in
> Bantustans controlled from the outside by Israel. What Israel has secured is
> official Palestinian consent to Israeli occupation, which continues in a stream-
> lined and more economical form than before.
>
> *(14)*

There could hardly be a more accurate description of the realities after Oslo, and the fact that this description is still valid is the measure of Said's foresight, a short while after the Oslo euphoria which he never shared.

Indeed, even thinking and writing about it as a 'conflict' normalises a misreading of the relationship between the two sides. As argued by many, a colonial power rela-tionship is not a 'conflict' between two equal sides – rather, it is a clash between the might of the militarised settler-colonial state and the disenfranchised, powerless and unarmed mass of the indigenous. Between such sides there cannot be co-existence – another misapplied term used by the Israeli Zionist left to obscure colonial power-relations. Indeed, Said discusses in detail what such putative co-existence might consist of – it should, in his judgement, include the understanding and acceptance by Arabs of the great tragedy of the Holocaust affecting Israeli Jews deeply, as well as the justified demands for reconciliation and reparations of the deep damage of the Nakba:

> This means that as Palestinians we demand consideration and reparations from them without in any way minimising their own history of suffering and gen-ocide. This is the only mutual recognition worth having, and the fact that the present governments and leaders are incapable of such gestures testifies to the poverty of spirit and imagination that afflicts us all.
>
> (208)

Such generous and penetrating understanding was far from the minds of Israel's leaders; Azmi Bishara dubbed the relationship between Israel and its occupied territories a 'relationship between a horse and its rider' (cited in Benvenisti 2007, 170). Between a horse and its rider any 'co-existence' is one of unilateral control and exploitation. Thus, any description of the 'conflict' which does not expose the real nature of the power relations inherent in a militarised occupation by a settler-colonial state, is one contributing to and justifying the coercive power of the *coloniser*.

Similarly, the phrase 'peace process' is another total misnomer, a propaganda term used by Israel and its partners to obfuscate and confuse the less informed, or the over-optimistic onlookers in the West, as well as the Zionist left inside Israel, always ready to believe, as well as spread the formulaic lies of, the Israeli propa-ganda machine. Indeed, Israeli propaganda could not function properly without its liberal apparatchiks – writers, filmmakers, choreographers, musicians, architects, lawyers and medics, artists and academics of every kind. Rather than use right-wing ideologues, Israeli propaganda (the so-called *Hasbara*) has for decades used the liberal edge of Zionism to spread its lies and distortions.

Of course, such a machine could operate neither by propagating the whole truth nor total lies. But liberal Zionists were always ready to engage in disingenuous simplifications of the situation in Palestine/Israel. They knew and understood the power-relations between the Zionist project and its Palestinian subalterns only too well; after all, any true intellectual would. But, like many intellectuals elsewhere, they were only too ready to support their 'own team' – by the use of ellipsis, lacunae, obfuscation and creative wording, they have spread the Zionist myths for seven decades, in the service of the society and the state which made them its powerful elite class, in what is otherwise not a typical class society. Such behaviour by national elites is so normative in recent as well as more distant memory as to merit no wonder or surprise.

An interesting feature of this recent 'betrayal of the intellectuals' (Benda [1928] 2007) is the fact that such elites are quite capable of encompassing a substantial contradiction – that of correctly judging the propaganda role they themselves fulfil on behalf of a less-than-liberal ruling political class, while believing that if international arbitration of such a regime is done by them – a 'liberal elite' – it somehow ameliorates the lies and misconceptions they spread. Thus they assist in hiding the true nature of the regime they support. An example given by Said is that of Connie Bruck, writing in the *New Yorker* about the process of the Oslo negotiations, and in contact with both Israeli and Palestinian sources. Describing how despite all the evidence she herself presents, Bruck still takes the Zionist line, in total contradiction of her own argument, Said ([1995]2007) comments:

> I mention all this about Bruck in order first of all to show that even when confronted with evidence of their own research and selection, supporters of Israel can override that evidence and conclude that some Zionists are fine people with a moral commitment. I recall feeling the same way when I first read Benny Morris's important book on the birth of the Palestinian refugee problem in which Morris – also a liberal Zionist – gives example after example of the concerted Zionist plan to drive out the Palestinians in 1948. Yet he too concludes, inexplicably, that there was no real plan, only a series of incidents that were the result of a general war.
>
> *(114–15)*

Said is not kinder to Palestinian intellectuals who concentrate on calling for unity while their country is whisked away from under their feet, as their priority of defending the PLO and PA (Palestinian Authority) is not one he shares – he prefers to defend Palestine and its people. An example Said quotes is clear evidence to the folly of such nationalist intellectuals:

> To say, as Mr. Ahmed Khalidi fatuously claims in a recent article, that it is irresponsible to ask for democracy in Palestine now, since we must wait for fifteen years before we can begin to think of democratic practices, is the rankest idiocy.
>
> *(117)*

Such debunking of authoritarian, anti-democratic arguments of the Palestine PLO-dominated elite will come to be seen as crucial, as such deeply entrenched tendencies take over the Israeli-sponsored Palestinian elite, making a mockery of the democratic energies of the First Intifada, which has indirectly but inexorably led to the Oslo negotiations.

That Israel had got the PA to do its dirty work controlling the Palestinian people, with the EU paying for this political manoeuvre which guarantees the continuation and intensification of the colonial project, is one of the bitter ironies of the colonial conflict in Palestine. Not only are the Palestinians facing one of the strongest armies in the world, which is itself supported by most of the rest of the world, but their own leadership has turned against them and refuses to hold elections which it knows it will lose. And all this before one even begins probing the corrupt network which the PLO employs as part of its project of controlling the Palestinians.

The functioning of the PA as a 'government' in control of the daily realities in Palestine was no better than their bungling of the Oslo negotiations. The main arm of this government comprises seventeen security organisations, armed and supplied by Israel, trained by the United States and the EU. This guarantees not only Israeli security but also the continued existence of the PA itself – the largest employer in the West Bank but one which produces almost nothing for the Palestinian population it is supposed to protect and provide for. While the PA's record of supplying basic services is a dismal one, with many privatised and serving their shareholders rather than the population, it is in the area of culture that this is seen most clearly.

Historically, left-wing revolutionary and nationalist movements have paid careful attention to the cultural aspects of the struggle for liberation. If in the nineteenth century such movements were mostly limited to the use of the printing press, this dramatically changed in the twentieth century. The Russian revolution is a case in point. Through its use of new technologies to attract and recruit the masses during (and especially after) the revolution via radio, revolutionary posters and theatre troupes and, perhaps most of all, the cinema, the Bolsheviks managed to build a powerful propaganda and agitation machinery no less important than the armed forces in protecting the young and fragile Soviet state.

What was a tool of market capitalism became an important and efficient armament in the service of a large and subsequently powerful state, and was used by the political and cultural elite to communicate with populations in Russia and beyond. The cinema sent a message of liberation, modernism, justice and radical change, and assisted in the creation of a new national, socialist identity in Russia by creating and projecting new ideas and aesthetics that fed the popular imagination. Eisenstein, Vertov, Kuleshov and others were instrumental in setting up the institutions of the Soviet film industry, including the world's first film school – the Gerasimov Institute of Cinematography (VGIK) – in Moscow where young filmmakers taught even younger students and developed a radical new cinematic language. This revolutionary lesson was well learnt in countries from Cuba to Egypt where, after revolutions in both countries, institutes of cinema were set up and film industries nationalised. Both countries also established production institutions and film schools, very much modelled on the Moscow studios and VGIK, and enjoyed proper support from the USSR for their nationalising efforts. Some African countries, such as Tunisia and Senegal, also followed this model after liberation and supported major cinematic authors as a result, including Ferid Boughedir and Moufida Tlatli in Tunisia and Ousmane Sembène and Djibril Diop Mambéty in Senegal.[1]

Palestine and film production

The PLO also seemingly learnt this important lesson and established a photographic department in 1968, which became the Palestine Films Unit (PFU) two years later. Despite the limited resources at its disposal and the very difficult conditions under which it operated, the PFU, under al-Fatah,[2] was responsible for some seventy films before its expulsion from Beirut in 1982, during the Israeli invasion of Lebanon. The invasion also brought the end of the Cinema Institute and the Production Unit of the Democratic Front for the Liberation of Palestine (DFLP), which was a separate film unit (Gertz and Khleifi 2008, 12). The films were viewed widely, especially in the Arab world, with some also screened in Europe which helped recruit European filmmakers to the Palestinian cause.[3] Most of the PFU output was documentary films, with only one narrative fiction film, *The Return to Haifa* (1982), ever produced. Even following the forced move to Tunisia (after being ejected from Beirut), the unit went on making films serving the Palestinian cause, albeit at a reduced rate. Of course, none of the films were seen in either Israel or the West Bank and Gaza, due to Israeli control. Filmmaking and film viewing in Occupied Palestine in this period were all but non-existent, with most of the cinemas closed down or destroyed by Islamic militants.

An important development took place during the First Intifada, which started in December 1987. This popular resistance through nonviolent direct action (NVDA) captured the imagination of many in the West and beyond, and many documentaries were produced during the first few years of the Intifada. While such films were not, in the main, produced by Palestinians, the process introduced many young Palestinians to the medium, through working as guides, fixers and translators for Western crews, and many took up media production later on.[4] This was important, as the pendulum of Palestinian film production would then move to Palestine itself, with young film-makers from both Israel and the West Bank and Gaza starting to leave their mark on the scene of cultural production. Significant here is the first Palestinian feature film, *Wedding in Galilee* (1988), by Michel Khleifi, a Palestinian with Israeli citizenship, residing in Belgium. The new filmmakers were working on their own, isolated from the now defunct PLO film unit and with the difficult task of raising production finance, typically resorting to the sympathetic attitude of some of the EU production funding programmes, as well as French, German and Belgian television channels. While this could not be termed an 'industry' there was clearly a new force at play, reflecting similar developments elsewhere (Naficy 2001).

The Oslo Accords of 1993 marked a change with the arrival of the PLO in Palestine. One would have expected that the PLO would not just continue film production but increase it by following the Soviet and Cuban models, building a national film institute and a film school in Palestine, and building a support system for the young Palestinian cinema.

The reality, however, was very different. The relationship with Israel, heavily constrained by the nature of the agreements and US pressure on the PLO and Palestinian National Authority (PNA), meant that any act or institution of cultural resistance was out of the question, and no proper support system for the arts was ever built by the PA's ineffectual and corrupt regime. Thus, it was at the very point of returning to Palestine that the PLO's work on cultural resistance was abandoned, impairing the struggle for liberation from Israeli occupation. This can be understood if one considers that the PLO prioritised its working relationship with the Israelis and the

United States over the continued struggle by its population. Thus, by institutionalising the popular struggle of the Palestinian people, the PLO and the then PNA acted as an Israeli adjunct serving Israel's security needs.

Thus, cultural resistance and cultural production of any kind were seen as anathema and left to the free market in Arafat's PNA; Arafat was never a Marxist, neither were any of his lieutenants. They all saw cultural production as having little to do with 'government', in the same way that most aspects of life in Palestine were excluded from the public domain and remained privatised to the detriment of society. Hence, many of the health, education and welfare systems in Palestine have never attained the status they enjoy in Western Europe and have stayed within the market economy of the PNA, corrupt as it is. In this context, it is hardly surprising that culture lacked any government support.[5]

This intentional distance from issues and difficulties of cultural production (and resistance) by the PNA and PLO, after 1993, had some interesting results. The PNA has not learnt from other national and anticolonial struggles, and this was deeply damaging to Palestinian society and its potential for resistance. Only a decade afterwards, in 2004, were the first hesitant moves to establish a Palestinian Film Festival undertaken; at a time when most capitals in the West already had well-established Palestinian film festivals of their own.[6] The whole structure of film culture – production, distribution, exhibition, research and criticism, lacked public support, and thus was rescinded. The PLO and PNA instead put all their propaganda eggs into the basket of the television arm of the Palestine Broadcasting Corporation (PBC). Despite its name, the PBC bears little resemblance to the UK's BBC and its poor production values and crude attempts to promote the PNA mean most Palestinians prefer Al Jazeera or Al Arabia, as proved by audience polls. This attempt to control the sophisticated Palestinian public sphere thus backfired – and no serious attempt to support the cultural sphere has been staged since.

The short spring of radical cinema in Israel

In the period immediately following Oslo, some exciting developments occurred both in Israel and the West Bank and Gaza, despite the depressing political environment. The seemingly promising Peace Process offered Israeli and Palestinian filmmakers some unique opportunities for nearly a decade, as the surge of optimism fired new productions, many dealing with history and memory of the conflict. This was possible due to a range of unique conditions.

In Israel – an affluent, Westernised society with ample public support for cultural production – funding for projects which could not possibly have taken place before was now available from a range of organisations, including the large Israel Cinema Fund and the Rabinowitz Film Fund, as well as some television channels and other smaller funding bodies. Before 1993, such funding bodies would not normally consider funding Palestinian film projects and Palestinian filmmakers were unlikely to request support from such bodies; now, all of a sudden, such attitudes where cast aside. A number of Palestinian filmmakers were encouraged to propose projects, and several were agreed by the funding bodies. For example, two documentarists, Nizar Hassan and Mohammad Bakri, had their films financed during this period and screened at Israeli film festivals and other venues. Hassan made *Isteqlall* (1994) and *Yasmine* (1996) during this period, both of which articulate a clear Palestinian perspective but were financed respectively by Keshet TV and the New Foundation for Cinema & TV (some of his other films were also partially funded by Israeli TV channels).[7]

The case of Mohamad Bakri is even more fascinating. Bakri, a successful theatre, film and television actor in Israel – gained international fame with his stage adaption of the Emile Habibi novel *The Secret Life of Saeed the Pessoptimist* (1974), which he performed in Hebrew, Arabic and German in Israel and Europe. Bakri made the documentary *1948* in 1998. The date is important – the fiftieth anniversary of the Nakba – and the film includes detailed evidence of massacres such as Dir Yassin during the 1948 war (Bresheeth 2006, 2001). For an Israeli organisation to fund such work was unprecedented. Bakri was also the producer of Ali Nassar's feature, *The Milky Way* (1997), and his later film, *In the Ninth Month* (2002). Even Elia Suleiman's first feature, *Chronicle of a Disappearance* (1995), received funding from the Israel Film Fund. While it would be an exaggeration to say these films received widespread distribution in Israel, they were seen by thousands of Israeli Jews, especially on television, and contributed to public debate about both the Nakba and contemporary relations between Israel and the PNA element of Palestine – a tiny area of the country.

At the same time, film policy was also inclined to enable Jewish-Israeli films which would not have received public support before. Though none of these were as interesting or radical as the films mentioned above – in contrast to the 1980s, when much more radical films were produced – the exceptions to this are important. In 1992, after the start of negotiations between the two sides in Madrid, Asi Dayan made *Life According to Agfa*, one of the most searing attacks on Israeli attitudes to Palestine and Palestinians, financed by the Israel Film Fund. Another exception is Raanan Alexandrowicz's *James' Journey to Jerusalem* (2003).[8] However, after 2007, as the direction changed, less than 4 per cent of films financed by the Israel Film Fund in the following decade, were made by Palestinians (Israel Film Fund 2018). Bearing in mind that Palestinians make up more than 20 per cent of Israel's citizenry, that figure is strikingly low. This suggests not only exclusion and censorship but also indicates an unwillingness on the part of Palestinian filmmakers to request Israeli funding as the BDS (Boycott, Divestment and Sanctions) movement grows. It is also clear that, in the current xenophobic atmosphere in Israel, to expect funding for Palestinian filmmakers, even though they are supposedly Israeli citizens with (almost) full rights, is a folly. After the passage of the *Nation State Law* in July 2018 (Green 2018), as Israel moved from *de facto* to *de jure* apartheid, it became clear that Israel's legal system will not even attempt to treat Arab Palestinian citizens, as well as their language and culture, as in any way belonging to the national *self* of Israel. As the official, legal *Other*, Palestinians can expect to be treated as second- or third-class citizens; and they do, while of course struggling against this racist legislation with the few remaining legal means at their disposal. It is also clear that the days of Palestinian MKs (Members of the Knesset) may be numbered, as another raft of apartheid legislation makes its way through the committees in the Knesset.

Thus, the door opened by some liberal curators in the early 1990s is now being slammed shut. The understandable but misplaced hopes for the Oslo Accords and the 'Peace Process' have been replaced by a militarised, nationalistic and extreme 'Jewish' culture and polity. In this context, there is no place for the crucial cultural exchange which the films and filmmakers discussed above attempted. With pretences of liberalism and democracy gone, possibly for decades, these simple civilised exchanges, limited as they necessarily were, are no longer possible. Over the last few years, the Culture Minister, Miri Regev, has tightened regulations conditioning financial support for the arts, so that no criticism of the state may be voiced in any form (Anderman 2018). The loopholes through which 'liberal' voices could be heard have been closed by an apartheid regime.

At the same time, European funds – the mainstay of Palestinian and Israeli filmmakers for decades, financing radical filmmaking as part of a projected peace process and cultural exchange – have recently stopped supporting such work almost entirely. The reasons are complex: from a rise of right-wing regimes in a growing number of EU countries (invariably friendly towards Israel and hostile to Palestine), to a reluctance to be seen as 'antisemitic' by funding any cultural expression critical of Israel, as the flawed IHRA (International Holocaust Remembrance Alliance) 'definition of antisemitism' is adopted by more states (Bresheeth 2018). This process of silencing both Palestine's narrative, as well as any criticisms of Israel, is likely to gain momentum in the medium term, due to Western governments' support for Israel. One only hopes that the BDS campaign may bring about a substantial change in public opinion, such that will force an about-turn in official positions.

Who is the audience of radical films about Palestine/Israel?

While some EU and European television channels were still supporting Palestinian projects and Palestine–Israel co-productions in the 1990s and early 2000s, such as *Route 181* (Eyal Sivan and Michel Khleifi 2004), questions were raised about the audience for such films.

Palestinian cinema is impressively lively for such a small, divided nation with such a large diaspora (51 per cent of Palestinians live outside Palestine). Indeed, the vivacity and complexity of Palestinian cinema is the envy of many larger and richer nations and now has a global reach. However, audiences are typically small, with films limited to arthouse and activist exhibition circuits. Nevertheless, many more people view Palestinian films abroad than in Palestine, where most of the viewing is on television screens due to the shortage of cinemas resulting from the lack of proper systems of support. Joseph Massad (2006) thus rightly raises the question: 'Who are these films targeting?' (39).

This is not an idle query. To produce Palestinian documentary or fiction with European funding, the films need to address audiences in these countries, rather than concentrate on Palestinian audiences *per se*. There is of course great value in reaching such audiences – with the EU consistently supporting Israel, even when Israel is carrying out war crimes in Lebanon or Gaza – a direct address of European audiences is crucial for making the case for Palestine, telling its story and promoting its narrative.

So, in comparison with the earlier, institutional PLO film production, which targeted mainly Palestinians and other Arabs, recent Palestinian cinema is largely seen outside Palestine, premiered at international film festivals and shown for the most part on European television channels with some limited screenings for political activists and cineastes. As a result, some Palestinian critics have argued that the leading Palestinian filmmaker, Elia Suleiman, directs his films towards overseas audiences. While such claims are far from justified, one can understand the sentiment – most Palestinians in Palestine are unable to see his films on the large screen they were made for, and clearly deserve. Such criticism may also be caused, to a degree, by the fact that recent filmmakers have also been harshly critical of the Palestinian administration. Elia Suleiman, Anne-Marie Jacir, Hani Abu Assad, Rashid Masharawi and especially Michel Khleifi do not shy away from their social and political responsibilities in this respect. Their films are not limited to an attack on Israeli policies and actions, but have much to say about current Palestinian society and its deep-seated problems. In his latest film, *Zindeeq* (2011), Khleifi voices a searing critique of Palestinian society in his hometown of Nazareth, a place seemingly in the grip of criminal gangs, where fear reigns every night, totally ignored and even abetted by the Israeli police and other state authorities. A more identifiable Nazareth can be seen in the more recent, sublime *Wajib* (2017) by Jacir, where the city and all its faults are depicted humanely and with humour. But *Wajib* is also not short on social and political critique, and we are left with a powerful dilemma at the end of the film: the conflict between the silent *Sumud* of the father, who continues to live under occupation in Nazareth, and his architect son who holds a more radical position against the occupation, but also prefers to live in Rome.

Like other critical films made by Palestinian filmmakers, *Wajib* was attacked by some commentators and faced a ban by Beirut film festival (though this was averted at the last minute). It seems that some Palestinians, especially those whose social and political capital lies with the PNA, are enraged by the courage and commitment of such films and interpret them as 'weakening the unity and fighting spirit'. We are again reminded of Said's ([1995]2007) critique of such hollow posturing on behalf of the corrupt elite around Arafat then, and Abbas now. This is despite the fact that it is exactly these kinds of films that continue and extend the political and cultural struggle against the occupation, Zionism and the iniquities meted out to Palestinians on a daily basis, and that it is the PNA that seems to collaborate with the Israeli authorities and do their bidding.

Ironically, such films – truthful, harsh and real as they are – seem to reduce the PNA's weak cultural inclination even further; the films that gain Palestine adherents and supporters elsewhere, supporting Palestine's narrative, are shunned or ignored by the PNA. For the same reasons, proper support for cinema is still wanting, five decades after the setting up of the PLO, and two decades after its return to Palestine. The more prizes are won by such films, the more they seem to be shunned in Ramallah.

Thus, on both sides of the conflict, in the colonising nation and in the colonised society, the powers that be are unhappy with their radical cinematic output, at a time when both Israeli and Palestinian films are praised elsewhere. In Israel, the debate flared up in 2013 when, out of five documentaries chosen for the Oscar, two came from Israel, at least notionally. These were the stunning *5 Broken Cameras*, by Emad Burnat and Guy Davidi, and *The Gatekeepers*, by Dror Moreh. In their different ways, both films attack and undermine the Israeli consensus, which supports the occupation, and their selection was presented by some in Israel as an anti-Israel plot, even an anti-Semitic plot (Segal 2013). It is clear that such films will not be produced in the future, now that the legislation has been amended. The *Jerusalem Post* went so far as to claim Moreh's film constituted 'an attempted coup d'etat by the retired Shin Bet heads' (Troy 2013). *5 Broken Cameras* received even more hostile reactions in the Israeli press. On the occasion of the film not winning the Oscar, the same paper reported: 'Bayit Yehudi chairman Naftali Bennett said Monday morning that he "didn't shed a tear" over the loss of what he referred to as an "Israeli anti-Israeli" documentary' (Jerusalem Post 2013).

Thus, as we have seen, the absence of financial and institutional support for Palestinian cinema has meant that filmmakers were able to be more independent, and to take a long and hard look at their own society as well as the Israeli occupation. The lack of support has led, ironically, to greater creative autonomy. In the case of Israel, the support system is now cutting its losses, making sure that filmmakers tow the racist, nationalist line required by all cultural production supported by state and public funding. In one case, in the colonised nation, the lack of left-wing support for filmmaking has meant that cultural resistance is alive and well. In the other, in the colonising nation, the qualified support is leading to the emasculation of the filmmakers' independence. In both cases, this stranglehold on cultural production is not just a plight affecting filmmakers, artists and writers, but a wider and deeper calamity for both societies. The voices of change pointing towards a just peace and common future are now crushed by governments on both sides, as well as by the EU and its media channels, thus making the production of new radical cinema of fact or fiction ever more difficult. Without a doubt, by silencing such cultural debate, the likelihood of a just, negotiated peace leading to the end of apartheid and equal society in Palestine/Israel has decreased significantly. While this may be seen as the political aim of the Israeli apartheid regime, it cannot be the true objective of the people, either in Israel or in Palestine.

Notes

1 Though it should be noted that neither Tunisia nor Senegal were able to support an industry on the Egyptian model – after all, the film industry in Egypt preceded the revolution by more than a decade (Shafik 1998, 11–15).

2 *Al Fatah* was the largest of the resistance groups, led by Arafat himself.

3 The most famous of whom were Jean Genet and Jean-Luc Godard, who made their own documentaries about the conflict and who have remained committed to the cause of Palestine ever since.

4 An example from my own experience: while working (with Jenny Morgan) on the BBC documentary *A State of Danger* (BBC2, 1989), we trained a number of Palestinians in film work. I later had the chance to send some donated video cameras and arrange for production training in the West Bank, based on the links we had established during film-making. Some of our production students became independent filmmakers.

5 This capitalist orientation is all the more pronounced via the lack of any socialist initiative on the part of the PNA, even of the very mild variety practised in India or many African states after liberation in the 1950s. Capitalism was never questioned and both social services and the utilities were privatised, in many cases owned by ministers of the PA (monopolies of gas, petrol, water, cement and food distribution are but a few examples of this).

6 The first call for submissions for the new festival went out in 2003, and the festival took place in 2004. This new initiative was not very successful, and more or less petered out, with little support from the PA.

7 I have written elsewhere at length about Nizar Hassan's films, and especially about *Ustura* (Legend). See Bresheeth (2006, 2001).

8 A film about an African teenager whose pilgrimage to the Holy Land is prevented when he is arrested as an illegal immigrant and subsequently exploited as cheap labour by an Israeli contractor.

References

Anderman, Nirit. 2018. 'Israeli Culture Minister Pushes to Nix for Festival Featuring Films that "Undermine Our Values"'. *Haaretz*, September 17, 2018. https://www.haaretz.com/life/.premium-regev-pushes-to-nix-funds-for-haifa-festival-over-film-that-undermine-va lues-1.6489212 (accessed September 24, 2018).

Benda, Julien. [1928]2007. *The Treason of the Intellectuals*. London: Routledge.

Benvenisti, Meron. 2007. *Son of the Cypresses: Memories, Reflections, and Regrets from a Political Life*. Berkeley and Los Angeles: University of California Press.

Bresheeth, Haim. 2001. 'Telling the Stories of Heim and Heimat, Home and Exile: Recent Palestinian Films and the Iconic Parable of Invisible Palestine'. *New Cinemas: Journal of Contemporary Film* 1, 24–39.

Bresheeth, Haim. 2006. 'The Nakba Projected: Recent Palestinian Cinema'. *Third Text* 20 (3/4): 499–509.

Bresheeth, Haim. 2018. "Zionism, Islamophobia and Judeophobia in Contemporary Europe and Beyond: Realities and Propaganda." *Journal of Holy Land and Palestine Studies* 17 (2): 193–220.

Gertz, Nurith and George Khleifi. 2008. *Palestinian Cinema: Landscape, Trauma and Memory*. Bloomington: Indiana University Press.

Green, Emma. 2018. 'Israel's New Law Inflames the Core Tension in Its Identity'. *The Atlantic*, July 21, 2018.

Israel Film Fund. 2018. 'Our Films'. Israel Film Fund (accessed September 21, 2018) http://intl.filmfund.org.il/films/

Jerusalem Post. 2013. 'Bayit Yehudi Rejoice at "5 Broken Cameras" Oscar Loss'. *Jerusalem Post*, February 25, 2013. https://www.jpost.com/Breaking-News/Bayit-Yehudi-rejoice-a t-5-Broken-Cameras-Oscar-loss

Massad, Joseph. 2006. 'The Weapon of Culture: Cinema in the Palestinian Liberation Struggle'. In *Dreams of a Nation: On Palestinian Cinema*, edited by Hamid Dabashi, 32–44. London: Verso.

Naficy, Hamid. 2001. *An Accented Cinema: Exilic and Diasporic Filmmaking*. Princeton, NJ: Princeton University Press.

Said, Edward. [1995]2007. *The End of the Peace Process: Oslo and After*. 2nd ed. London: Granta Books.

Segal, H. 2013. 'Anti-Israel Festival'. *Yediot Ahronot*, January 14, 2013. http://www.ynet news.com/articles/0.7340.L-4332078.00.html

Shafik, Violet. 1998. *Arab Cinema: History and Cultural Identity*. Cairo: The American University in Cairo Press.

Troy, Gil. 2013. '"The Gatekeepers": Speaking Spooks' coup d'etat'. *Jerusalem Post*, April 30, 2013. https://www.jpost.com/Opinion/Columnists/The-Gatekeepers-Speaking-spooks-coup-detat-311628

11

SCRATCH VIDEO REVISITED

Nick Cope

Introduction

During the summer of 1984, the Fridge Nightclub in London became the hub for a loose alliance of young video makers to gather and screen work, showcasing new video production techniques and practices that were politically astute and radical in both form and content. Domestic video formats introduced into Britain in 1978 were becoming readily available, affordable, technically sophisticated and widespread by the early 1980s, and facilitated easy and cheap recording of broadcast television. Re-editing and re-contextualising this footage became the modus operandi of this newly emerging genre that came to be known as Scratch Video. Championed by a small coterie of critics and curators, Scratch was, however, swiftly recuperated into gallery contexts and mainstream media. Both praised and criticised at the time, more recent re-evaluations recognise Scratch as a profound and radical exemplar in innovative sound and image compositional practice. Overtly political in a politically polarised time, Scratch has been described as a 'carnival of resistance' (Evans 2005, 5), and this political quality, together with its visionary aesthetic – Scratch anticipated both the creative possibilities afforded by digital media and the Internet, as well as sampling and remix technologies and practices – has led to it being dubbed 'the one true British Avant-Garde of the twentieth century' (Cubitt 2009, n.p.).

However, despite Scratch's re-evaluation and entry into the canon of UK video art, several aspects of the movement remain overlooked. In revisiting Scratch and examining its appraisals, this chapter will cast new perspectives on the role and significance of Scratch for British radical film culture and history. In particular, I will argue that Andy Birtwistle's (2010) recognition of Scratch as an exemplar of affective audiovisuality, a form of visual music, poses a radical challenge to its critics, and foregrounds a previous failure to consider sound as a critical element of the address of moving image practice. Seen in this light, Scratch emerges also as a major early contributor to what Vernalis, Richardson and Gorbman (2013) have called the 'new audiovisual aesthetics'.

History

Shortly after the 1981 riots in Brixton, South London, the founders of the legendary London-based punk rock venue the Roxy Club, Andrew Czezowski and Susan Carrington, opened their new club, The Fridge. Located above the Iceland frozen food store in Brixton Road, the club integrated moving image culture into its visual design, featuring 'a pyramid of broken TVs showing John Maybury videos as part of a radical décor that included beat-up fridges and (fake) dead cats hanging from its ceiling' (de Florence 2009, n.p.). French artist Bruno de Florence created the installation of twenty-five old television sets, stacked up and chained together by the dance floor, known as 'The Video Lounge'. Twice a week he ran screenings where several sources of video could be sent simultaneously to the TVs, creating the first-ever regular venue for video in a nightclub, and by 1984, pioneering the creation of what came to be known as Scratch Video.

De Florence's nights drew together an eclectic mix of young video makers. Their influences, practices and engagement with technologies diverged from the structuralist and formalist concerns of much video art and experimental film practice that had dominated British video art for the previous fifteen years. Instead of shooting their own material, Scratch artists re-edited and re-contextualised off-air television recordings, sometimes using image processors to affect the colour, texture, size, shape and montage, often in parodic form with 'Reagan, Thatcher and the "military industrial complex" as main targets' (Rees 2011, 105). In this way, Scratch was a major departure from what had come before it, and signalled a new and exciting potential opportunity for video artists. As Birtwistle (2010) puts it, the radical implications of the new technologies meant that:

> For the first time ever, the sounds and images of broadcast television became permanently available to almost anyone who wanted to record them. This not only provided Scratch artists with the material content of their work, but also signalled a change in the relationship between the producers and consumers of television. In short, the VCR prompted and supported a culture of audiovisual appropriation that found its most immediate manifestation in Scratch.
>
> *(244–5)*

The term Scratch was first applied to records coming out of New York's hip hop scene, where artists such as Grandmaster Flash showcased new styles of scratching, looping, repeating and mixing records, sounds and music. As with Scratch video, it was technological innovation – DJ turntables, among other things – that made possible the scratching and remixing in hip hop. David Toop (1991) describes listening to Scratch records as akin to 'an electronic blip-storm of cartoon voices, commercials, bursts of movie and TV dialogues, scratches, funk fragments, power chords, brass stabs, frantic percussion breaks': an account of an aural experience not so different from that which might greet the eyes and ears on encountering de Florence's video installation at The Fridge (184). Scratch artist George Barber (1990) credits journalist Pat Sweeney with coining the term Scratch Video in 1984, 'comparing it to New York's Hip Hop scene' (116). The combination of off-air video recording and advances in edit suite technologies meant that video material could be looped, repeated and mixed in methods analogous to and informed by how hip-hop artists were approaching record production. Audio could be edited independently of images with technology opening up new opportunities to explore the juxtaposition of music, sound and moving image. 'Editing was central to Scratch .... The first wave of "decent" technology did indeed help delineate an aesthetic and make achievable the first truly edit based video form' (Barber 1990, 115).

Dissemination, recuperation and decline

Scratch made a big impact partly because of the highly enthusiastic reviews it received from key advocates writing in the popular cultural press. Andy Lipman was Scratch video's first propagandist and, as editor of the video column in London's listings magazine, *City Limits*, Lipman made it his business to get to know all the artists screening work at The Fridge.[1] His first article on the movement, 'Scratch and Run', made the front cover in October 1984. Extolling the radical potential of Scratch, he noted the connection to hip hop and emphasised the 'inter-active response to the one-way arrogance of broadcast television' through a fluidity of video editing, 'more akin to sound-mixing than montage film techniques, with a healthy critique of the mass media':

> Hip-hop video, image break-dancing: television does a body pop. Broadcast TV is scoured for arresting images and fed into video editing systems like shredding machines. The fusion of funk rhythms and visuals on collision course crumble original context. Reassurance and sweet reason, television's facade disintegrate before your bombarded eyes .... Video scratching is an interactive response to the one-way arrogance of broadcast television .... If television is our shop window on the world, scratch has just chucked a brick through it and is busy looting 30 years of goodies, with abandon.
>
> *(Lipman 1984, 18–19)*

Lipman lists a diverse collection of individuals and groups working with video, drawing reference to underlying themes of political oppositional practices, strategies of questioning and subverting broadcast television, and a loose alliance of alternative and 'industrial music' practices and practitioners, video artists, arts organisations and pop cultural remixing; specifically naming work by Nocturnal Emissions, Duvet Brothers, Kim Flitcroft and Sandra Goldbacher, Paul Maben/Protein Video, George Barber, Derek Jarman, Cerith Wynn Evans, Richard Heslop, The Anti

Group, Psychic TV/Genesis P-Orridge, Doublevision and IKON, Clive Gillman, Graham Young, Steve Hawley, Jez Welsh and Nick Cope. Becoming 'an evangelist' for the form (Franklin 2014, 121), Lipman continued to champion Scratch throughout its short life, and is a key figure in its move from the relative obscurity of club screenings to its impact on the contemporary video art scene and mainstream broadcast media.

In December 1984, in partnership with de Florence, Lipman curated a series of screenings at the Institute of Contemporary Arts in central London, the first Scratch gallery screenings. *Scratch Television: Watch This Space* featured work by many of the above-mentioned artists, myself included, as well as Peter Savage, Graham Young, Bob Cuthbertson and Slack Video. Its impact was swift and further gallery screenings followed. As writer and programmer, Michael O'Pray, commented, Scratch was filling a void in a 'fragmented and rather tired area' (O'Pray 1986, 34). The recently formed Film and Video Umbrella (FVU) was initiated in 1985 by O'Pray and David Curtis, film officer at the Arts Council, to curate touring programmes of historically influential works, and to create a platform for contemporary talents innovating with film and video. For its second programme, Mark Wilcox, Alex Graham and O'Pray curated *Subverting Television*, intended as an early snapshot glimpse of the 'nascent "scratch video" movement' (FVU 2018, n.p.).

A further programme of Scratch works selected by O'Pray and Tina Keane was included in *The New Pluralism: British Film and Video 1980–85* at the Tate Gallery, London, in April 1985. Scratch briefly made it onto television, with Lipman curating *Scratch Now! The State of the Art* as part of *Channel 5: A Showcase for Video*, a project that ran throughout September 1985 in London to accompany screenings of the UK Channel 4 television series, *The Eleventh Hour*, that same month. Three TV episodes covered contemporary British video art, with one episode dedicated to Scratch presented by Lipman and fellow video critic, Sean Cubitt. Scratch faced a number of challenges in its encounter with broadcast media; technical broadcast quality thresholds have long been a hurdle for non-broadcast quality formats to negotiate in order to be screened, and a further hurdle was copyright clearance (Dovey [1986]1996).

While domestic video formats facilitated the ease of recording off-air footage, it was developments of the semi-professional (though lower than broadcast standard) U-matic video format and the Sony Series 5 U-matic video editing suite that impacted on how Scratch artists could manipulate and montage their source material. These could facilitate video editing accuracy to within one fifth of a second or more, still very rough by contemporary standards but a significant advancement on previous technologies at the time. The U-matic format was a significant improvement on home video formats, where editing was a very haphazard and inaccurate affair, often resulting in visual noise at the intersection of cuts. Moreover, the new U-matic technologies were becoming cheaper, easier to use and more accessible, occupying a space between expensive broadcast television facilities and the new domestic formats. Significantly, a handful of art colleges and local community video projects were investing in this equipment, and through these the Scratch video artists were accessing the means of production and creating their work. The intersection of technology with the educational and community media contexts of the time was a crucial – yet mostly overlooked – component of the context in which Scratch emerged.

Concurrent with the inroads Lipman had been making in his exposure of Scratch to the gallery, video art and TV broadcast sectors, George Barber was exploring the potentials of the new domestic formats for independent distribution, to significant effect. In 1984 and 1985 Barber compiled two collections, *The Greatest Hits of Scratch Video 1 & 2*, and self-distributed by mail order on VHS cassette. Barber garnered significant press coverage, including a feature in the national *Sunday Times* magazine, and sold around 800 copies of the cassettes – significantly more than many other video distribution projects of the time (Knight and Thomas 2012, 111). The first thirty-minute volume brought together works by Barber, The Duvet Brothers (Rik Lander and Peter Boyd-Maclean), Kim Flitcroft and Sandra Goldbacher, John Scarlett-Davis, Jeffrey Hinton and John Maybury. The second saw work by Gorilla Tapes (Gavin Hodge, Jean McClements, Jon Dovey and Tim Morrison) join further work by Barber, Flitcroft and Goldbacher and the Duvet Brothers. Together, they established a canon of Scratch works through the comprehensive collection of pieces and the publicity the tapes received.

However, soon after these canonising volumes were released, Scratch video began to wane, with some commentators at the time attributing this to the speed with which the style and techniques of Scratch were recuperated into mainstream visual culture. In the month before *The Eleventh Hour* broadcast, O'Pray, Lipman and Cubitt, accompanied by artists George Barber and Tim Morrison, screened the *Subverting Television* selection at the Edinburgh Television Festival for an audience of television executives. Rees (2011) would later note the 'immediate impact' of the work 'on astonished TV executives', and the alarming speed with which its devices were appropriated into televisual culture (105). Indeed, John Walker recalled that even as early as September 1985, 'the opinion was voiced that the fashion for Scratch was over because it had already been recuperated by the mass media' (Walker 1987, 158), arguably evidenced by Paul Hardcastle's pop record and Scratch-style video ('19') reaching number one in the UK pop charts. Even Lipman, Scratch's first flag-waver, became its pallbearer, declaring 'Scratch: Dead on Arrival' and that 'Scratch video has not only arrived, it's already mainstream' (Lipman 1985b, 7–9). Whilst the Duvet Brothers toured their *Live Multiscreen Scratch* multi-monitor show nationally and internationally for three years between 1984 and 1987, most of the other artists involved moved on to other projects. Following the FVU tours, no further significant screenings took place for over twenty years; Scratch becoming a short-lived, albeit highly significant, cultural phenomenon.

Critical reception and reappraisal

Initial critical reaction in the 1980s was partisan, harsh and damning. Critics tended to concentrate on the swift recuperation of Scratch techniques by broadcasters, and to dismiss the engagement with new technologies of post-production as empty techno wizardry. These critiques were largely rooted in a formalist avant-garde position derived from the conceptual traditions of semiology and structuralism that had dominated critical discourse in the art world as well as its institutions of funding and distribution since the 1970s. As such, the critiques were deeply suspicious both of a video art that engaged with populist tendencies (Welsh [1984]1999), and of the dangers of techno-centric practices (Hawley [1988]2002). The visual pleasure and centrality of music to Scratch was anathema to contemporary ideas regarding the shape and form that critical political visual discourse ought to take, and Scratch techniques were dismissed as boys playing with their toys (Elwes 1985). However, Lipman was not alone in his defence of the form. John Walker, in the first major study of the relationship between visual arts and pop music, addressed Elwes' criticisms by arguing that the minimal, conceptual video of the 1960s and 1970s had failed to engage audiences. Instead, he argued that, 'If video-makers want to communicate with a wider public, then visual pleasure had to be used – as it is in advertising – firstly to attract attention and secondly to sugar the ideological pill' (Walker 1987, 157). Adding that entertainment and education need not be mutually exclusive, Walker countered Elwes' assertion that, in Scratch's montage of dole queue imagery and techno music, 'we are left wondering whether to debate the evils of unemployment or get up and dance' (Elwes 1985, 6–7).

Lipman (1985a) continued to eulogise Scratch and its pioneering challenge by the new generation of artists in 'Taking TV Apart', a booklet accompanying *The Eleventh Hour* broadcast, but he also acknowledged the criticisms of Scratch – its lack of critical analysis, its celebrations of the imagery it sought to undermine, its dependency on received imagery and a supposed failure to pose positive alternatives to the empty values it exposes. However, he notes that the criticism is 'motivated by a resentment towards the populist appeal of Scratch' and, in a far-sighted claim over the significance of the movement, he argues that it

> misses the point about the practice of Scratch, regardless of the end product, which anticipates the inter-active era of electronic networks, where the combination of video and computer promises to allow the exchange and re-processing of information, into new visions to suit individual taste. Unlike the one-way system of current broadcast media, there could be a network resembling the telephone system, where calls, or programmes, or computer software could both be made and received by each individual. Such developments raise fundamental questions about the status of the 'artist' and art objects. Scratch takes the broadcast media as its paintbox, the video recorder as its palette, and the TV screen as its canvas.
>
> *(Lipman 1985a, 10)*

In this visionary response, Lipman clearly anticipates the development of the Internet and the explosion of creative possibilities forged by convergent digital media, and outlines the radical proposal in Scratch that he found so appealing. Furthermore, Scratch anticipated important debates that would emerge around sampling technologies, plunderphonics, online mash-up culture and file sharing, including its 'inherent challenge to copyright law' that Dovey ([1986]1996) explored in his account of clearing Gorilla Tapes' work for broadcast (283–90), and which hindered the wider exposure of Scratch at the time.

From the late 1990s, reappraisals of Scratch began to appear in emerging video art histories.[2] Re-evaluations of perspectives and more positive acknowledgements of its import and impact followed. Welsh (1992) described Scratch as a form that irretrievably changed the face of video art, which in turn shaped the development of pop video, youth TV and videographics, and emphasised the seismic shifts in the perception of Scratch's cultural value:

> Sour faced avant-gardists were keen to dismiss Scratch as 'decadent' and 'ideologically suspect' or to point out that it was unoriginal …. But these criticisms were misdirected and short sighted …. Scratch Video … changed the way television looks … [and] has even influenced the way Hollywood writes its scripts.
>
> *(Welsh 1992, 136)*

By 2005 Elwes had re-appraised her views, addressing Scratch at some length and recognising its importance politically: 'scratch must take the credit for being the last UK video movement that was allied to a collective social and political consciousness, before the 1990s made the selling of the artist the central purpose of art'

FIGURE 11.1 Original programme notes from Scratch Television, the first gallery screenings of Scratch, ICA London, December 1984. Courtesy of Institute of Contemporary Arts, London.

(Elwes 2005, 116). This is echoed by Rees (2007), who acknowledges that the 'short-lived but very effective' movement 'was also the most explicitly political video art in ten years' (161).

The most significant re-evaluation of Scratch comes from Birtwistle (2010), who recognises Scratch as a profound and radical exemplar in innovative sound and image compositional practice and a radical challenge to its critics. By exploring previously neglected and under-theorised aspects of film and video sound, Birtwistle claims Scratch as a form of visual music, or cinesonics, locating the form in new and emerging contexts of affective cinema and audiovisuality. Birtwistle maintains that Scratch was pioneering forms of audiovisual practice ahead of critical discourse, and as such posed a radical challenge to critics at the time, for whom:

> Scratch simply did not make sense; they were unable to situate the affective and sensational dimensions of the form's audiovisuality within existing critical and theoretical frameworks. All the critics of Scratch could see were insufficiencies, and it has taken more than two decades for this moment to be affirmed as a radical departure from the critical and creative agenda set in motion by the linguistic turn of structuralism.
>
> (272)

The lack identified by Birtwistle in the critical culture of 1980s video art helps to explain oversights that have occurred in the historical record with regard to video practices engaging with music as a key component. The late 1970s and early 1980s saw the emergence of 'a new kind of media' in the wake of punk, centred around an alternative culture arising from a DIY infrastructure of independent record labels, distribution and record stores (Welsh [1984]1999, 270). Some of these labels and post-punk groups pioneered independent media production and distribution practices that to-date have received scant attention in video art histories (see Cope 2018).

The relationships between and across cultural forms and communities such as music and film are a rich and under-explored aspect of radical media cultures more generally. Scratch arises from, was influenced by, and operated in the networks spawned through the independent music sector as much as through video art. Music could be looked to for models of composition and structural organisation, as well as distribution, and the music press used as a means of publicity and promotion. Andy Lipman (1984) name-checks Ikon and Doublevision in his *City Limits* article and Al Rees (2011) makes evident the connections between the Scratch generation of filmmakers, their roots in a 'punk-era revision of the underground' and the encounters of Ken Russell, Kenneth Anger, Derek Jarman, Genesis P-Orridge of Throbbing Gristle and William Burroughs. Rees observed a fusing of Jarman and P-Orridge 'tendencies' with younger filmmakers 'drawn to their world of free play, extremist imagery and a hallucinatory "dream-machine" cinema', resulting in a 'new punk underground', who led a 'rebellion against the structural avant-garde which preceded it' (86). While many emerging histories of film and video maintain a separation of address of genres and practices, Rees links these histories, recognising the intertwined networks, practices and cultures at play. Revisiting

Scratch thus yields a further potential lesson for contemporary radical film cultures. What can those involved in radical film practice today learn from their counterparts in other media, and vice versa? These relationships, and their value, can serve to enrich and empower those involved, and strengthen the cultures they are involved in building.

Aside from this handful of (usually brief) references scattered across the histories of (UK) video art published from the 1990s onwards, Scratch appeared largely forgotten. This began to change in the mid-2000s following the *Rewind* project, one of the first major efforts to restore and archive early British video. This project resulted in some of the first Scratch screenings since the 1980s. As the programme notes observed, until then Scratch had been 'generally forgotten about in contemporary culture' (Rewind 2018, n.p.). Curated by *Rewind*'s archivist, Adam Lockhart, the programme sought to include both the better known canon of work compiled by Barber as well as other works from the time including the Japanese/ German collaboration between Hada and Hiller, and my own rarely screened and more ambient piece *Suffer Bomb Disease* (1985).

With the *Rewind* project based in Scotland, many of its screenings and activities have been based in the region, breaking the London-centric focus of much of the earlier Scratch screenings. However, in May 2008, Seventeen Gallery in London curated a retrospective exhibition, *Scratch!*, which ran for a month and featured work by Gorilla Tapes, Goldbacher & Flitcroft, Barber and the Duvet Brothers. Encapsulating the problems of a reductive and limiting approach to radical film history that so often obscures as much as it reveals, the exhibition claimed these artists as the entirety of the movement and short-sightedly located the genre as a purely London-based phenomenon.

These screenings and the very much ongoing re-appraisal of the impact of Scratch demonstrate what is at stake in the 'rediscovery' of radical film histories.[3] It also illustrates how those of us involved are engaged in contemporary – rather than historical – struggles over the meaning, history and significance of the work and its significant value for audiences today.

Notes

1 Lipman had been involved in community video work since 1980, project co-ordinating the Grierson Award-winning documentary 'Framed Youth' in 1983, recognised by Ieuan Franklin (2014, 118) as 'a high watermark in the history of both community video and the realization or fulfilment of Channel 4's remit'. The documentary arose from a South London community video project co-ordinated by Lipman with Philip Timmins, which facilitated a group of twenty-five gay and lesbian young people to acquire and share video production skills both behind and in front of the camera. Launching the careers of both musician Jimmy Somerville and artist and filmmaker Isaac Julien amongst others, the film, Franklin notes, 'can be regarded as an early example of *scratch video*' (his emphasis) through its use of a collage of found footage including cartoons, news clips and TV drama excerpts, and inspired Lipman to become 'an evangelist for the art of the video remix' (118). He would later go on to propose and produce Channel 4's *The Media Show* and sadly died in 1997 at the age of 45.
2 A number of media art histories appeared with the new millennium, including Rees (1999), Elwes (2005) and Curtis (2007).

3 As indicated by academic engagement, such as Cope (2012, 2018) and Goldsmith (2015), and screenings of my own and others' work at the UK's Media, Communications and Cultural Studies Association conference in 2015, the *Up Down Top Bottom Strange and Charm* International Arts Festival in 2016 and Sheffield Doc Fest in 2018. Will Fowler curated a major BFI programme, *This Is Now: Film and Video after Punk – Rediscovering Underground Film 1979–85* in 2015 (yet once again there was a predominantly London-centric slant to the work selected). The 2019 London Short Film Festival also celebrated Scratch in its opening event, *All That Scratching Is Making Me Itch*, returning Scratch once more to the ICA.

References

Barber, George. 1990. 'Scratch and After: Edit Suite Technology and the Determination of Style in Video Art'. In Paul Hayward, ed. *Culture Technology and Creativity in the Late Twentieth Century*. London: John Libbey.

Birtwistle, Andy. 2010. *Cinesonica: Sounding Film and Video*. Manchester: Manchester University Press.

Cope, Nick. 2012. *Northern Industrial Scratch: The History and Contexts of a Visual Music Practice*. Thesis (PhD). University of Sunderland. Available from: https://sure.sunderland.ac.uk/3287/ (accessed October 12, 2017).

Cope, Nick. 2018. 'Nothing Here Now but the Recordings: The Moving Image Record of Joy Division and the Factory Video Unit'. In Martin Power, Eoin Devereux and Aileen Dillane, eds. *Heart and Soul: Critical Essays on Joy Division*. London: Rowan and Littlefield.

Cubitt, Sean. 2009. 'Scratch Video'. Scratch Video Installation, Street Level Gallery, Glasgow, March 16–21, 2009. Live Webcast from Australia, March 20, 2009: transcription by Nick Cope from QuickTime Movie recording.

Curtis, David. 2007. *A History of Artists' Film and Video in Britain*. London: BFI.

de Florence, Bruno. 2009. *Video Lounge* [online]. Available from: http://www.deflorence.com/?p=283 (accessed March 12, 2019).

Dovey, Jon. [1986]1996. 'Copyright as Censorship: Notes on "Death Valley Days"'. In Julia Knight, ed., *Diverse Practices: A Critical Reader on British Video Art*. Luton: University of Luton Press/Arts Council England, 283–290.

Elwes, Catherine. 1985. 'Through Deconstruction to Reconstruction'. *Independent Video*, 48, November, 21–23. Available from: http://fv-distribution-database.ac.uk/PDFs/Channel5-850900.pdf (accessed July 15, 2018).

Elwes, Catherine. 2005. *Video Art, A Guided Tour*. London: I.B. Taurus.

Evans, Gareth. 2005. 'The Boy from Georgetown'. In Steven Bode and Nina Ernst, eds. *George Barber*. London: Film and Video Umbrella (online, with slight amendments). Available from: http://www.luxonline.org.uk/artists/george_barber/essay(1).html (accessed October 12, 2017).

Film and Video Umbrella. FVU. 2018. 'FVU Touring Programmes 1985'. *Film and Video Umbrella* (online). Available from: https://www.fvu.co.uk/projects/fvu-touring-programmes-1985 (accessed July 11, 2018).

Franklin, Ieuan. 2014. 'Talking Liberties: *Framed Youth*, Community Video and Channel 4's Remit in Action'. In Christopher Pullen, ed. *Queer Youth and Media Cultures*. Basingstoke: Palgrave.

Goldsmith, Leo. 2015. 'Scratch's Third Body: Video Talks Back to Television'. *View: Journal of European Television History and Culture* (online), 4 (8). Available from: http://ojs.viewjournal.eu/index.php/view/article/view/JETHC097/210 (accessed May 2, 2019).

Hawley, Steve. [1988]2002. 'Spin, Tumble, Freeze: Technology and Video Art'. Undercut 16. In Nina Danino, and Michael Maziere, eds., *The Undercut Reader*. London: Wallflower Press.

Knight, Julia and Thomas, Peter. 2012. *Reaching Audiences: Distribution and Promotion of Alternative Moving Image*. Bristol: Intellect.

Lipman, Andy. 1984. 'Scratch and Run'. *City Limits*, 5–11 October, 18–19. Available from: https://nickcopefilm.files.wordpress.com/2013/09/northern-industrial-scratch-final-web.pdf pp. 114–115 (accessed October 12, 2017).

Lipman, Andy. 1985a. *Video: The State of the Art*. London: Channel 4/Comedia.

Lipman, Andy. 1985b. 'Scratch: Dead on Arrival?' *IPPA Bulletin*, December, 7–9. Available from: http://uodwebservices.co.uk/documents/Duvet%20Brothers/DB039.pdf (accessed March 12, 2019).

O'Pray, Michael. 1986. 'Scratching Deeper'. *Art Monthly* 95, April, 34. Available from: http://www.duvetbrothers.com/cuttings.htm (accessed March 12, 2019).

Rees, Al. 2007. 'Experimenting on Air: UK Artists' Film on Television'. In Laura Mulvey and Jamie Sexton, eds. *Experimental British Television*. Manchester: Manchester University Press.

Rees, Al. 2011. *A History of Experimental Film and Video*. 2nd edition. London: BFI Publishing.

Rewind. 2018. *Artists' Video in the 70s and 80s* [online]. Available from: http://www.rewind.ac.uk/rewind/index.php/Welcome (accessed July 16, 2018).

Toop, David. 1991. *Rap Attack 2: African Rap to Global Hip Hop*. London: Serpent's Tail.

Vernalis, Carol, Richardson, John and Gorbman, Claudia, eds. 2013. *The Oxford Handbook of New Audiovisual Aesthetics*. Oxford: Oxford University Press.

Walker, John A. 1987. *Cross-Overs: Art into Pop/Pop into Art*. London: Comedia.

Welsh, Jez. [1984]1999. 'Post-modernism and the Populist Tendency'. Undercut 12, summer 1984 1984. In Margaret Dickinson, ed., *Rogue Reels: Oppositional Film in Britain, 1945–1990*. London: BFI, 190–196.

Welsh, Jez. [1992]1996. 'One Nation Under a Will (of Iron), or: The Shiny Toys of Thatcher's Children'. Kunstforum International, 117, Germany. In Julia Knight, ed., *Diverse Practices, A Critical Reader on British Video Art*. Luton: University of Luton Press/Arts Council England.

Filmography

Death Valley Days, 1984. Video. Luton: Gorilla Tapes. Available from: https://lux.org.uk/artist/gorilla-tapes (accessed October 12, 2017).

Doublevision presents; Cabaret Voltaire, 1982. Video. Nottingham: Doublevision.

Doublevision presents; Cabaret Voltaire, 2004. DVD. London: Mute Records.

A Factory Complication, 1982. Video. Manchester: Factory/Ikon.

A Factory Video, 1982. Video. Manchester: Factory/Ikon.

Joy Division 'Here are the Young Men', 1982. Video. Manchester: Factory/Ikon.

Paul Hardcastle '19', 1985. Directed by Jonas McCord, Bill Couterie/Ken Grunbaum. London: Chrysalis Records. Available from: https://www.youtube.com/watch?v=hRJFvtvTGEk (accessed July 12, 2018).

TGV: The Video Archive of Throbbing Gristle, 2007. DVD. London: Industrial Records.

The Greatest Hits of Scratch Video: volumes 1 and 2, 1984. Video. London: George Barber. Available from: http://www.luxonline.org.uk/artists/george_barber/the_greatest_hits_of_scratch_video.html (accessed October 12, 2017).

23 Skidoo – Seven Songs, 1984. Video. Directed by Richard Heslop. Nottingham: Doublevision. Available from: https://vimeo.com/46603784 (accessed July 16, 2018).

View From Hear, 1984. Video. Directed by Nick Cope. Sheffield: 391/Image Factory. Available from: https://nickcopefilm.com/391-view-from-hear-videos/ (accessed December 16, 2017).

Films online

A selection of Scratch videos available on YouTube, including work by George Barber, The Duvet Brothers and Gorilla Tapes: https://www.youtube.com/playlist?list=PLB31727C7B91E565C (accessed June 6, 2017).

A selection of Nick Cope's Scratch video and other related work: https://nickcopefilm.com/2013/09/17/sheffield-scratch-and-super-8/(accessed June 6, 2017).

12

A FUNNY THING HAPPENED ON THE WAY TO UTOPIA – THE WORKSHOP DECLARATION (1982–1989)

Andy Robson

The Workshop Declaration (1982–1989) was a radical intervention within the UK film and television industry, both on a structural and organisational level. Formulated in March 1982 by the Association of Cinematograph, Television and Allied Technicians (ACTT), the main film and television trade union in the UK, together with Channel 4, the British Film Institute (BFI), the Regional Arts Associations (RAA) and the Independent Filmmakers' Association (IFA), the Workshop Declaration was a far-reaching arrangement that aimed to nurture a film practice radically different from the mainstream film and broadcasting industry. Crucially, this was not a conventional agreement negotiated between a union and an employer's organisation. It was a statement of principles adopted by the ACTT to allow its members to engage in non-commercial film and video work in an effort to create a permanently funded regional network of film and video workshops that would actively engage with local communities long-term.

To be franchised by the union, funding would be provided to a film workshop that would consist of a minimum of four full-time members on an equal fixed wage (£10,088 in 1982). The Declaration stipulated that the regional workshops would operate on a non-commercial and non-profit distributing basis, with cross-grade working – as opposed to the rigid specialism of director, editor, camera, sound, etc. – encouraged. Crucially, to strengthen and maintain the sector, copyright on all productions would be retained by the workshop. The Declaration was underpinned by 'integrated practice' whereby the practice of the filmmaker would not be confined to production alone but significantly extend to exhibition and distribution activities. Filmmakers would therefore participate with the community on a long-term, multi-dimensional level, the impact of which would generate a unique film and video culture. However, despite being a profoundly radical agreement that nurtured and produced some of the most politically provocative films ever broadcast in Britain, the wider impact of the Workshop Declaration has largely been overlooked by film and media scholars for much of the last thirty years.

The films and videos cultivated under the Workshop Declaration are, however, barring a select few, routinely dismissed and discussions of integrated practice within an industrial context are widely derided. The landscape of the film and television industry has of course drastically altered since the 1980s. Memories of cooperative collective bargaining may seem positively bygone from today's perspective, and collective decision-making based on the shared use of cumbersome film and video equipment may seem a distant concept for a generation of film- and video-makers using affordable, individualised and self-standing digital audio-visual paraphernalia. Additionally, the mechanisms that implemented the Workshop Declaration, namely the closed-shop system of the trade union movement, have been dismantled and nullified, and national and regional funding policies supporting the Declaration have been redrawn and realigned. Since the global economic crisis in 2008 and the austerity measures instituted by the UK government impacting arts funding, many film practitioners and researchers have revisited previous eras of cine-activism for inspiration.

However, the Workshop Declaration has largely been discounted from these discussions on account of histories focusing predominantly on the complications that ultimately led to the decline of the workshop movement. This is jarring given that the 1980s witnessed a higher level of state funding for film activities than the decade before, with provision being dispersed over a wider geographical area. In comparable times of austerity, the Workshop Declaration is significant for contemporary film practitioners as it increased the volume of independent moving image work distributed and exhibited outside of conventional channels, while simultaneously remedying workplace isolation and unemployment discontinuity in the sector. Furthermore, it provided a multi-funded framework that ultimately led to a body of work that confronted the beginnings of the neo-liberal project in Britain, enabling both filmmaking and political activism to merge and give voice to the 'enemy within' (miners, trade unions, women of Greenham Common), while concurrently increasing the inclusion of BAME, LGBTQ+ and female filmmakers in the film industry.

This chapter aims to counter this dismissive discourse on the Workshop Declaration, while also positioning integrated practice as an increasingly relevant and applicable model for today's DIY film, video and online culture. The Workshop Declaration, including its productions, exhibition spaces and distribution networks, would be an appropriate example within Eshun and Gray's (2011) discourse of the *militant image*. Eshun and Gray explore a terrain of '*ciné-geography*' that revisits the archives of oppositional filmmaking that have been overlooked. Such an endeavour encompasses a series of encounters with 'practices and formulations that are often deemed embarrassing and foolhardy, if not altogether discredited by contemporary historiography' (Eshun and Gray 2011, 1). *Ciné-geography* denotes not just specific films made in this era but also the 'new modes of production, exhibition, distribution, pedagogy, and training made possible in these historical formations' (Eshun and Gray 2011, 1).

This re-evaluation of the Workshop Declaration is motivated by a case study on an integral member of the workshop movement, the Newcastle-based Amber Film and Photography Collective. Amber is significant within this *ciné-geography*. The collective was pivotal in the inception of the Workshop Declaration, and now past its fiftieth year, has continued to integrate production, exhibition and distribution activities across its work despite fluctuating funding conditions. The research provided access to Amber's extensive paper archive, presenting the opportunity to explore key documents related to the Workshop Declaration within Amber's extensive collection, an era spanning 1974–1994. Crucially, the term *ciné-geography* also refers to the 'afterlives' of the militant image, for example the digital platforms, formats, applications, files and torrents that offer potential for the workshop model to be reworked online (Eshun and Gray 2011, 1).

ACTT

The Workshop Declaration was officially endorsed on March 25, 1982, by its signatories at an ACTT Film Production Branch meeting in Soho Square, London. More accurately, however, the Declaration originated eight years prior to that date and, crucially, outside of London. Its core impetus came from a small group of regional filmmakers and campaigners, for whom the London-based film industry was inaccessible and altogether irrelevant to their regional film activities.

Roy Lockett, the Deputy Secretary-General of ACTT, an integral figure with the inception of the Workshop Declaration, declared in *Action! Fifty Years in the Life of a Union*, an anniversary tribute to ACTT, that the Declaration was an unparalleled achievement for the film and television industry:

> For less than the budget of one smallish feature, a network of vigorous production units has emerged, with strong regional roots and functions, ranging from exhibition and research, to education and production. With strong links to the labour movement and an abrasive radicalism, the workshops are the nearest any organisation has come to building a national film culture from the bottom up … breaking out of the erratic lottery of one-off productions.
>
> *(Lockett 1983, 167)*

The UK film workshop movement emerged in the late 1960s, forged out of the radical political confrontations of time; opposition to the Vietnam War, second-wave feminism, global student protests and the cine-activism that occurred in Paris in May 1968 where the filmmakers, trade unions and the labour movement momentarily converged. The working methods of the London Filmmakers Co-op, founded in London in 1966, and its non-hierarchical, collective management structure and integration of production, distribution and exhibition, was a key blueprint for the developing movement. Intrinsic to that method was the long-term engagement pursued by the film and video workshop with their chosen community. Workshops, such as Amber in the North East of England, began to form reciprocal relationships with a chosen regional community. Alternative film and video output was produced with that community, who in turn would then form an audience for that product.

The original collaborative funding structure was negotiated through new agreements and codes of practice designed to meet the aspirations and working practices of the developing workshop sector. This was not only an unprecedented advancement for the industry, it was also a cultural and structural breakthrough within ACTT. Since its foundation in 1933, ACT (later adding Television in 1956), functioned both as a trade union negotiating appropriate terms and conditions for its members and as a guild representing the different craft skills in the film and television industries. ACTT operated a pre-entry closed shop meaning that only ACTT members of the union could be considered for employment. Regulated admission meant there was never any alternative labour force, and therefore provided the ACTT with leverage in any negotiation with employers. Industrial checks on arrangements were rigorously upheld to guarantee there was a balanced pool of labour that ensured members' employment (Reid 2017, 251).

Despite a dominant commercial focus, ACTT also had a latent cultural brief that was actively concerned with all cultural aspects of films, broadcasting and recorded material, particularly the implications of the communication industry on the public. In 1984, Lockett produced a Background Paper for a TUC Arts Policy Discussion, detailing the ACTT's cultural evolution. The new arrangement was a consequence of the recruitment of many regional film workers previously excluded from the union's infrastructure. Now that the work of these workshops was recognised, the Workshop Declaration would prevent further casualisation within the sector. Additionally, it provided the workshop sector with democratic control of their own organisations, the retention of copyright, annual funding of integrated practices built around workshop production, and 'the freedom to engage in radical, socialist, feminist and community-based production outside the commercial parameters of the mainstream industry' (Lockett 1984, 1).

Channel 4

The Declaration was initiated eight months before Channel 4's first broadcast in November 1982. The newly formed channel viewed the workshops as a distinctive production sector that would deliver programmes for minority audiences and fulfil its original remit for innovative and experimental programming. The channel assigned a dedicated department, the Independent Film & Video Department, led by commissioning editor Alan Fountain, to oversee the workshop sector. Marking a major shift in the commissioning process, workshops would be financed over one to three years. Contrary to traditional one-off commissions, workshops were free to decide what films to make and had editorial control on the final cut of their work. Not only was this arrangement conducive to the channel's need to generate a distinctive product, it also afforded filmmakers time and space for experiment outside the demands of the market led economy. The workshops received equipment and salary subsidies from the channel, and in return the workshops produced a 'programme of work', consisting of several film and video productions that would evolve slowly over time. Once the work was near completion the channel would agree a price for the production under the buyback formula, a method based on a ratio of money to each minute of documentary and fiction produced, designed to generate further investment for the workshop model and practice within the sector.

In its first year of broadcasting, the channel contributed £875,000 to the workshop sector. Of this, £430,000 went to eight workshops franchised under the Declaration, facilitating their programmes of work over one or three years (Amber Film and Photography Collective [£48,000], Birmingham Film Workshop [£59,000], Cinema Action in London [£90,000], Four Corners in East London [£25,000], Frontroom [£96,000], and Newsreel in London [£19,000], North East Films [£19,000] and Trade Films in Gateshead [£14,000]). A further £86,000 was shared between eight film workshops, to nurture their practice towards being fully franchised (Bristol Co-op [£5,000], Changing Images [£4,000], East Anglia Film Co-op in Norwich [£5,000], Lusia Films in London [£3,000], New Cinema Workshop in Nottingham [£2,000], Poster Collective in London [£15,000], South Wales Women's Collective [5,000] and Manchester's Workers Film Association [£8,000]). And, an additional £30,000 was divided between ten developing video workshops. Moreover, the BFI contributed to the Workshop Declaration via the creation of the Regional Production Fund (RPF) in 1982. A fixed yearly rate of £220,000 was allocated to regional film and video workshops franchised by the ACTT. Benefitting from the fund in 1982 were Birmingham Film and Video Workshop, Trade Films, Leeds Animation Workshop and Sheffield Film Co-op.

Between 1982 and 1991 Channel 4 broadcast over seventy workshop productions in dedicated programme slots, *The Eleventh Hour* (1982–1989) and *People to People* (1983–1987). By 1986/87 fifteen workshops were franchised and a further four new workshops were receiving development funding. The workshop infrastructure was clearly burgeoning and integrated practice had expanded to areas of training, archiving, research and film education within communities. For instance, in 1986/87, Edinburgh Film Workshop Trust produced five films and videos, and provided training with weekly video and animation sessions. Likewise, Four Corners, in the London borough of Tower Hamlets, in addition to their four productions of that year, offered video projects for women and the unemployed. As well as making eight productions, Trade in Gateshead were collecting films made across the North East for preservation within a regional archive. Video making within the community was also supplied by workshops such as Chapter in Cardiff and Albany Video in Deptford. Similarly, in addition to their productions of that year, Sankofa and Ceddo ran regular training and community screenings in North London. The mid-1980s marked a productive peak with three innovative, award-winning workshop productions: Amber's *Seacoal* (1985), Black Audio Film Collective's *Handsworth Songs* (1986) and Birmingham Film and Video Workshop's *Out of Order* (1986). Following this success, it was announced that 'the hour of the workshops had arrived', due to the sector's growing skills and confidence that owed much to the infrastructure put in place by the Workshop Declaration (Petley 1988, 25).

However, concurrently the Workshop Declaration was viewed as anachronistic and unfashionable within the industry. Criticism focused principally on the output of the workshops. With some exceptions, productions were dismissed as 'bad work promoted as art', characterised by amateur, self-indulgent and conventionally dull documentaries (Fitzgerald 1988, 163). Even as early as 1985, christened *British Film Year*, a government-backed attempt to revitalise Britain's flagging cinema attendances and industry output, the workshops were routinely undervalued as merely a training ground or a route of promotion to the mainstream industry. Integrated practice or the alternative structures provided by the Workshop Declaration were downgraded in favour of the dominant forms of the film industry. Within the promotional material of *British Film Year*, the alternative, oppositional, social practices of the workshop movement were completely disavowed. Martin Auty underlined this disparaging tone declaring the workshop movement represented 'a sop to the collective conscience of the BFI, ACTT and Channel 4 by maintaining a tradition of independent filmmaking long after the audiences for such work have disappeared' (Auty 1985, 68). He also revealed an institutional resentment within the BFI towards the workshops for draining the resources from the Production Board to the point where the BFI could fund only one to two feature-length productions per year.

The Workshop Declaration operated over seven years, from 1982 to 1989. Its demise was signalled with the introduction of the Broadcast Act 1990, which drastically changed the broadcasting landscape. It initiated a new commercial agenda of competition, with an increased focus on audience figures. Both the BFI and the RAAs had received extensive cuts by the Conservative government, leaving Channel 4 as the sole funder of the Workshop Declaration. Channel 4, now under pressure to sell its own advertising, forced the Independent Film and Video Department to pursue a new venture, ironically titled *Television with a Difference*. Returning to a conventional one-off commissioning process, the new scheme effectively spelled the end of the revenue funding for the workshops.

Television with a difference

In preparation for this transition, Alan Fountain produced the discussion report, *Workshop Policy in the 1990s*, in April 1989, and distributed it amongst the film and video workshops. Instigating the rhetoric within discussions of the Workshop movement that would follow, the paper predominantly focused on the problems of the Workshop Declaration, whereby noteworthy achievements are treated as irregularities within a largely inadequate collective body of work. Fountain proclaimed the 'strikingly original agreement' had produced 'a steady flow of award-winning programmes and films which might not have been made outside the workshop or some similar agreement' (Fountain 1989, 2). He listed the Black Audio Film Collective's *Handsworth Songs* and *Testament* (1988), Amber's *Seacoal* and *Byker* (1983), Cinema Action's *Rocinante* (1986), Frontroom's *Acceptable Levels* (1983) and Birmingham Film and Video Workshop's *Out of Order* in this category. 'Some sharp and unusual documentaries from the workshops' are also acknowledged including Edinburgh Film Workshop Trust's *Northern Front* (1986), Newsreel's *Nambia: Tell The World* (1985) and *Welcome to the Spiv Economy* (1986), Steel Bank Film Co-op's *Please Don't Say We're Wonderful* (1986), Trade Films' *Farewell to the Welfare State* (1986) and Sheffield Film Co-op's *Bringing It All Back Home* (1987) (Fountain 1989, 2).

Fountain also recognised examples of workshops contributing 'to the formal development of programme making', noting Birmingham Film and Video Workshop's *Giro* (1985), and *Girl Zone* (1986), Amber Films' *T Dan Smith: A Funny Thing Happened on the Way to Utopia* (1987), Sankofa's *Passion of Remembrance* (1986) and, again, Black Audio's *Handsworth Songs* (Fountain 1989, 2). He commended the alternative arrangements that contributed to a wider, more diverse film culture by nurturing new voices, from significantly underrepresented directors, producers and technicians. Fountain considered the growth of the black and Asian film workshops (Ceddo, Sankofa, Black Audio Film Collective and Retake) as a significant achievement of this commitment. Equally, he draws attention to the work the Birmingham Film & Video Workshop achieved with young people and Red Flannel's activity with women in the Welsh valleys that would not have transpired without the stability of regular workshop funding.

Despite confidently stating that the workshop productions made a vital contribution to the political and aesthetic diversity of Channel 4, Fountain nevertheless underlined the inbuilt difficulties arising from the Declaration. A major concern for Fountain was that, by 1989, Channel 4 was the sole funder of workshop movement. Fiscal cuts to the Declaration's other signatories had a profound impact on the original aspirations of the workshop movement. A key issue for Fountain was that the long-term funding structure tended to draw the channel into contractual relations that often exceeded its own screen requirements, and therefore prevented it from funding workshops new to the movement. This produced a static workforce, with too little money to generate growth. Fountain argued that the franchised workshops, protective of the limited funds they did receive, inadvertently morphed into small institutions that were unable to accommodate or seek the next generations of creators. These problems in the sector compounded to the extent that some of the workshops' mode of practice had become indistinguishable from a conventional commissioning process.

Much of this analysis was supported and extended by Fountain's Deputy Commissioning Editor at the IFVD, Rod Stoneman (1992), in 'Sins of Commission', published in the film studies journal *Screen*. Significantly, Stoneman devalued the benefits of integrated practice, arguing the only genuine example of workshop practice, in terms of the effective fusion of production, exhibition and distribution was the *Miners Campaign Tapes* (1986), the video work made collectively by several workshops in support of the miners during their strike of 1984/85. Stoneman acknowledged that Channel 4 was culpable in this respect as it forced the groups to concentrate their efforts on production, as the promise of transmission to large audiences seemed to sideline the workshops' other commitments to distribution, exhibition, training and archiving (Stoneman 1992, 136).

The production-based relationship with Channel 4 effectively misrepresented the wider impact of the workshops. But to see the work in terms of product alone would distort the wide-ranging activities associated with integrated practice that was central to workshop process. From its origins in the late 1960s, the workshop movement had imperatively understood the importance of securing an audience for its productions. Workshops had developed and maintained various localised exhibition sites and distribution strategies throughout the country, ensuring the films and videos produced were viewed by the local community.

Throughout the 1980s the yearly BFI handbooks gave a full listing of every workshop in operation across Britain, both franchised and non-franchised, and provides a far more positive degree of evaluations of workshop productions and practice. The 1987 edition casts the Declaration's influence further by describing how the sector was 'the backbone of regional independent production in this country' and 'rapidly gaining international recognition' (BFI 1987, 47). It lists Amber's *T Dan Smith: A Funny Thing Happened on the Way to Utopia*, its third major film in two years, Cinema Action's *Rocinante*, Sankofa's *The Passion of Remembrance* and Black Audio Film Collective's *Handsworth Songs* as examples of the diverse range of productions cultivated by the Declaration, produced within a framework of integrated practice embracing exhibition, distribution and production:

> Not all workshops carry out all these activities as equal priorities, but the general understanding of the crucial interdependence between these factors within an alternative audio-visual culture, means that the workshops developed a special relationship to their audience with which they work.
>
> *(BFI 1987, 328)*

Ironically, the 1989 edition, published in the same year as Fountain's *Workshop Policy in the 1990s* report, declared 'in less than twenty years the workshops have moved from the margins to the centre of British audiovisual culture' (BFI 1989, 349). Completely contrasting with Auty's view, the Workshop Declaration is not positioned as an unnecessary irritant that diverted funding money away from the conventional British film industry but as a vital component within it. Interestingly, attention is also paid to the expanding workshop model that attracted several local authorities interested in developing alternative media industries 'due to the growth in new delivery and distribution' of the developing systems of cable and satellite (BFI 1989, 349). Following this enthusiasm for the new working methods under the workshop model the article optimistically concludes, 'the film and video workshops are likely to be a permanent element in the fast-changing audiovisual ecology' (BFI 1989, 349). Despite that forecast, in the space of eight years, workshop sector members began the decade as independent, innovative and experimental filmmakers, positioned by a vibrant new channel to deliver minority audience television, and ended it industrially outmoded and culturally extraneous. With added irony, by the late 1980s, the sector was being scrutinised by the same neoliberal ethos and value for money logic that had affected the miners and local authority workers, the very groups the workshop sector had supported.

Digital afterlife

The predominant failure narrative surrounding Channel 4's relationship with the Declaration, dominated by discussions on production, serves to disguise its wider *ciné-geography*, the exhibition and distribution strategies deployed by the workshops. These forgotten audience-building initiatives of the 1980s provide an untapped wealth of knowledge for today's independent film and video makers and wider cultural and political activists working online. The demise of the workshop movement inevitably contributed to workshop material becoming unavailable and workshop-related collections are therefore still waiting to be born within a contemporary context. Collective filmmaking has largely been sidelined by the dominance of the auteur-led textual analysis within scholarly research. Consequently, this has led to a limited historiography, but fittingly the Declaration's regeneration may arrive through the developing field of distribution studies, illuminating areas that previous discourses have chosen to ignore.

Julia Knight's extensive research has focused on the distribution activities of many organisations within the UK independent film sector's 'third circuit' of the 1970s and 1980s. Knight's findings propose that the models engaged by these organisations provide effective parallels for contemporary online practitioners seeking to circulate their product to a wider audience. Knight argues that digital technology carries the conviction that once work is uploaded, the internet will instinctively proliferate the delivery of a more diverse moving image culture to a wider audience (Knight 2007, 19).

Knight's findings reveal that similar utopian assertions were made with preceding technological revolutions such as the VHS and DVD. The new formats, comparable to potentials of the Internet, raised hopes that alternative distribution models could be deployed to circumvented established distribution networks. While there were notable breakthroughs within the workshop sector such as the *Miners Campaign Tapes*, the potential for VHS or DVD to expand the audience or non-mainstream moving image work remained limited. However, there are important lessons for the contemporary era within these historical precedents as online distribution initiatives experience the same issues and confront similar imitations. The proponents of video distribution can provide the historical framework with which to better understand both the potentials and limitations of online moving image distribution. The affordability of digital film equipment coupled with the accessibility for users to engage in socially networked, cloud-based, multi-platforms has not only increased the amount of product being circulated but has intensely accelerated the transformation of conventional distribution and exhibition channels within the media industry. The leap from analogue to digital has effectively streamlined the process of integrated practice, converging production, exhibition and distribution activities. Now, with cheap production costs, online engagement has provided contemporary film and video activists with the capacity to connect with unlimited number of viewers.

Instead of devising completely new distribution approaches, it is essential to excavate initiatives outlined and referenced earlier with other film and video technological advancements such as 16 mm, U-matic, and VHS. The lifespan of the Workshop Declaration was entirely brief; however, due to the high level of financial state support for the sector in the 1980s, a healthy stream of alternative product was produced, exhibited and distributed. The Declaration enabled the production of a large amount of non-broadcast work within the sector. Separate to the celebrated *Miners Campaign Tapes*, workshops using brand new video equipment produced tapes focusing on key concerns facing their chosen communities. These videos, shot on high band U-matic, were duplicated onto VHS and distributed rapidly across the given region, quickly addressing the pressing issues facing their communities in an open and accessible manner. The tapes would then be disseminated and discussed in targeted audience groups, who would be encouraged to debate openly to develop a tactical counter-response. This overlooked period of video activism has largely been ignored due to the ephemeral nature of its process. Indicative of the non-commercial ethic underpinned by the Declaration, the tapes were made with and alongside a chosen community and given away to the same community for free. This filmmaking approach was in complete opposition to the established norms of the mainstream film industry, further evidenced by the workshops' non-compliance with copyright and indifference in assigning individual credits. Investigating the archives and collections of workshops within this *ciné-geography* would provide a deeper understanding of integrated practice and would offer a pre-digital model for today's online video activists who are eager to connect with grassroots groups and distribute productions to targeted audiences.

Conclusion

The Workshop Declaration not only countered the realities of the under-funded, non-waged conditions that epitomised the independent sector in the 1970s, but also extended the production, exhibition and distribution potentials of non-mainstream moving image work in the 1980s. It was nurtured by a collective rejection of the artistic individualist mode of expression in favour of responsibility to a specific constituency. By being rooted and responsive to a local community, the workshops were able to offer product that was more attuned to the ongoing concerns of the region and were well placed to provide a wider perspective than the fleeting viewpoints offered by the mainstream broadcasters. Producing, exhibiting and distributing work in a permanent residency with a constituency, the workshops were able to challenge representations, widen the diversity of the country's national film culture and sustain an audience within an evolving regional film and video infrastructure. Incorporating the targeted communities within every aspect of the filmmaking process, the workshops enabled marginalised groups to have an unprecedented input into what was transmitted and screened, making the UK film and television industry arguably more democratic and accountable to its audiences than at other time in its history (Wayne 1990, 12). The model may no longer be applicable to state-funded provision but the workshop model is suitable in a contemporary discussion around DIY online audience building. Fundamentally, by identifying the relationship with a community as the foremost component within its approach to filmmaking, the workshop model reminds contemporary online video practitioners that, regardless of the unlimited access and expedite distribution systems provided by the Internet, strategic, labour-intensive community work is required before any radical production can have significant impact with a targeted audience.

References

ACTT. 1984. 'Grant-Aided Workshop Production Declaration' in *Rogue Reels: Oppositional Film in Britain, 1945–90*, edited by Margaret Dickinson, 163–167. London: BFI.

Auty, Martyn. 1985. 'But Is It Cinema?' in *British Cinema Now*, edited by Martyn Auty, and Nick Roddick, 57–70. London: BFI.

BFI. 1987. *British Film Institute Film and Television Handbook*, 47. London: BFI.

BFI. 1989. *British Film Institute Film and Television Handbook*, 349. London: BFI.

Eshun, Kodwo and Ros Gray. 2011. 'The Militant Image: A CineGeography'. *Third Text* 25 (1): 1–12.

Fitzgerald, Teresa. 1988. 'Shoptalk', *Sight and Sound*, summer: 163–169.

Fountain, Alan. 1989. 'Workshop Policies in the 1990s: A Discussion Document'. London: Channel 4. Source: Film and Video Distribution Database, University of Sunderland.

Knight, Julia. 2007. 'DVD, Video and Reaching Audiences: Experiments in Moving Image Distribution'. *Convergence: The International Journal of Research into New Media Technologies* 13 (1): 19–42.

Lockett, Roy. 1983. 'Tomorrow Today' in *Action! Fifty Years in The Life of a Union, Association of Cinematograph Television and Allied Technicians*, edited by Peter Avis, 159–165. London: Pears Publication.

Lockett, Roy. 1984. 'Background Paper for a TUC for an Arts Policy Discussion'. London: ACTT. Source: Amber Film and Photography Collective.

Petley, Julian. 1988. 'Declarations of Independence'. *Monthly Film Bulletin* 55 (648): 24.

Reid, Ian. 2017. 'Trades Unions and the British Film Industry, 1930s–80s' in *The Routledge Companion to British Cinema History* edited by I. Q. Hunter, Laraine Porter and Justin Smith, 251–261. Routledge: London.

Stoneman, Rod. 1992. 'Sins of Commission'. *Screen* 33 (2): 127–144.

Wayne, Mike. 1990. 'Work in a Void'. *Independent Media*, May99: 12–13.

PART III

Festivals and exhibition

13

FILM, INTERRUPTED

Alternative screening practices for a radical film culture

Elena Boschi

Debates about political film and radical film culture have been largely centred on texts, their oppositional content, style and other textual characteristics, which are often assumed to be the main sources of their political value. As a result, less emphasis has been placed on production, distribution and exhibition contexts, and the way screening practices can shape our experiences of radical films has received limited attention. In the UK context, the work of the Radical Film Network (RFN) has contributed to a shift towards thinking about production, distribution and exhibition of politically and aesthetically radical film, as is clearly stated in the sub-heading of the call for papers of the RFN's first conference where the initial version of this project was presented. At the time, I had been thinking about how screening practices, especially debates about radical films, could be changed to promote participation, bringing together insights from film studies scholarship (Casetti 2009, 2011; Kassabian 2008) and recent work on anxiety and militancy (The Institute for Precarious Consciousness; IPC 2014a, 2014b), drawing on what I had read about the exhibition practices associated with Third Cinema in the Latin American context (Solanas and Getino 1969; Chanan 1997; Stam 2014; Wayne 2001). In the model I proposed, participants would discuss films during breaks within, not just after the screening, in small groups. The interrupted screening was a theoretical model waiting for its practical realisation, which I managed to orchestrate on more than one occasion in the following years with a little help from the Radical Film Network, and other supportive organisations and filmmakers.[1] In this chapter I will draw a connection between the ideas behind the interrupted screening, the historical exhibition practices that have inspired it, and its practical application in the contemporary context of UK film culture.

I would like to start with a provocation: while the model I outline below was devised with overtly political films in mind, its application might benefit our experiences of radical and not-so-radical films alike. Mike Wayne (2001) makes a related point in the introduction to his book *Political Film*: 'In order to [refute the claim that Third Cinema is dead], Third Cinema has to be developed as a theory, as a *critical* practice which is inspired by and tries to be adequate to Third Cinema films. But not only them' (2). Despite being developed through and for overtly political films, some of which could be associated with Third Cinema, the interrupted screening might help us to open up to scrutiny films that generally are not subject to much critical debate in their exhibition contexts. I'm talking about films that would make the majority of our readers cringe, for being ideologically compromised and generally lacking a critical dimension or, worse, for a radical posturing that conceals a rather more questionable outlook. Avoiding such films can let their problematic and simplistic perspectives become common sense as their message seeps into people's minds without being questioned, not by a leading figure like a curator or a filmmaker, but by a community of participants who don't just watch a film, but bring their own experiences to it. Conversely, a not-so-radical experience can leave politically and aesthetically radical films and their potential unfulfilled. Films featuring challenging content and style don't necessarily produce a radical experience for the viewers, who may remain just that unless they're given an opportunity to participate in the film more fully. While chances to discuss films after a screening are often already available at the kind of event where radical film culture thrives, their format doesn't always allow for significant participation and these debates may reflect and perpetuate power imbalances despite the organisers' best intentions.

Wayne clarifies Tomás Gutiérrez Alea's call for an 'open' spectacle, a useful notion for understanding not only film texts but also people's experiences of film:

> The spectacle must be open in the sense that it encourages the spectator to understand the world as complex and to understand that only through their participation in the world after the cinematic spectacle has finished can the inequalities and injustices of this complex world be addressed. So a dialectical cinema offers a 'path', a 'guide to action', rather than specific or easily achieved solutions. The metaphor of a journey, of travelling, is apt. [...] The openness of Third Cinema is primarily an openness towards history as a site of possible action, which means that the film itself is only a staging post on a journey that takes place beyond the cinematic spectacle.
>
> (Wayne 2001, 149)

These are all important ideas for the development of a critical practice at the stage of exhibition. But why wait until after the cinematic spectacle and why not embed participation in the screening when we can 'open' the film and start the journey right there, in the cinema? If film is a 'detonator', as Solanas and Getino (1969) aptly defined it, waiting until after the cinematic spectacle has ended feels like wasting a great opportunity. Letting the journey begin in the breaks during a screening has another significant advantage. In the small-group discussions, participants could find new and old fellow travellers, providing support in the contemporary setting, where anxiety permeates our lives and, as the IPC argue, is effectively preventing militancy – which, in the context of radical film culture, might block 'political mimesis' (Gaines 1999). The model I propose is no magic panacea. Interrupting films won't always make them better for the audience, who won't all necessarily turn into participants, and may make some people uneasy, as it is an unfamiliar experience. It's not perfect and it's a work in progress, so it will need to be adapted depending on the different circumstances and the cultural contexts where it's applied. However, the interrupted screening has the potential to create favourable conditions for participation by more people, some of whom wouldn't normally take active part in a post-film debate, which I believe makes it an interesting model to think about, use, and adapt for those working on/in radical film culture and beyond.

The ideas that have shaped the interrupted screening come from different places, but they share one feature. They're all very much about contemporary aspects of the way we watch films, engage with other texts and the world around us. They also track crucial changes in these engagements that form the theoretical basis for the interrupted screening model, so I'm going to start by discussing these ideas. Francesco Casetti and Anahid Kassabian's work explores recent shifts in the way audiences engage with film through social media, often without the continued attention taken for granted in contemporary film viewing, while The Institute for Precarious Consciousness seeks to bring consciousness raising back into practices other than film viewing. Despite being quite different and seemingly unrelated, combining their insights on new viewing practices with new challenges for radical politics in the twenty-first century has highlighted the opportunity and the necessity for screening practices loosely based on how Solanas and Getino's *The Hour of the Furnaces* (1968) raised questions and was stopped, so that the audience could debate the questions.

In *Film Cultures*, Janet Harbord concludes her chapter about 'Aesthetic Encounters' with a crucial observation for radical film studies:

> [A]esthetic engagement with film can provide one of the potentially transformative features of culture, shifting perspective, denaturalizing time, confronting the viewer with differences. Yet it is not possible to state the conditions or contexts of this happening, nor to specify the textual form in advance.
>
> *(Harbord 2002, 135)*

In this passage Harbord makes a very important point for anybody thinking about radical film. While acknowledging the power of film viewing, she notes the difficulty in pinning down what it is that triggers aesthetic engagement with film. The same could apply to the idea of radical engagement with film, which can't be planned. Textual forms can't guarantee a radical film experience and neither can context, but Harbord emphasises the fluid possibilities despite the social value certain texts and contexts are given. She talks about sites of exhibition including the multiplex cinema, the arthouse independent cinema, the art gallery and the home, but doesn't discuss the practices happening in these sites.

Casetti focuses instead on the practices surrounding films watched outside their canonical sites of exhibition in the relocation of cinema. While radical films are not always watched outside the movie theatre, what has been happening in these other spaces has brought about significant changes for film viewing as we knew it. The practices developed outside the movie theatre are often brought back to the motherland, as Casetti calls it, through re-relocation:

> If traditional spectators once modelled themselves on films, spectators now model films, or remodel them onto themselves, thanks to a combination of precise practices which invest the object, the modalities and the conditions of vision. The effect is that the spectators become the active protagonists of the game. They are no longer asked to be present at a projection with eyes open; instead, they act.
>
> *(Casetti 2011, 6)*

These changes are interesting for our purpose: audiences modelling films, remodelling films onto themselves, through the practices Casetti calls *performance* (doing something), which are replacing *attendance* (being present) in the era of the relocation and re-relocation of cinema. Casetti (2011) identifies various new types of 'doing', including relational doing, which he locates 'especially outside the film theatre, where spectators watch films by themselves and are often motivated to construct a group with which to share their own experience' (7). He talks about spectators sharing their individual experience on their smartphone via social media, presumably while watching the films. But what about people sharing directly? It's been happening in the scheduled and unplanned interruptions which often punctuate our film experiences at home in the company of other people, in the cinemas where intermissions halfway through films are still common, in other sites of exhibition where pausing films is a possibility – for example, the art gallery setting now often invites *performance* through interactive installations.

In her article on inattentive engagements, Kassabian (2008) discusses a range of situations in which music is present alongside other stimuli and becomes subject to secondary or simultaneous attention. She also notes how multitasking isn't a new phenomenon, but began in the early twentieth century, with radio and Muzak, and continued from TV to the world wide web, smartphones, video games, etc. (119–120). If we combine these insights with Casetti's view that watching films outside the movie theatre has increased audiences' *performance* after relocation, it becomes clear that our experiences of film also involve secondary or simultaneous attention. The changes Kassabian talks about aren't only affecting our encounters with music. Attention spans are changing and, whatever we think of it, it is an issue we're not necessarily thinking about in our practice, as curators, programmers, or as teachers. While I ask students to put away their phones during a screening in class, pre-empting relational doing which would otherwise punctuate the class screening, I am interested in finding ways of harnessing those kinds of disruptions in the film experience. The relational doing happening during films, in the dead times between fragments of films or after isn't necessarily radical. Think, for example, about students checking Facebook during a screening, or about commercial breaks on TV, an interruption aimed at feeding consumerism. There is, however, radical potential in the interruptions which break *attendance* and, I argue, can promote *performance*, providing a space where we could begin to cultivate radical film experiences. The old-school relational doing I'm talking about, pre-web-2.0, already happens where radical film culture is lived through debates, usually following the screening of a full film. But are these practices fulfilling the potential the films may offer? Often following a rigid, hierarchical model, these events generally feature visible experts providing knowledge, introducing the screening, leading debates and Q&A after the films, usually watched in their entirety. The relational doing happening at most radical film events is therefore quite regimented. After participating in such events as audience many times, I was asked to do a brief introduction, screening and Q&A for Gay History Month at the University of Liverpool LGBT Network, and I found the setup vaguely frustrating. The event attracted a substantial crowd who, I think, liked the film, but I had hoped the screening would fuel the relational doing which I imagine happens after or perhaps while the LGBT Network punters watch a historical lesbian romance at home together. Interestingly, relational doing was relocated outside the austere Victorian theatre space and stimulating conversations started at the cafe after the event.

I started to think about how I could combine these two experiences, how I could bring those lively debates back to the motherland and the other non-theatrical venues where people watch radical and not-so-radical films. In addition to thinking about the relocated experiences Casetti describes, the acclaimed radical open text of *The Hour of the Furnaces* (Fernando Solanas and Octavio Getino, 1968) came to mind. As Robert Stam reminds us

> At key points, the film raises questions [...] and proposes that the audience debate them, interrupting the projection to allow for discussion. Elsewhere, the authors appeal for supplementary material on the theme of violence and liberation, soliciting collaboration in the film's writing. The 'end' of the film refuses closure by inviting the audience to prolong the text.
>
> *(Stam 2014, 273–4)*

These radical practices developed in the very risky setting of revolutionary Argentina where gathering to watch *The Hour of the Furnaces* was dangerous. In their manifesto, 'Towards a Third Cinema', Solanas and Getino talk about the insights they gained from what happened when they were screening *The Hour of the Furnaces*:

> Each showing for militants, middle level cadres, activists, workers, and university students became – without our having set ourselves this aim beforehand – a kind of enlarged cell meeting of which the films were a part but not the most important factor. We thus discovered a new facet of cinema: the participation of people who, until then, were considered spectators. At times, security reasons obliged us to try to dissolve the group of participants as soon as the showing was over, and we realised that the distribution of that kind of film had little meaning if it was not complemented by the participation of the comrades, if a debate was not opened on the themes suggested by the films.
>
> *(Solanas and Getino 1969)*

Their final point, I argue, has great relevance for radical film more broadly, not only for open texts which, like *The Hour of the Furnaces*, have those spaces for participation already built into the structure of the film.

While fearing for one's life – like in the initial setting where *The Hour of the Furnaces* was shown – is an experience that will be unfamiliar to most of us, a subtler anxiety permeates our lives in the neoliberal order, as the IPC (2014a) brilliantly explain in their piece 'We Are All Very Anxious'. The IPC argue that the dominant affect that holds contemporary capitalism together, effectively preventing militancy, is *anxiety* – doing the job *misery* did for the modern era and later *boredom* for the 1960s–1970s.

> Today's public secret is that everyone is anxious. Anxiety has spread from its previous localised locations (such as sexuality) to the whole of the social field. All forms of intensity, self-expression, emotional connection, immediacy, and enjoyment are now laced with anxiety. It has become the linchpin of subordination.
>
> *(IPC 2014a)*

Aside from the fact that films about social issues often feature anxiety-inducing content, which can undoubtedly influence our experiences, it's important to think about the ambient anxiety the IPC are talking about, as its effects don't spare the intensity, self-expression, emotional connection, immediacy and enjoyment that those of us working with radical film seek to promote.

With this in mind, it's worth considering another crucial point the IPC have made about current approaches: 'Current militant resistance does not and cannot combat anxiety. It often involves deliberate exposure to high-anxiety situations' (IPC 2014a). For these reasons, dangerous experiences like those of the activists gathering to watch and discuss *The Hour of the Furnaces* at the time of its initial release would be similarly ineffective. However, the strategy the IPC identify to overcome this all-pervasive anxiety shares its basic principle with the way audiences encountered *The Hour of the Furnaces* in late-1960s Argentina. For the IPC, coming together in 'affinity groups [...] can provide a pool of potential *accomplices* [and] create the potential to shift the general field of so-called public opinion in ways which create an easier context for action'.[2] While there are obvious differences between the two historical moments, there are also clear parallels between the aim of the IPC's proposed strategy and the conditions these screenings created for Solanas and Getino's documentary. Their words about the situation outside the liberated space surrounding their film are worth quoting at length:

> Outside this space which the film momentarily helped to liberate, there was nothing but solitude, noncommunication, distrust, and fear; within the freed space the situation turned everyone into accomplices of the act that was unfolding. The debates arose spontaneously. As we gained in experience, we incorporated into the showing various elements (a mise en scene) to reinforce the themes of the film, the climate of the showing, the 'disinhibiting' of the participants, and

the dialogue: recorded music or poems, sculpture and paintings, posters, a programme director who chaired the debate and presented the film and the comrades who were speaking, a glass of wine, a few mates [teas], etc.

(Solanas and Getino 1969, 16)

The words used here to describe the world outside their liberated space could easily have been written about the all-pervasive anxiety the IPC are talking about. Moreover, Solanas and Getino's emphasis on everyone becoming accomplices is another significant overlap, and there are clear parallels between their concern with 'disinhibiting' participants and the IPC's main goal to dissolve anxiety. In Solanas and Getino's account there's no clear indication of group sizes in the screenings they're talking about. However, given the limited participation that a single large-group debate usually promotes, small-group discussions, which the IPC suggest for consciousness raising, could allow for broader participation. In 'The Changing Geography of Third Cinema', Michael Chanan quotes Joris Ivens, saying:

We realised that the most important thing was not the film and the informa-tion in it so much as the way this information was debated. One of the aims of such films is to provide the occasion for people to find themselves and speak of their own problems. The projection becomes a place where people talk out and develop their awareness. We learnt the importance of this space: cinema here becomes humanly useful.

(Ivens quoted in Chanan 1997)

There are clear parallels between, on the one hand, the IPC's goals and, on the other, what Ivens, and Solanas and Getino, say about cinema's radical potential. Alliances between people, whether general or built in the cinema, and audiences 'doing' alongside texts are two key aspects in the writing about Third Cinema.

The model I propose seeks to combine the IPC's drive towards new con-sciousness raising experiences where alliances can fight anxiety, on the one hand, and practices taken from the radical film experiences developed in the context of Third Cinema exhibition, on the other. In a context where new viewing practices often break *attendance* and promote *performance*, not only in relocated experiences but also back in the movie theatre (Casetti 2011) and audiences are often engaging with films inattentively for various reasons (Kassabian 2008), pausing a screening and talking about the film may not seem like such a bizarre proposition after all. Embedding interruptions in a screening, and thereby giving people some time to talk, becomes part of a collective experience, and starting to undo their back-ground anxiety can produce the right climate for organising change – an elusive outcome that those of us working to promote radical film culture often struggle to achieve. The interrupted screening doesn't offer itself as a handy pre-packaged 'solution' for all radical film curators. Rather, it's a set of suggestions on how to put this into practice that began as theoretical reflections and was later refined through a few practical applications, but fundamentally remains a work-in-progress that will continue to change in the hands of whoever decides to apply it. I will now outline the practical aspects of putting on an interrupted screening with some reflections on what I have observed in the events I have organised so far.

At the time of writing I have planned and run eight interrupted screenings, three within larger events and five as standalone events. The choice of the film needs to be addressed first. I started out using documentaries as the clear focus on a specific issue means they are generally easier to show in this format. However, after doing one screening with a fiction film about Cuba for the Havana Glasgow Film Festival, I think fiction films are worth exploring further despite being challenging. Showing *La Película de Ana* (Daniel Díaz Torres, 2013) in the context of a Cuba-themed film festival probably made it easier, as the event attracted a small crowd who had prior knowledge of and interest in Cuba, which kept the conversations going without much need to facilitate, despite the unavoidable initial awkwardness after the first interruption.

Another issue is where to interrupt the film and how often. In *The Hour of the Furnaces* the structure was predetermined by the division of the film into numbered chapters, each with a title. At various points during the film, direct quotes and facts presented using intertitles offered clear cues for debate.[3] This is a rare and, one could argue, rigid structure for a debate about a film. For documentaries which already had clear sections, like *Africa Is a Woman's Name* (Ingrid Sinclair, Bridget Pickering and Wanjiru Kinyanjui, 2009), a film about three women making a difference in their communities in Africa, the interruptions matched the three sections. For other documentaries, we tried to respect the implicit structure while choosing stopping points that would provoke discussion. It's worth noting that stopping the film after pending questions have been addressed isn't always good, as this doesn't let people debate the questions independently of the film itself. Some comments I have observed in the group discussions for the first screening of *We Don't Like Samba* (CIS Berlin 2014), a documentary on the social struggles in Brazil after the World Cup and Olympics foreign investment started pouring into the country, have made me reflect on the value of talking about certain aspects the film had not yet addressed. Having breaks after a minimum 15 minutes and maximum 30 minutes, and letting participants discuss each part for about 10 minutes seems to have worked in the events organised so far, as the participants haven't made negative comments on this aspect. Regarding how the interrupted screening changed the way participants experienced the film, a few people mentioned that the format helped them remember what happened in the film in more detail and aided concentration. One last thing a curator needs to think about in the pre-event phase is letting prospective participants know about the format, which needs to be introduced clearly not only on the day of the event but also in the publicity materials that will be disseminated ahead of it. Finally, it's important to ensure that the filmmakers and/or the distributor are not against the film being shown with interruptions.

There are other issues to think about in preparation for the screening day. Choosing a suitable venue is perhaps the most important aspect in the pre-event phase, as is setting it up in a way that will make this unusual experience work well. Given the importance of non-theatrical spaces for the development of the film viewing practices discussed by Casetti, using venues other than the classic cinema space was a natural choice. However, his point about these viewing practices having made their way back into the motherland also made me want to do an event in the traditional context of a cinema with fixed seats. Wherever possible, choosing venues with non-fixed seating makes the arrangement more conducive to a collective experience in the small groups. Arranging any movable seats in short, slightly curved rows of five/six seats, with room between one row and the other, allows participants to close the row into a half circle during breaks, so that people face one another while talking, and straighten the row again, so that people face the screen again when the screening resumes after a break. While this does limit the venue's capacity, it is highly likely to facilitate discussion as anybody who has ever taught a seminar will know. Using a traditional theatre space isn't ideal, but a few basic adjustments can adapt fixed seating for small-group discussions. Marking nearby seats for participants (e.g., two/three contiguous seats and another two/three contiguous seats right behind them) allows people to turn to face those behind them to talk during breaks. The small groups cannot be too near each other, which again means sacrificing capacity, but these are necessary adjustments for small-group conversations, as some distance is needed to keep them separated.

Solanas and Getino (1969) talk about 'noncommunication' outside the freed space of the showing, which evokes not only the ambient anxiety the IPC discuss, but also the way communication generally works during post-screening debates, aimed towards the front where usually a moderator manages interaction between members of the audience, on one side, and panel members, on the other, and sometimes among members of the audience. However, where people in the audience talk to each other during post-screening debates, this doesn't usually involve close interaction and exchanges are generally limited. Some comments in the feedback I have gathered point out the interactivity of the interrupted screening, while others mentioned feeling more connected with other participants, less passive, more active, etc. For one participant the discussions created a less isolating, more shared experience. Another, at the interrupted screening of *We Don't Like Samba*, organised for the Radical Film Network Festival and Unconference at Flourish House in Glasgow, said that the event helped them to meet people with similar interests and pointed out its value for political consciousness raising and organising. While those attending this event would be more inclined to engage in this before coming to an interrupted screening, I still find the comment encouraging, as the interrupted screening was a catalyst of some sort for something happening outside the space of Flourish House. It is worth noting that feedback forms cannot capture anything happening after the event, which makes measuring its effects quite challenging. This also justifies the relative lack of comments on what may have started while talking about the film at the event.

Besides briefly introducing the interrupted screening in the publicity materials, it's important to give some context about it, as well as saying what will happen during the screening and the breaks. While I have only done this in person at the beginning, it's possible to replace this with a short explanation on a leaflet alongside basic information about the film. Introducing the format might have helped to contain anxiety about this very unfamiliar experience, as the vast majority of participants said they had never experienced a similar event. Despite talking about the format before the start, some participants did say they felt uneasy during the initial break, but this issue resolved itself after the ice had been broken. One participant said that the interrupted screening did not work for them and suggested giving people the opportunity to join a different group, which I think could be offered at the organisers' discretion.[4] Despite not finding the event enjoyable, the participant still answered 'yes' to the question 'Would you participate in another interrupted screening?', like everyone who completed a feedback sheet after the events that have been held until now.

As the facilitator of these events, after the initial introduction I just directed breaks, pausing the film when necessary, reminding people it was time to talk, and letting them know the film would resume shortly – more than once when people were deep in conversation and carried on talking! Some comments asked for more direction, more structure, even questions to guide their discussions. While *The Hour of the Furnaces* did include questions, I think providing questions might guide the process too tightly and potentially limit the spontaneous interaction between participants. At the end of the film, after the final small-group discussion, I usually ask each group to share something they talked about with the other groups, opening a short large-group discussion to close the event. By then the awkwardness that might happen when starting a single post-screening debate has disappeared and it's often difficult to stop talking.

This brings me to the issue of time. The interrupted screening obviously requires more time than a traditional screening, even with a Q&A at the end, which might cause issues we need to consider as curators. The maximum film duration I have worked with so far was 100 minutes for *La Película de Ana*, with most documentaries averaging at about 60 minutes. Three breaks plus some general discussion after the last round of small-group discussions generally adds 35–40 minutes to the event duration. With an hour-long documentary, the added time was still within what most participants and venues would consider normal. However, with longer films this might cause issues. Introducing the interrupted screening for the first time using a film that doesn't exceed 90 minutes (ideally shorter) would allow us to gauge participants' response to this format with a standard duration event. Including questions in the feedback sheet about whether people would participate in a longer event would help us to plan future events. With most standard Q&As lasting between 15 and 30 minutes, replacing the Q&A at the end with breaks during the film wouldn't add too much time to the event's overall duration. Giving evidence of what the interrupted screening would bring to the film event and planning time carefully would reassure venues where discussions are limited to post-screening Q&As and programming schedules are tight. Ultimately, collective engagement with film on a deeper level requires time and negotiating this with exhibitors and participants is a challenge worth taking up.

Much like those conversations, this chapter is a work in progress and remains open. Starting from ideas about our engagements with film and other media, I have outlined significant changes which I believe offer opportunities for radical film screening practices. By letting these changes into the spaces where we experience radical film, I argue that the anxiety that keeps us from taking action in the face of neoliberalism can be defused. To do this, I have proposed a model loosely based on the screening practices of Third Cinema to promote audiences' participation not only after a screening has ended, but also in the breaks during the film, something we're becoming used to when seeing films outside the movie theatre, with a different attention from what is normally expected at a screening. Finally, I have outlined the interrupted screening model in more detail, bringing some insights from feedback I have gathered since I started running these events in 2015. While I haven't yet had the opportunity to do this with fiction films that are not overtly political, I believe the interrupted screening could work for these films, as it would offer an opportunity to open them to challenge problematic and simplistic aspects. The current political situation in the world calls for adaptable tools people can use to stop dangerous divisions growing among us. The solitude, non-communication, distrust and fear that Solanas and Getino mentioned in their manifesto are currently being exploited for the dangerous pursuit of right-wing political agendas across Europe and beyond. Radical films are a powerful resource to fight on these fronts. My hope is that the interrupted screening can be used to amplify their power and let more people engage with them and, crucially, with each other. If not now, when?

Notes

1 I am particularly grateful to CIS Berlin, Roger McKinley at FACT Liverpool, Susan Forde, Richard Warden, the organisers of the Radical Film Network Festival and Unconference in Glasgow, Kathy Kamleitner, Barbara Orton, Eirene Houston, Savera UK, the organisers of the Radical Film Network Conference in Tolpuddle, and all the people who participated in the interrupted screenings that have been held so far for their collaboration and support.
2 The IPC take feminist consciousness raising as a model for their method, but also quote other similar processes including critical pedagogy in Latin America, *autocoscienza* (literally self-consciousness) in Italy, 'testifying' in the civil rights movement, and 'speaking bitterness' in revolutionary China (IPC 2014b).
3 Part 1, 'Neocolonialism and Violence', begins with footage showing violent repression in the streets, accompanied by a crescendo of indigenous percussion instruments, and intertitles including a quote from the Argentine intellectual Raúl Scalabrini Ortiz that reads 'The history they taught us is false. The hopes of wealth they give us are false. The international perspectives they present to us are false. The economic beliefs that were spread are false. The freedom proclaimed in the texts are not real.' Later, chapter 9, 'Dependence' 'Neocolonialism and Violence', ends with a montage showing animals being slaughtered intercut with still images of commercials, wealthy men and women wearing expensive clothes and driving new cars, accompanied by a slow-paced musical piece with a smooth female voice singing non-verbal lyrics. Intertitles are used during and after the montage. The first intertitle reads 'Every day we export more to receive the same', the second 'Every day we work more for less' and the third 'Argentina's external

debt exceeds six billion dollars'. After the montage, the intertitles provide the following information: 'The foreign monopolies and their local allies control almost all the national economy. All the meat industry, energy, oil, cereal commerce, the chemical industry, the production of cellulose, 70% of tungsten, 92% of lead, 98% of zinc. Sulphur, silver, gold. The press agencies and all the mass media.' The facts and the quotes shown in this kind of intertitles raise questions about specific issues, as does the voiceover narration, therefore providing a precise direction for the conversations after the interruptions.

4 One of the goals of an interrupted screening is to make people talk to people they wouldn't normally talk to, whether because of their different nationality, social class, gender, etc. With this in mind, letting someone switch group because differences among people in the group cause issues could defeat the purpose of the event. However, if this were to result in someone feeling threatened, it could reinforce anxiety rather than undoing it as the IPC suggest. Therefore, it's crucial to think about these issues ahead of the event, make a decision, give explanations if need be, and communicate it to the audience in the introduction.

References

Casetti, Francesco. 2009. 'Filmic Experience'. *Screen* 50 (1): 56–66.

Casetti, Francesco. 2011. 'Back to the Motherland: The Film Theatre in the Postmedia Age'. *Screen* 52 (1): 1–12.

Chanan, Michael. 1997. 'The Changing Geography of Third Cinema'. *Screen* 38 (4): 372–388.

Gaines, Jane M. 1999. 'Political Mimesis'. In *Collecting Visible Evidence*, edited by Jane M. Gaines and Michael Renov, 84–102. Minneapolis, MN: University of Minnesota Press.

Harbord, Janet. 2002. *Film Cultures*. London: Routledge.

Institute for Precarious Consciousness. IPC. 2014a. 'We Are All Very Anxious: Six Theses on Anxiety and Why It Is Effectively Preventing Militancy, and One Possible Strategy for Overcoming It'. *Plan C* April 4, 2014. https://www.weareplanc.org/blog/we-are-all-very-anxious/ (accessed December 20, 2018).

Institute for Precarious Consciousness. IPC. 2014b. 'Anxiety, Affective Struggle, and Precarity Consciousness-Raising'. *Interface* 6 (2) November: 271–300. http://www.interfacejournal.net/wordpress/wp-content/uploads/2015/01/Issue-6_2-IPC.pdf (accessed December 20, 2018).

Kassabian, Anahid. 2008. 'Inattentive Engagements: The New Problematics of Sound and Music'. *Cinema Journal* 48 (1) Fall: 118–123.

Solanas, Fernando and Octavio Getino. 1969. 'Towards a Third Cinema'. *Cinéaste* 4 (3) Winter 1970–71: 1–10.

Stam, Robert. 2014. 'The Two Avant-Gardes': Solanas and Getino's Documenting the Documentary: Close Readings of Documentary Film and Video, edited by Barry K. Grant and Jeanette Sloniowski, 254–268. Detroit, MI: Wayne State University Press.

Wayne, Mike. 2001. *Political Film: The Dialectics of Third Cinema*. London: Pluto Press.

14

RE-THINKING HUMAN RIGHTS FILM FESTIVALS

A radical perspective

Anthony Killick

This chapter focuses on the spatial and cultural reproduction of human rights and activist film festivals within the context of neoliberalism and austerity. With regards to the UK, for example, over the past couple of years both the Joseph Rowntree Foundation and the UN have released reports detailing how the government's austerity policies have led to increasing child and pensioners poverty, forcing disabled people into work via changes to welfare policy (Joseph Rowntree Foundation 2017) and reducing the prospects for women's equality (United Nations Trade and Development 2017). The filmmaker Ken Loach, who made *I Daniel Blake* (2016), has called such policies 'conscious cruelty' (Taylor 2015), while more recently, Philip Alston, the UN's Special Rapporteur on extreme poverty and human rights, has called austerity in the UK a 'political choice' that is 'cruel and misogynistic' (Ward 2018). It is clear, therefore, that although the discourse of 'human rights' usually refers to the 'distant suffering' of Others (Tascón 2015), austerity is a human rights violation that manifests within the 'developed', liberal democratic urban environments in which many activist and human rights film festivals take place, but pay much less attention to. This chapter looks at the ways in which festival organisers operating within the boundaries of the neoliberal city have produced spaces that aim to be antithetical to neoliberalism, both in the way they organise space, and in the subject positions they aim to foster. Its main case study is the Liverpool Radical Film Festival (LRFF; for which I was an organiser from 2014–16), but the chapter also draws on interviews carried out with organisers of the Workers Unite Film Festival (New York) and my perspective owes a great deal to conversations with the organisers of Subversive Film Festival (Zagreb).

The main argument presented here is that the assertion of human rights from a left internationalist perspective (Blackburn 2011) entails countering the effects of austerity through forms of (primarily) local action on the part of activist film festival organisers and their desired audiences. Here we must be wary of the fact that human rights and activism are terms that have been co-opted by neoliberal interests in order to perpe-tuate militarism and the expansion of markets, particularly (for the purposes of this chapter) within the localised urban environment. Indeed, in this latter respect it should be noted that the dynamic nature of neoliberalism is such that it not only permits certain 'activist' and 'countercultural' forms and lifestyles, but that it *needs* them in order to renew itself through endless processes of 'growth', such as the commodifica-tion of culture and the gentrification of working class neighbourhoods. The problem addressed here is that scholars writing about activist and human rights film festivals have so far failed to address the fact that liberal democracies rooted in capitalism not only tolerate but *require and assimilate* opposition in order to expand markets and pre-sent the appearance of a properly functioning democracy (Winlow et al. 2015).

Research on activist and human rights film festivals must, therefore, provide a more thorough analysis of what is meant by 'activism' and precisely what 'social change' or forms of 'human rights' it engenders. This is not to offer a fatalistic critique of activism, nor to destroy the possibility of effective opposition to capital in the neoliberal period, but to stress how deeper thinking is required in order to understand the difference between resistance to neoliberalism and the 'resistance market'.

As well as a left internationalist conception of human rights and an understanding of neoliberalism as a system of dynamic subsumption, this theoretical framework also draws on critical urban theory (Brenner 2012), and aims to make a contribution to the incorporation of geographical and socio-cultural questions around 'spatial scales of social theorising and political action' (Harvey 1994: 41) into the field of critical film festival studies (Winton and Turnin 2017). Thinking about neoliberalism as manifest in the urban environment allows us to look at the ways in which activist and human rights film festivals both challenge and are subsumed by the global phenomena of neoliberalism *within their specific localities*. Sonia Tascón's (2015) concept of the 'huma-nitarian gaze' correctly identifies a position whereby the (generally white, north-wes-tern) spectator is distanced from the (generally black, globally southern) on-screen subject due in part to forms of representation that are rooted in a universalist and Westernised 'humanitarianism'. However, this chapter outlines a local/global frame-work that draws on left internationalist ideas, and looks at how film festival organisers aim to create audience positions that facilitate an understanding of neoliberalism as a global issue, the localised, imminently felt effects of which can be met with practical responses 'on the ground'.

Human rights and left internationalism

Samuel Moyn's (2010) book on the history of human rights and its discourse, *The Last Utopia*, is an important work within the field. However, this chapter bases its conception of human rights on Robin Blackburn's (2011) critique of Moyn. The distinction between these two theorists is important, as it broadly exemplifies the difference between a liberal and a socialist understanding of human rights. According to Moyn, human rights 'emerged in the 1970s seemingly from nowhere' (Moyn 2010: 3). Blackburn's critique is that Moyn overemphasises the

1970s as a breakthrough decade for human rights discourse, and neglects a long history of struggles taking place over the past few hundred years that clearly involve the rights of humans, in particular anti-colonialist movements dating back to the Haitian revolution and the actions of radical slavery abolitionists working in the 1700s and 1800s. Moyn's oversight of this history detracts from a contemporary understanding of human rights:

> [Moyn] apparently does not regard the anti-racialist component of much anti-colonialism and anti-imperialism as a dimension of the 'human rights' package – wrongly, in my view. The struggle against apartheid South Africa was an icon of the anti-imperialist movement and surely had an absolute claim to the banner of human rights.
>
> *(Blackburn 2011: 135)*

Blackburn also points out Moyn's dismissal of internationalist socialist and anti-racist movements in the 1960s and 1970s as simply 'the starkest counterpoint to later human rights activism' (Moyn as quoted in Blackburn 2011: 135). In fact, according to Blackburn:

> That period witnessed a proliferation of movements that helped dramatically to widen notions of 'human rights': women's liberation, gay liberation, the hopes of 'socialism with a human face' in Czechoslovakia, the overthrow of dictatorship in Portugal and Spain, the European surge of trade union mobilisations.
>
> *(Blackburn 2011: 135)*

Thus Moyn's oversights risk an annulment of history, specifically the significant human rights gains made by Haitian revolutionaries, slavery abolitionists and the Socialist Left in the post-war period, particularly, for example, insofar as the Universal Declaration of Human Rights was interpreted by the non-aligned movement as 'incorporating significant social and economic rights [which] summarised the results of nearly a century of labour struggles' (Blackburn 2011: 134). This critique bears significance when it comes to the organisation of activist film festivals that are guided by a broadly similar internationalist outlook on human rights. For example, Andrew Tilson, the director of the Workers Unite Film Festival (WUFF), perceives a distinction between WUFF and human rights film festivals insofar as the latter screen films that are outward-facing, focussing on abuses taking place in Other nations while omitting localised struggles and labour perspectives that may facilitate solidarity between audiences and the subjects on screen. According to Tilson, this is part of a broader tendency within human rights film festivals to avoid questions around labour rights.

> It's fascinating that you can have 25–30 films at a human rights film festival and not a single one will be about labour issues ... to me that's criminal because obviously so often the two overlap, and actually the crux of a lot of these labour issues is a basic attack on human rights ... what I've seen is that

human rights film festivals tend to particularly focus on individuals, or ethnic groups, classes of people under attack, but rarely separate them out as workers or remotely discuss the idea of labour rights. WUFF obviously focuses on these issues, and we also tie as much of our labour struggle discussion to a link to human rights abuses happening concurrently with a strike or other labour action … Human rights festivals … often leave out the work and employment based component of the whole issue – such as the threats to health and safety in Indian sweatshops and how they fight back against this exploitation.

(A. Tilson, personal communication, August 2017)

Here it can be seen that labour struggles are the thread of commonality that Tilson uses to collapse the distance between audience and on-screen subject, that mode of separation exacerbated by the humanitarian gaze. For Tilson, it is the fostering of the spectator as a *worker* that encourages solidarity between the New York based audience and (to use his example) workers in Indian sweatshops. This understanding of workers' rights *as human rights* echoes Blackburn's argument that the latter should be understood from an internationalist perspective. According to Blackburn:

Human rights must prove itself, not just at one time and in one place but across a range of different contexts …. Social and economic demands with a progressive character – the right to work, pensions, basic income, minimum wages, shorter working week, universal healthcare etc. – can sometimes be advanced through the language of rights, even if over the past twenty years 'HRD' has more often been tethered to the liberal imperial masthead …. 'Human Rights' can serve as a valuable watchword and measure. But because inequality and injustice are structural, constituted by multiple intersecting planes of capitalist accumulation and realisation more needs to be said – especially in relation to financial and corporate power and how these might be curbed and socialised.

(Blackburn 2011: 137–8)

Thus Tilson and Blackburn offer conceptions of human rights that are grounded in left internationalism. However, there is a tension that exists within this school of thought that has often been theorised as the question of whether activism should be directed towards local or more globalised aspects of struggle (Harvey 1997), and it is crucial to understand this tension in thinking about how it is addressed by anti-neoliberal film festivals through their practices, as developed within localised contexts. According to Harvey, activist forms can be theorised in terms of a discernible spectrum:

From tangible solidarities understood as patterns of social life organised in affective and knowable communities to a more abstract set of conceptions that would have universal purchase [which] involves a move from one level of abstraction to another capable of reaching out across space.

(Harvey 1997: 33)

However, in the move from tangible to abstracted forms of resistance 'something [is] bound to be lost' (ibid), namely, the concern with a place-based politics that is built on local class and gender familiarities. The problem, according to Harvey, 'is not only the level of abstraction at which the world view of socialist politics gets constituted, but of the very different structures of feeling that can attach to those different levels of abstraction' (Harvey 1997: 36). To further extrapolate the issue, we are not only dealing with the levels of abstraction, but also 'the kind of abstraction achievable given different ways of acquiring knowledge in the world' (Harvey 1997: 37). The episte-mological value of film exhibition, that is, film as a producer of certain kinds of knowledge, is such that activist and human rights film festival audiences can potentially develop an understanding of the relation between local and global forms of anti-neo-liberal resistance. As Tim Ingold notes:

> The local is not a more limited or narrowly focussed apprehension than the global, it is one that rests on an altogether different mode of apprehension – one based on an active, perceptual engagement with components of the dwelt-in world, in the practical business of life, rather than on the detached, disinterested observation of a world apart. In the local perspective the world is a sphere … centred on a particular place. From this experiential centre, the attention of those who live there is drawn ever deeper into the world, in the quest for knowledge and understanding.
>
> *(Ingold 1993: 41)*

It is not the intention of this chapter to argue for the efficacies of one or another form of activism. Rather, it is to analyse human rights and activist film festivals as a relatively new form of resistance through which reconciliations between local and global con-cerns could be made. Although this perspective requires an understanding of practical engagements with political issues at the local level, it is not one of a reactionary or regressive parochialism. Murray Bookchin (2015) argues that too narrow a focus on the concerns of a locality can engender a damaging 'localism' that actively negates knowledge of the wider world. His ideas around confederalism and interdependence aim to re-constitute power at the municipal (as opposed to state) level, while stressing the need for co-operation among different municipalities. At the same time, con-sidering abstracted issues, theories and questions 'does not entail the abandonment of class politics for those of the "new social movements", but the exploration of different forms of alliances that can reconstitute and renew class politics' (Harvey 1997: 41). This has been the task of the festivals mentioned in this chapter, one of which I will now analyse in greater depth.

LRFF organisational practices

I joined the LRFF organising team in 2014, having moved to Liverpool from Bristol, where I had worked on the Bristol Radical Film Festival since 2012. I therefore had close access to the LRFF organisers and was able to conduct in-person, semi-structured interviews with them. My physical proximity to the subject meant that I was able to utilise a method of what Toby Lee (2016) calls 'deep hanging out'. In his study of the Thessaloniki International Film Festival (TIFF), Lee draws on the theories of anthropologist, Clifford Geertz, who stresses the importance of long-term immersion in order to capture the tiniest ways of being in the world enacted by the subject/s, which then serve to illuminate their relations to objective structures. These relations influence the forms of practice that are subsequently developed within localised contexts. Lee's navigation of a series of interwoven habitus enables him to 'put flesh on the bones of institutional structures' (Lee 2016: 125). That is, through the ethnographic work of 'being there', he was able to situate the festival within Greece's social and political climate. While there is no space in this chapter for an in-depth analysis of Liverpool's recent sociopolitical history (see Wilks-Heeg 2003; Meegan 2003; Belchem and Biggs 2011; Frost and North 2013) it is important to note that in the years since 1987 (with the defeat of the Militant-led Labour council by the parties emerging wing of neoliberal 'moderates') the model of regeneration within Liverpool has largely consisted of private-sector led development and the use of cultural strategies to attract inward investment. The implementation of the neoliberal 'creative economy' (Hesmondhalgh et al. 2015) has focussed almost entirely on developing commercial businesses within the city centre. Although this has undoubtedly allowed the city to improve in many ways, areas outside of the centre are still heavily neglected. The UK's 2015 Indices of Multiple Deprivation found that Liverpool is the fourth most deprived local authority area in the country (it had previously been the first) while the most severe deprivation is found in the 'inner core' which surrounds the city centre (Liverpool City Council 2016).

Yet Liverpool has a history of autonomous activity among residents who have frequently been dissatisfied with regeneration efforts across parties and throughout different periods. Thus there have been various community-led regeneration strategies that have taken place between the period of de-industrialisation and the present one of private-sector led regeneration. Kenn Taylor notes that:

> The radical spirit that has over the years fuelled protests, riots, strikes, occupations and takeovers, remains. As do the skills in organising, protesting, publicising and delivering action [...] the failure time and again of ... grand plans and ideologies dreamt up by outsiders to improve the lives of the poor in Liverpool ... has helped create a mistrust of such ideas ... fostering instead a do-it-yourself mentality where disenfranchised communities have taken matters into their own hands.
>
> *(Taylor 2011: 160–2)*

This DIY mentality has become a cornerstone of numerous arts projects around the city (Killick 2017), and it is in this spirit that LRFF was founded and developed. The history of the festival has been described in greater depth by Steve Presence (2017), and by myself (Killick 2017), but for the purposes of this chapter my analysis begins in 2014, the year I joined the LRFF team. At that point the festival had been running since 2012 under the name Liverpool Radical Documentary Film Festival, and was now undergoing a transition in both its membership and practice. Some founding members had decided to take a step back from the festival, while others, such as myself, were beginning to get involved. The first thing that struck me about the festival was the fluidity of its core programming team. Having got in touch with members through its Facebook page, I was invited to a meeting at The Casa, a space in the city centre that had been converted into a bar by a group of dockworkers, who had pooled their redundancy money after the 1995 strike (Marren 2016). At that point the core group consisted of Steve Eye, the festival's one remaining founder member, Grace Harrison, a curator with an interest in avant-garde film, Hayley Trowbridge, who at the time was a PhD researcher at Liverpool University, and Darren Guy, an editor of the grassroots activist publication, Nerve, who had recently developed an interest in screening radical film as an intervention in neoliberal space. Harrison had become involved in the organising team simply by attending the first year of the festival and talking to some founding members who had since left, while Trowbridge became involved through her production of a series of micro-documentaries on women in Liverpool, which had been screened at a previous edition of the festival. At that meeting there was one other attendee, who like myself had never been to an LRFF team meeting – Will Mcleod, a freelance photographer who worked part-time in a bookmakers. It became clear to me, given the location and the informal nature of the conversation that followed, that members of the public were free to join the programming team on request, and that anyone who happened to have been in The Casa at that point could have become involved with the festival there and then.

I mention this as a pointer to the loose and informal organisational practices that characterise LRFF. Although at the time I thought this to be indicative of disorganisation, it soon became clear that the festival's openness to new volunteers and its relaxed approach to 'productivity' propagated a social relation among members of the organising team that is interdependent while allowing each member an almost complete autonomy in their programming choices. As this case study will show, LRFF resists incorporation as an official company or organisation for the very reason that members feel this would detrimentally affect the social relations upon which the festival functions. As Trowbridge explains, to do so would involve the implementation of more rigid working structures, wherein 'we might end up being more of a conventional organisation … but if we pushed down that path we'd lose the solidarity that we have. The mutual support, the trust' (personal communication, April 2017). This perspective on working practices is put in play through the festival's division of labour, wherein, as Trowbridge explains:

> Everyone does everything. Everyone organises. Everyone programs films and proposes events …. Everyone leads discussions. Everyone books film makers. Everyone helps out with the marketing, whether it's social media or it's updating the website, whether it's putting the programs out, whether it's word of mouth …. Everyone sets up gear. Everyone does tech stuff … so there are no 'roles' I guess is what I'm saying.
>
> *(Personal communication, April 2017)*

The purpose of the festival, then, is not to pull together a team of cultural gate-keepers, but to offer membership of the festival's organising team to the wider public as a potential means of community engagement. In this way the very core of LRFF – its organisational structure – is geared towards countering the 'loneliness epidemic' that has become a central feature of social life in the neoliberal period (Monbiot 2016). Members of the public are invited to organise screenings, and make use of the social and cultural capital accumulated by the festival over its previous editions. The festival also abstains from involvement with large funding bodies. For the organising team, this has become a defining point of the festival's identity. According to Trowbridge, it is crucial to LRFF maintaining a particular form of social relation among its members.

> We don't go for mainstream funding. We don't have the organisational status that would allow us to go for mainstream funding, and nor do we want that. That's not because we don't want to be accountable or to produce accounts …. It's about if we formalise everything then this becomes a job, or it becomes something like a big grant guzzling, funding hungry organisation …. And actually we've always been pretty radical in how we get things done and how we organise.
>
> *(Personal communication, April 2017)*

Guy echoes the reluctance to view festival organisation as a paid role.

> When there's money involved … when someone's getting paid, there's always a danger of people starting to get jealous and refusing to do things that they said they'd do because someone else is getting paid for doing stuff …. It's okay that it's been done on a shoestring [budget].
>
> *(Personal communication, April 2017)*

The closest LRFF has come to developing an 'official' structure is setting up a bank account, and organisers consciously negate this form of 'productivity'. Indeed, the suggestion that an organisation could or even should be 'less productive' is almost blasphemy at a time of fierce competition among various groups for different pockets of funding. LRFF's 'politics through practice' (Trowbridge, personal communication, April 2017) mean that organisers choose not to enter this game because they simply have no interest in it. This small example of the way the team organises itself has an impact on the kinds of screening spaces that characterise LRFF, and the subsequent local/global positionality of its audiences.

LRFF screenings: text, space, audience

Given LRFF's shoestring budget, screening venues are often negotiated with individuals and organisations with some access to a space on a basis of mutual benefit. The structure of the festival was such that it had previously run one-off events over the year at the behest of individual organisers, with the annual, core LRFF programme taking place over a series of two weeks in the middle of November. However, at the initial meeting in 2014 it was decided that two weeks was too long a time commitment for organisers, and that to avoid ill-health and burnout (especially given the freezing November weather and the fact that many screenings took place in spaces without adequate heating facilities) the annual festival should be reduced to a weekend programme that would be situated in venues within the city centre, while one-off screenings would continue to take place throughout the year in areas outside of the centre such as Toxteth and Kensington. The idea of this two-way navigation between city centre and periphery was to 'take radical film to new audiences … rather than expect them to come to us' (D. Guy, personal communication, April 2017) while at the same time maintaining a non-commercial presence in the city centre. Screening venues therefore vary, and include spaces like abandoned warehouses, independent cafés, and public or community spaces that are threatened with closure. In almost all cases the festival uses its own equipment, which is usually a laptop connected to a projector, some speakers and a portable or makeshift screen. As well as carrying out an activist function by bringing attention and/or financial benefit to the space (always through donations, as LRFF has never charged entry for its events), the films screened also usually bear some form of historical or close theoretical connection to the venue. The set of practices deployed by LRFF aims to establish a spectator positionality whereby audiences engage with the political issues of their dwelt-in locality, while at the same time maintaining an awareness and understanding of the global nature of politics and solidarity. This local/global, internationalist position serves to break down the distancing effects of Tascón's humanitarian gaze.

For example, in 2015 LRFF was held at the Pagoda Chinese Arts centre on Duke Street, a street close to the relatively new Liverpool One shopping centre, but which has yet to see any of the benefits of regeneration. Despite Liverpool City Council's highlighting of Pagoda as an example of how 'the cultural sector has proven that it can support attempts by diplomatic and business interests to develop and consolidate international relationships and trade' (Liverpool City Council 2013: 12), one year later the council revoked all of the centres' funds. In an effort to help it stay open, LRFF rented the space for £300, constructing a screen that was large enough for a community hall out of some donated wood and sheets of white fabric. Many of the screening fees throughout the festival were waived by filmmakers. Perhaps the most prominent of these 'solidarity screenings' was the film *Sleaford Mods: Invisible Britain* (Hannawin and Sng 2015), which brought an audience of around 150 people to Pagoda, and was followed by a panel discussion with the filmmakers and representatives from Reel News, a video activist newsreel based in London, as well as members from activist groups working in Liverpool, including the Blacklist Support Group (BSG), which provides a platform for blacklisted construction workers. Also included on the panel were JENGba (Join Enterprise Not Guilty by association), who campaign against a specific piece of UK criminal legislation that 'allows for a group of people to be convicted of a crime regardless of which person committed it … 80 per cent of people convicted are from black and ethnic minority backgrounds' (SMIB 2015). The aim here was to garner support for JENGba, and also to encourage people to attend an upcoming BSG protest event.

The debut feature documentary of two independent filmmakers, *Invisible Britain*, follows the British electro-punk duo, Sleaford Mods, as they tour the 'invisible' cities of the UK; that is, 'the neglected, boarded up and broken down parts of the country that many would prefer to ignore' (SMIB 2015). The cultural geography represented here is not that of 'global cities' such as London, Manchester and Edinburgh, but the comparatively ignored and neglected spaces of Colchester, Wakefield and Northampton. Some of the 'invisible' venues in which the Sleaford Mods play can be likened to the 'invisibility' of the Pagoda Chinese Arts Centre that is exemplified by the revocation of its public funds. At the same time as following the band, the film presents a range of different working class cultural groups, campaigns and spaces from around the country, some of which are similar to LRFF. This connection between festival and on-screen space advances the consecration of working class habitus and, potentially, a nationwide cultural geography that is also a geography of protest. The increased visibility of such spaces to working class audiences has the potential to generate new social, cultural and political opportunities that are off the table within the 'mainstream' spaces of, for example, A-list film festivals, which for the most part are not areas to which the working class have access. In one sequence the film highlights the debate around 'Joint Enterprise', and the LRFF panel was joined by a mother of someone sentenced to life in prison under the legislation. The anger felt by many working class people towards this piece of legislation meant that, as well as offering the possibility of realising potentialities through dialogue, the discussion following the film also took on a cathartic dimension, while noting the European-wide and even global implementation of austerity. In this sense both the film and the festival provide opportunities for 'invisible' people to speak, since the spaces in which they will be listened to are increasingly maligned within the neoliberal city. While the film outlines the various different localised contexts in which austerity is being administered and fought against throughout the UK, the discussion that followed led to some audience members signing up to attend the BSG protest.

Conclusion

I give the above screening example not as a way of 'proving' that a specific subject position has been fostered (difficult, if not impossible). Rather, the aim of this chapter has been to show some of the ways in which activist film festivals are informed (whether consciously or not) by an anti-austerity politics that is locally situated while being conscious of its international dimensions. The 'politics in practice' enacted by LRFF aims to create spaces that are antithetical to neoliberalism, in the hope that audiences would understand that its localised manifestations can be fought against through practical actions that can also be understood as part of a global project of defending human rights.

References

Belchem, J. and Biggs, B. 2011. *Liverpool: City of Radicals*. Liverpool: Liverpool University Press.
Blackburn, R. 2011. 'Reclaiming Human Rights' in *New Left Review* 69, 126–138. https:// newleftreview.org/II/69/robin-blackburn-reclaiming-human-rights

Bookchin, M. 2015. *The Next Revolution: Popular Assemblies and the Promise of Direct Democracy*. London: Verso.

Brenner, N. 2012. 'What is Critical Urban Theory' in *Cities for People not for Profit*, edited by N. Brenner, P. Marcuse and M. Mayer, 11–23. London: Routledge.

Frost, D. and North, P. 2013. *Militant Liverpool: A City on the Edge*. Liverpool: Liverpool University Press.

Harvey, D. 1997. *Justice, Nature and the Geography of Difference*. Oxford: Blackwell.

Hesmondhalgh, D., Oakley, K., Nisbett, M. and Lee, D. 2015. *Culture, Economy and Politics: The Case of New Labour*. London: Palgrave.

Ingold, T. 1993. 'Globes and Spheres: The Topology of Environmentalism' in *Environmentalism: The View from Anthropology*, edited by K. Milton, 29–41. London: Routledge.

Joseph Rowntree Foundation. 2017. 'UK Poverty 2017: Country Reaches Turning Point after Rise in Child and Pensioners Poverty'. https://www.jrf.org.uk/press/uk-poverty-2017-country-reaches-turning-point.

Killick, A. 2017. 'Building a Small Cinema: Resisting Neoliberal Colonisation in Liverpool'. *Achitecture_MPS* 11 (1) doi:10.14324/111.444.amps.2017v12i3.001

Lee, T. 2016. 'Being There, Taking Place: Ethnography at the Film Festival' in *Film Festivals: History, Theory, Method, Practice*, edited by M. de Valck, B. Kredell and S. Loist, 122–138. Oxon: Routledge.

Liverpool City Council. 2013. 'Liverpool Culture Action Plan 2014–2018' [online] Available: https://liverpool.gov.uk/media/8911/liverpoolcultureactionplan2013.pdf. Accessed April 13, 2020.

Liverpool City Council. 2016. 'Indices of Multiple Deprivation'. http://liverpool.gov.uk/council/key-statistics-and-data/indices-of-deprivation/

Marren, B. 2016. *We Shall Not Be Moved: How Liverpool's Working Class Fought Redundancies, Closures and Cuts in the Age of Thatcher*. Manchester: Manchester University Press.

Meegan, R. 2003. 'Urban Regeneration, Politics and Social Cohesion: The Liverpool Case' in *Reinventing the City: Liverpool in Comparative Perspective*, edited by R. Munck, 53–77. Liverpool: Liverpool University Press.

Monbiot, G. 2016. 'Neoliberalism Is Creating Loneliness'. *The Guardian*, October 12, 2016. Accessed April 13, 2020. https://www.theguardian.com/commentisfree/2016/oct/12/neoliberalism-creating-loneliness-wrenching-society-apart

Moyn, S. 2010. *The Last Utopia*. London: Harvard University Press.

Presence, S. 2017. 'One Screening away from Disaster: Precarity and Commitment in the Radical Film Network's Community Exhibition Sector' in *Community Filmmaking: Diversity, Practices and Places*, edited by C. Chapain, R. Comunian and S. Malik, 210–226. New York: Routledge.

SMIB. 2015. *Sleaford Mods: Invisible Britain* [documentary], Paul Sng, Nathan Hannawin, UK.

Tascón, S. 2015. *Human Rights Film Festivals: Activism in Context*. New York: Palgrave Macmillan.

Taylor, K. 2011. 'From the Ground Up: Radical Liverpool Now' in *Liverpool: City of Radicals*, edited by J. Belchem and B. Biggs, 159–172. Liverpool: Liverpool University Press.

Taylor, Diane. 2015. '"Conscious Cruelty": Ken Loach's Shock at Benefit Sanctions and Food Banks'. *The Guardian*, November 23. https://www.theguardian.com/film/2015/nov/23/ken-loach-benefit-sanctions-jeremy-corbyn-food-banks

United Nations Trade and Development. 2017. 'Beyond Austerity: Towards a Global New Deal'. http://unctad.org/en/PublicationsLibrary/tdr2017_en.pdf

Ward, Victoria. 2018. 'UK's Welfare System Is Cruel and Misogynistic, Says UN Expert after Damning Report on Poverty'. *The Telegraph*, 16 November. https://www.telegraph.co.uk/news/2018/11/16/welfare-system-cruel-misogynistic-un-expert-warns-damning-report/

Wilks-Heeg, S. 2003. 'From Global City to Pariah City? Liverpool and the Global Economy, 1850–2000' in *Reinventing the City: Liverpool in Comparative Perspective*, edited by R. Munck, 36–52. Liverpool: Liverpool University Press.

Winlow, S.*et al.*2015. *Riots and Political Protest: Notes from the Post-Political Present*. Oxon: Routledge.

Winton, E. and Turnin, S. 2017. 'The Revolution Will Not Be Festivalised: Documentary Film Festivals and Activism' in *Activist Film Festivals: Towards a Political Subject*, edited by S. Tascón and T. Wils, 83–103. Bristol: Intellect.

15

FRAMES OF COUNTERPOWER

The politics of film programming

Ezra Winton

Introduction – screening stories of audience counterpower

> The curators at festivals or broadcasters have a responsibility – I mean, it's their job. Films are made all the time about other cultures, and it's something that festivals have to do on a regular basis: to assess whether a film is entertaining, whether it's honest, whether it's helpful. This should be something that festivals should be thinking about with every single film that they program. Who is the audience and who are the storytellers and do they have a right to tell the story they're telling? Do they understand the responsibility they carry? Does the storyteller understand the responsibility, and do the programmers?
>
> *(Alethea Arnaquq-Baril)*[1]

Film programming and curation – which includes the selection, screening and reception context of films – is a dynamic site of political power involving great privilege and responsibility, as Inuk filmmaker Arnaquq-Baril (*Angry Inuk*) insists. The selection (and its dejected bedfellow, rejection) and placement of films for public reception is all too often either elided in studies of media, cinema and cognate fields, or is denuded of its politics – whereby characterisations, especially those found in festival studies, turn on agnostically apolitical, innocuously industrial or purely artistic processes of curation. This is a curious condition, given that literature and research in and of the art world abounds with deep probing of the politics of programming (see Balzer 2014), and that film programmes, not unlike gallery programmes, are carefully evaluated, regulated, placed, staged and cared for within the context of both the institution's agendas and curator's lived experiences, prejudices and competencies. The study of documentary has similarly overlooked the politics of programming and curation, which is doubly curious given the genre's consistently articulated association with social and political issues by industry, filmmakers, audiences and researchers alike. At university departments across the globe scholarly analyses of film texts continue to flourish faster than Netflix's streaming market share, while the ways in which those same films are valued, chosen, positioned and contextualised in culture and society evade analogous levels of enthusiastic inquiry. Yet, in this era of digital media/art abundance – the age of curators or 'curationist moment' (Balzer 2014, 9) and 'age of access' (Rifkin 2000) as it were – what happens between a film's production wrap and the space of audience reception is of incredible consequence to questions of politics, including those concerning representation, ethics, activism, and especially power and 'counterpower', or 'the capacity of a social actor to resist and challenge power relations that are institutionalized' (Castells 2007).[2] To support this opening credo, I offer the following illustrative example.

In 2014 during a screening taking place as part of the annual VIBGYOR international short and documentary film festival in Thrissur, India, an angry mob stormed the screening venue and attempted to shut down the projection of *Ocean of Tears* (Billal A. Jan), a 27-minute Kashmiri film about human rights violations (including violence) suffered by mostly Kashmir women at the hands of Indian security forces.[3] Mark Achbar was attending the festival for a screening of the documentary he co-directed with Jennifer Abbott, *The Corporation* (2003). He recalls a frenetic, chaotic scene:

> A few minutes after it [the projection of *Ocean of Tears*] had started, the BJP [Bharatiya Janata Party] protesters interrupted the screening, yelled nationalist slogans, and tried to tear down the projection screen. They were a few feet from me. I just kept taking pictures [see Figures 15.1 and 15.2].
>
> Then I saw something I'd never seen at a film festival. A large portion of the audience got up on the stage [Figure 15.1], as if to defend the projection screen, and in an impressive show of solidarity, raised their fists and shouted down the intruders in unison for several minutes until the police finally escorted them from the theatre back to the street. The screening continued – to much applause.
>
> *(Achbar 2014)*

What this episode highlights (aside from the troubling march of Indian politics toward fascism and organised grassroots resistance against it)[4] is the severity of the stakes that are at play when certain films are shown in certain public contexts by certain organisations or people. Each context changes with each film, each screening organisation, each political regime in which that film circulates and each public or film culture to which it is shown. In some cases, the stakes are enormous and measured in actual harm (both physical as in this anecdote, and cultural as in one of the cases discussed at greater length below), and thus these politics of programming reveal a vigorously articulated rebuke to claims of both cinema's 'passive audiences' as well as the enduring industrial and academic conjuring of apolitical screening spaces.

FIGURE 15.1 VIBGYOR festival attendees move from their seats to the stage to protect a screening of *Ocean of Tears* from censorship by the BJP (at left) in 2014. Photo courtesy of Mark Achbar.

FIGURE 15.2 VIBGYOR festival attendees block a member of BJP from censoring a screening of *Ocean of Tears* in 2014. Projection screen can be seen behind the stage at right. Photo courtesy of Mark Achbar.

Capital programming vs community programming: TIFF and The Yes Men

If we start from the premise that curate, as its Latin roots suggest, is 'to care for', we may then pivot to the screening context of cinema, and ask: Who cares for films and filmmakers publicly; how do they care for them (and why); and how are impacted communities, publics and audiences cared for? In my forthcoming book (Winton Forthcoming) I differentiate between two film curating approaches, philosophies and value-sets: capital programming and community programming. As a film scholar, critic and curator who has been programming political film (mostly documentary) for two decades, I fully acknowledge that these categories are not certain, air-tight encasements: they are instead suggestive, porous containers meant to provide a frame through which we might better formulate questions of politics, representation and ethics concerning the selection, rejection, ordering and placement of film texts in wider culture and society.

In terms of film festivals, there is a constant push for 'new' content, for 'discovery programming', and for standing out as unique in a sea of many similarly constituted institutions (current estimates suggest the world is teeming with upwards of 5,000 film festivals – with new film fetes emerging each and every day).

Yet looking at the highly controlled content delivery and ordering system in operation at a commercial festival like the Toronto International Film Festival (TIFF) where more than one third of the institution's $42 million operating budget comes from sponsors (TIFF 2017, 65) it would appear the festival conforms to the film festival circuit's conventional operational logic, which is a market logic of mostly known, or predicted, differentiation (films you can bank on). Sean Farnel has estimated (Winton 2013a, 133) that, during his tenure at Hot Docs as head programmer, around 90 per cent of programming was constituted from known films, and around 10 per cent was composed of 'cold submissions' (no a priori knowledge of the film selected).[5] I call this kind of film curation 'capital programming' for the manner in which it capitalises on recognised products that have sold well on the market (the festival circuit), or will sell well based on previous programming knowledge (of the filmmaker, distributor, the issue, etc.). Capital programming's directive is measured by quantifiable variables: increased audiences, increased budgets, increased media imprints, increased social media buzz, etc.

Capital programming is distinct from 'community programming' (Zielinski 2008), where programmers work with communities of peers, artists, activists and festival publics to represent the diverse interests in the field while foregrounding community building that is informed by – and at times led by – stakeholder and impacted communities on and off screen (for instance a stakeholder Indigenous community would have equal or lead say in how an Indigenous film is programmed at a settler-run, curated and funded screening institution). Capital programming, as a manifestation of commercial populism, services a popular conceptualisation of the 'average audience' member, who associates with and appreciates liberally mainstream, commercially attuned cultural products more than outside-the-playing-field, lower budgeted and radical-voiced works (see Figure 15.3). This is unless the filmmaker's cultural capital ensures a packed house regardless, such is the case with exceptional indie and arthouse directors with large cinephile fan bases. Festivals attend to their own interests to raise the popularity of their events. This is in order to grow numbers in audience and therefore revenue or capital (cash, in-kind and sponsor investments). 'Average' (whose etymology is concerned with the economics of equalising between gains and losses) here of course is meant to invoke and reflect the 'average' population, the vast middle demographic who adhere or acquiesce to governing hegemonic value systems from gender binaries to unjust economies to 'universal' rights (that is, most of us in most societies). In this way, capital programming contributes to the cultural reinforcement

FIGURE 15.3 In the Hot Docs 2013 programme the festival saluted its audience on the occasion of twenty years in operation. From the likely thousands of audience images Hot Docs selected for this commemoration, the one above is revealing for the conveyance of class, among other things. Image courtesy of author.

of political and economic hegemonic and unjust systems that help hardwire audiences through processes of normative enculturation. Or, as Castells (2007), in his discussion of power and counterpower, summarises:

> Throughout history communication and information have been fundamental sources of power and counter-power, of domination and social change. This is because the fundamental battle being fought in society is the battle over the minds of the people. The way people think determines the fate of norms and values on which societies are constructed.
>
> *(238)*

Film programming is not an innocuous act and indeed has its role in reinforcing or rejecting dominant norms and values. Or, to borrow from Richard Fung, festival programming also 'programs' audiences (Fung 1998).

The community vs commercial duality exists indeed across multiple communication platforms and culture industry sites. There have also been numerous complaints that large cable companies have cut back on community programming and moved to create programme formats that mimic those of commercial broadcasters (Skinner 2010, 228). With the case of publicly funded film platforms like TIFF in the fiction realm and Hot Docs in the non-fiction camp, commercially oriented festivals may allocate the resources of production (of the festival – mainly industry and screening events) to ensure their programming fits with their specific brand (in an effort to differentiate in a saturated market place of festivals, at least in urban centres like Toronto where audiences are able to frequent over 100 film festivals per year). Yet mimicked formats are replete along the festival circuit – from industry markets to sidebar programmes to awards, to sponsors (a quick tally of Toronto festivals sponsored by Canada's top five banks is very telling) to the programming of the same films. This mimicry and focus on what commercially 'works' (what appeals to the vast but moneyed middle) has over time ushered in the festival equivalent to the bankable Megaplex blockbuster: 'the festival film'.

As non-fiction festival hits and commercial champs, *docbusters* (coined by documentary filmmaker and entrepreneur Morgan Spurlock and summoning commercially successful non-fiction films – see Winton Forthcoming) are ultimately situated and marketed as commercial products, often sharing discursive, promotional and programming space with Hollywood films. As a commercial enterprise seeking to increase ticket sales, TIFF programmes a smaller selection of documentaries per year, which are carefully placed among the festival's larger fiction programme (which in turn is made up of Hollywood, world cinema and indie film fare). In a 2018 podcast, TIFF's documentary programmer, American-born Thom Powers, postulates that we just might be in the 'golden age' of documentary, signalling both a willingness to ignore the pronounced struggling status of the vast bulk of non-fiction cinema, and to champion capital programming that props up safe crowd-pleasing films like *Won't You Be My Neighbor* (Morgan Neville, 2018, $22.6 million USD box office gross) and ethically suspect filmmakers like Werner Herzog.[6] TIFF's description of the podcast is revealing for the way it positions documentary in the market: Powers discusses how "documentary" went from a dirty word to a financially viable genre, how Netflix helped expand the art form, and the technological innovations that have changed the genre for the better.[7] Here one encounters the essential reducibility of capital programming for documentary: in order to clean the genre up we must turn to the polishing mechanisms of the market, which with the help of one of the largest, tax-avoiding, inequitable media corporations on the planet (in 2018 alone, Netflix co-founder Reed Hastings earned $36 million USD),[8] is dusting off the embattled mode of audio-visual storytelling to help its products make millions. The implication is of course that documentary was a dirty word among those seeking to capitalise on the genre, seeing little opportunity for exchange value on the marketplace, until commercial hits like *One Direction: This is Us* (Morgan Spurlock, 2013, $68.5 million USD box office gross), *Amy* (Asif Kapadia, 2015, $23.7 million USD box office gross) and *Jackass 3D* (Jeff Tremaine, 2018, $171.1 million USD box office gross) have proven the naysayers wrong. That the list of top-grossing documentaries is brimming with hagiographies of celebrities and boy bands is not surprising.[9] Nor is it a news flash to discover that large film festivals like TIFF pepper their programming with docbusters and debuts by doc-celebs like Michael Moore. It is disconcerting however, when a major world leader in film culture and industry like TIFF differentiates its programming, toggling towards the possibility for community-oriented, politically active curation, only to foreclose on this possibility and flex institutional musculature to ensure capital is returned to its rightful, protected and lofty position.

I refer to the festival's reaction to an event that took place at TIFF 2014, when the festival programmed the newest documentary by co-directors Igor Vamos and Jacques Servin, eponymous members of international prankster/activist group The Yes Men, and Laura Nix. *The Yes Men Are Revolting* ($50,190 USD total box office) follows Mike Bonanno and Andy Bichlbaum (Vamos' and Servin's character names) as they expose corporate malfeasance in relation to the world's worsening climate crisis, while collaborating with climate justice activists like Gitz Crazyboy at Alberta's oil sands industrial project. In the film, Crazyboy strikes a serious tenor to the political antics of Mike and Andy as he recounts the ways in which the massive environmental devastation the oil sands reap negatively impact nearby First Nations communities, including his own. In a TIFF news release dated July 29, 2014 the documentary is described as delving into 'the topical exploration of the environment' (TIFF 2014) but searches on the TIFF site for any mention of the film or its three co-directors proves to be unfruitful. Perhaps tiff.net has a terrible search function (it does). Perhaps TIFF would rather forget that it ever programmed the film (it likely does). As a feature documentary dedicated to advancing progressive politics around climate crisis, and featuring politically radical voices critiquing corporate capitalism while celebrating direct action in many forms, *The Yes Men Are Revolting* is a refreshing politicised programming choice for a corporate friendly festival like TIFF. Still, The Yes Men come with a 'global brand' that is recognised, and have made international news headlines repeatedly for their outrageous, radical pranks, so perhaps programmers at TIFF still saw this entertaining activist film as bankable, especially considering The Yes Men activists were in attendance. But what they didn't bank on was that the activism would accompany the film in the social spaces around the festival, including in an actual bank a mere three 350 metres from TIFF headquarters.

The bank in question was the Royal Bank of Canada, or RBC. The action involved Gitz Crazyboy very loudly and publicly closing his account at the King West RBC branch, due to the Canadian institution's colossal financial investment in, and support of, the Alberta oil sands extraction project.[10] As he made the proclamation, activists streamed in to the branch and a dance party erupted – much to the discomfort of staff. TIFF management got wind of the action, took offence and threatened to cancel the screening of the film, which was the world premiere at one of the world's leading film festivals. The problem? RBC is the main corporate sponsor of TIFF. The issue? The requisite polite, grateful filmmaking guests invited to the festival were misbehaving and making a major sponsor look bad. The action had all the hallmarks of a Yes Men stunt and was organised by a local climate justice group. Fifty people flooded the tiny branch and chanted in unison 'HE CLOSED HIS ACCOUNT!' while balloons and streamers filled the air and a boom box carried by one activist/party reveller added to the cacophonic frenzy. Making a cameo in the city were even two activists (one of whom was Mike) in corporate 'survivaball climate suits' featured in the film (Figure 15.4) and which

FIGURE 15.4 Activists don 'survivaball' outfits around the corner from the RBC branch near TIFF, and await the signal to enter the branch for the ensuing dance party held in celebration of Gitz Crazyboy closing his account due to the bank's financing of Alberta's devastating tar sands project. Image courtesy of author.

are meant to (quite ridiculously) allow corporate executives to adapt to climate crisis-induced rising sea levels by way of inflatable all-in-one work outfits. From the position of this observer it was a zealous, inclusive and joyful action that managed to highlight RBC's immoral role in supporting the oil sands while celebrating a direct action against one of Canada's most powerful (financial) institutions.

Rather than facilitating diverse cultural and political responses to political issues featured in a programmed documentary, TIFF reinforced its strategy of managerial control and commercial enclosure, constraining the possibilities and potential for artistic expression, cultural diversity and political action. Rancière (2004) comes to mind here, as the scholar's concept of the 'distribution of the sensible' can be used to describe the role of commercial festivals in contemporary culture and politics as status-quo enforcers. The Yes Men were on the one hand granted screen space to act un-sensibly, but when those disruptive actions spilled off the screen and into the greater socio-cultural and economic spaces of the festival, notably impacting sponsor image and proving (temporarily) unmanageable, the institution's containment muscles contracted; and just as Rancière's cultural 'police' re-set a given dominant agenda, TIFF aggressively adhered to its well hewn capital programming values, and valued its top corporate sponsor (whose values are at significantly pronounced odds with anyone fighting to reverse the climate crisis) over its programmed film and invited film guests.

TIFF, like so many commercial mainstream film festivals, acts less as a space and platform for alternative culture and politics but rather as an outpost of the global entertainment industry, where off-screen comfort and sensibility are safeguarded and the socio-political status quo is protected against radical and activist contamination. This points to ways in which a politics of programming includes not just the selection of films, but presentation, placement and the screening environment as well. The policing of wider contextual currents around the screening of a politically charged documentary at TIFF also draws insight into the festival's values mandate regarding community engagement, which I would characterise as *community containment*, whereby audiences and publics resistant to the (commercial) values of the festival's capital programming are marginalised (and threatened with eviction) while sensibly behaving members of the festival community are rewarded and held as positive examples.

TIFF's handling of The Yes Men's activism at the festival in 2014 is indicative of what Abercrombie and Longhurst (1998) call the 'Incorporation/Resistance Paradigm', whereby audiences are either incorporated into dominant ideology (in this case a liberal framework that infers political action is best confined as entertainment without implicating audiences or encouraging diverse activation, including the direct, collective confrontation of major financial sponsors[11]) through participation (attending festival screenings devoid of politically transformative actions) or they are resistant to incorporation (in this case, by staging actions against the festival's top sponsors, in the wider social spaces connected to TIFF). A politics of programming that celebrates and builds on documentary cinema's resistance roots and connected activism (on and off screen) should include opportunities for radically political, transformative screening contexts, where for instance political actions related to film subjects are encouraged and supported, or at the very least tolerated. After all, RBC's promotional copy for their TIFF sponsorship has it right, at least in theory: 'Proudly supporting the infinite possibilities of film' (see Figure 15.5). Documentary's political possibilities are potentially radically transformative. To quash that potential is to perform a disservice to the makers, subjects, stakeholder publics and audiences alike.

Theorising radical curation

The TIFF/Yes Men incident draws attention to the need for institutions and organisations that mindfully care for radical filmmaking and its activating effects. This might be called a form of radical curation, and the above example highlights its opposite, along with three linked concepts I connect with commercially oriented film programming and exhibition sites (and therefore with capital programming): agnostic curation, the liberal festival possessive and screen ethics. The first gestures towards depoliticised screening spaces and the idea that *a film is a film is a*

FIGURE 15.5 TIFF's biggest corporate sponsor, RBC, proclaims that it 'Proudly supports the infinite possibilities of film.' That is, unless of course those possibilities include off screen activism directed against RBC and its nefarious financial activities. Direct action doesn't make for good popcorn-eating events, apparently. Image courtesy of author.

film, or, put differently, the liberal conceit that entering into socio-political considerations of who made what and that when one evaluates the structure and ethical dimensions of that relationship they are entering superfluous and unfairly anti-artistic territory (or relatedly it harkens the much trotted out – especially in these days of global white supremacist invigoration – precept of 'politically correct'). That film programmers should actually care about, research and evaluate who funds and who makes films in which conditions, and especially documentaries – where the context is so much more sensitive to real lives and consequences – is a prickly suggestion, one that continues to reveal the deep cleavage between so-called defenders of free speech and avant-garde art and those calling for more ethical filmmaking and programming. With regards to settler film productions and curation that advance settler colonial projects, Bruno Cornellier (2016) has analysed this attitude as part of 'the white possessive', a concept he borrows from Goenpul scholar Aileen Moreton-Robinson (2015), which describes the learned and highly structured hierarchal affordances and privileges white settlers are naturalised into, from possessing Indigenous lands, to bodies, to images, stories and social spaces. But these affordances and privileges are not innate – they are learned through structured processes of enculturation that is maintained through the exercise of power, especially through the influence of society's most dominant institutions. While many film festivals may seem suitably categorised in an 'alternative media' camp, larger players like TIFF and Hot Docs are dominant institutions in their own field (cinema generally, documentary particularly), and as settler-formed and run institutions they continue to uphold settler hierarchies of power for the most part, and therefore legacies of domination and control all too often go unchecked under the guise of edgy art, the consistently articulated acknowledgement of festivals as alternative exhibition platforms (to more traditionally dominant commercial television, Hollywood and the Megaplex) and the exceptional radically voiced documentary film. Not all films are created equal, a dictum that should be incorporated into a politics of programming that acknowledges the systems of domination in which it operates, and whose host institution's purported values should be matched by their actions. Chelsea Vowel (Métis) calls the denial of these structured inequities in the settler context the 'myth of the level playing field' (Vowel 2016, 124).

Confronting agnostic curation also involves addressing the liberal festival possessive, which as the cultural compendium of economic neoliberalism, flattens politics into modes of comfortable reception and reshapes diverse political discourse and action into a liberal framework where individual action, the market and Western-designated universal rights are the order of the day. In the liberal possessive framework, one in which oppressive power is identified and counterpower is mobilised only on screen (never in the festival's social spaces), 'capitalism is a form of power that is intimately stitched into the fabric of everyday life and which animates and is animated by a host of social institutions' (Haiven 2018, 33) including film festivals. The liberal possessive is as such part of a programming cocktail at commercial festivals that normalises systems of domination and exploitation like capitalism. Even when those systems are challenged on screen in structural, radical ways, commercial festivals, like all commercial exhibition sites, preclude any possibility for collective mobilisation and resistance in response to screened subjects. Champions of the liberal festival possessive also grant impunity to corporate sponsors, and when confronted by audiences opposed to these allegiances, deploy discourse that almost always articulates a noble agnosticism: 'It's not our job to do politics,' and privileges the individual client: 'It's up to each audience member to decide if they want to do something.'[12] In this way agnostic curation elides and even supports unjust power imbalances replete in the film world instead of addressing them and working toward a fair, more just playing field; and the liberal festival possessive provides the extended agnostic, non-confronting, entertainment reception space for programming, even in the case of curated progressive and radical documentaries.

Lastly, screen ethics: my term that captures the position that the ethical dimension of film (and especially documentary) is not limited to the relationship between the filmmaker and the subject or other cultural workers. Screen ethics implies that content should not be divorced from context, and that ethical considerations should include the ways in which films are made *and* the ways in which films circulate and are embedded/deployed in wider cultures and society. With this in mind, when we ask what are the ethical concerns around a film like *Check It* – a documentary shown at festivals including Hot Docs and produced by a marketing firm that has threatened legal action against activists for using the term 'radical media', which the company has trademarked[13] – we are including questions of representation, reciprocal relationships between makers and subjects and audiences, as well as curation and screenings of the film. Screen ethics, which gathers making, showing and experiencing under one principled roof, is therefore a tool to wrench apart capital programming's component parts, which include agnostic curation and the liberal festival possessive. The ethical gathering of film production with film circulation and exhibition forces a closer look at a series of relations that move outward from a film's inception to its reception, from intent to content to context, and keeps company with Bill Nichols' call for a 'documentary code of ethics'[14] by supporting festival best practices and protocols.[15]

Conclusion: let's talk value and values

When film exhibition sites create alternative platforms for cinema that at times privilege radical and progressive political perspectives, yet foreclose on related activist incursions, or choose to turn a blind eye to the problematic political economy behind a production, there comes a values disconnect. Recently at Cinema Politica, an alternative political film exhibition network for which I serve as Director of Programming, our programming team voted unanimously (curatorial decisions are made by consensus) in favour of selecting a work, but with a caveat that we would look further into who made it and their relationship with the subject, and to research one of the film's sponsors, Lush cosmetics. Recognising that films are not always 'independently' produced, that independent filmmakers sometimes go bankrupt and/or take money from private entities to produce their work, we have a process of proceeding with caution in such scenarios where a corporate sponsor is made visible to us as programmers. In this case we realised that Lush has led anti-sealing campaigns, and this articulated value-set is at odds with those of Cinema Politica: notably that we support Indigenous, and in this case, Inuit right to self-determination, sovereignty and cultural heritage. That means for us, we cannot support a film that, despite its exceptional technical aspects or radical political content, has been supported by a corporation whose values are at odds with ours (personally as programmers, and collectively as an organisation). We then wrote a letter explaining this to the filmmakers, which was returned with a very compassionate and generous reply that acknowledged the act of adhering to those values.

Films may have value on a market, and may be evaluated with such value in mind when considered in regimes of capital programming. That value may be expressed in terms of box office, streaming views, ticket sales or media imprints. That value may be predetermined as programmers carefully track productions across the festival circuit, nurturing relationships with filmmakers that will land them a docbuster or festival hit in their own institution. De Valck and many other festival scholars have also talked of the value that is added to films when they are programmed at large, notable festivals. This value is measured in part by laurel leaves – a currency not worth any use value with a high inflation rate and that is proudly displayed on movie posters across the globe. 'Value-adding' is also thought to increase a film's capital potential (social, cultural, economic, symbolic capital) in order to transform festival screening revenues (where filmmakers are for the most part not remunerated from ticket earnings) into distribution revenues (where many estimates posit less than 10 per cent of all festival films find gainful distribution). But, beyond capital and economic value, films and their contexts also reflect and embody *values*, those intangible qualities that give shape to how we see the world and how we behave in the world. And, how we tell and care for stories. Tasha Hubbard, an Indigenous filmmaker based in the Canadian prairies, connects value to story here:

> Indigenous people have not been seen as having value, and that translates to our stories. And so, a lot of our stories implicate Canada and implicate those who benefit from injustice. And that's the majority of Canadians. So that's an uncomfortable truth, and sadly not enough people are courageous enough to face that. And I think storytelling has potential to create some cracks in that kind of a wall. You know, we joke about Trump's wall, but we have our own walls here in this country, and they're pretty high. So how do we get through that so that people see the value and see the strength in Indigenous stories. We've been taught so much over the years and over the decades, through residential schools or various policies, that we aren't valued. I make films and I think a lot of us are in the same position, where we want to share our stories with each other too, because, again we're always taught only stories by white people have value. We need to go back to valuing our own stories too.
>
> *(Hubbard 2018)*

While Hubbard isn't addressing the programming and curating of those stories or films, she is pointing to the relationship between value and values. When a person or their stories isn't valued by a society, that society is likely to move through the world with values that reflect that ignorance and prejudice. When a documentary is screened that challenges such historical undervaluing and consequential injustice, not only does the value of such stories have the potential to shift, so do the values the audience member carries. This is the powerful potential of political and radical cinema – to change minds, and following Castells, to change behaviour and eventually systems of domination and oppression. Yet, if the spaces where such transformation are given a chance to evolve are stamped out by other value(s)-sets (those that privilege corporate sponsors, profit, growth, harmful companies), then the power of film, and especially documentary, is limited in its capacity to nourish counterpower. If the care-takers of film – the curators, programmers and festival managers – aren't up to the task of transforming our exhibition institutions to match the values they and their documentaries champion, then it's up to the rest of us to do the job, whilst keeping busy at building alternatives across geographies, cultures and diverging value-sets. That's a frame worth looking, and working, through.

Notes

1 Source: http://ezrawinton.com/2015/12/22/curating-the-north-documentary-screening-ethics-and-inuit-representation-in-festival-cinema/
2 The full quote reads: 'I understand power to be the structural capacity of a social actor to impose its will over other social actor(s). All institutional systems reflect power relations, as well as the limits to these power relations as negotiated by a historical process of domination and counter-domination. Thus, I will also analyze the process of formation of counter-power, which I understand to be the capacity of a social actor to resist and challenge power relations that are institutionalized. Indeed, power relations are by nature conflictive, as societies are diverse and contradictory' (Castells 2007, 239).
3 See also Shweta Kishore's Chapter 8 in this volume.
4 For a thorough and rousing documentary account of the history and contemporary situation regarding Hindu nationalism, fascism and the ruling elite in India, be sure to view Anand Patwardhan's IDFA-award winning opus *Reason* (2018, India, 241').
5 For more on hot vs cold programming, see this Indiewire article that caused a flurry of online debate when Sundance Director of Programming Kim Yutani admitted there were no real surprises at the 2019 edition of the festivals because, 'We track these things so far in advance.' Source: https://www.indiewire.com/2018/11/sundance-film-festival-tough-odds-indie-gatekeepers-1202024241/
6 https://www.tiff.net/the-review/tiff-long-take-ep-79-golden-age-of-documentary-film/
7 https://www.tiff.net/the-review/tiff-long-take-ep-79-golden-age-of-documentary-film/
8 https://www.broadcastingcable.com/news/netflix-ceo-hastings-pay-jumps-to-36m-in-2018
9 For a lengthy discussion on the politics of 'popular documentary' see Winton (2020).
10 In the following short video, Eriel Tchekwie Deranger, from the Rainforest Action Network, explains why RBC should be called out (and shut down) for their involvement in the Alberta Tar Sands project: https://bit.ly/2BVrkd2
11 For more on audience implication and impunity, see Winton (2013b).
12 See Winton (2013a), 233.
13 Source: https://patrickmccurdy.wordpress.com/2011/05/12/radical-media-uk-ad-firm-threatens-activsts-with-legal-action-over-the-use-of-term-radical-media/

14 Source: https://www.documentary.org/content/what-do-about-documentary-distortion-toward-code-ethics-0
15 Some festivals are taking the lead on this, notably the Ann Arbor Film Festival and the imagineNATIVE Film & Media Festival.

References

Abercrombie, Nicholas and Brian Longhurst. 1998. *Audiences: A Sociological Theory of Performance and Imagination*. London: Sage Publications.

Achbar, Mark. 2014. (Filmmaker) in discussion with author. March.

Balzer, David. 2014. *Curationism: How Curating Took Over the Art World and Everything Else*. Toronto: Coach House Books.

Castells, Manuel. 2007. 'Communication, Power and Counter-power in the Network Society'. *International Journal of Communication* 1, 238–266.

Cornellier, Bruno. 2016. 'Extracting Inuit: The of the North Controversy and the White Possessive'. *American Indian Culture and Research Journal* 40 (4), 23–48.

Fung, Richard. 1998. 'Programming the Public'. *GLQ: A Journal of Lesbian and Gay Studies* 5 (1), 89–93.

Haiven, Max. 2018. *Art After Money, Money After Art: Creative Strategies Against Financialization*. London: Pluto Press.

Hubbard, Tasha. 2018. (Filmmaker) in discussion with author. October.

Moreton-Robinson, Aileen. 2015. *The White Possessive: Property, Power, and Indigenous Sovereignty*. Minneapolis: University of Minnesota Press.

Rancière, Jacques. 2004. *The Politics of Aesthetics: The Distribution of the Sensible*, London: Continuum International Publishing Group.

Rifkin, Jeremy. 2000. *The Age of Access: The New Culture of Hypercapitalism Where All of Life Is a Paid-for Experience*. New York: TarcherPerigee.

Skinner, David. 2010. 'Minding the Growing Gap: Alternative Media in Canada'. In *Mediascapes: New Patterns in Canadian Communication*, 3rd edition. Toronto: Nelson Education, 221–236.

TIFF. 2014. 'TIFF News Release, July 29, 2014'. Online: http://media.tiff.net.s3.amazona ws.com/emails/pdf/TIFF%20DOCS_2014.pdf

TIFF. 2017. 'TIFF Annual Report 2017'. Online: https://assets.ctfassets.net/22n7d68fswlw/ 5JZoRb4Of6euOQEYYScCgw/04c3889a8c325cb766884c86e38e043a/TIFF_Annua lReport17_digital_72dpi.pdf

Vowel, Chelsea. 2016. *Indigenous Writes: A Guide to First Nations, Métis and Inuit Issues in Canada*. Winnipeg: Highwater Press.

Winton, Ezra. 2013a. 'Good for the Heart and Soul, Good for Business: The Cultural Politics of Documentary at the Hot Docs Film Festival.' PhD Dissertation, School of Journalism and Communication, Concordia University, December.

Winton, Ezra. 2013b. 'Upping the Anti- Documentary, Capitalism and Liberal Consensus in an Age of Austerity'. *POV Magazine* 92, Winter. Online: http://povmagazine.com/arti cles/view/upping-the-anti

Winton, Ezra. 2020. 'Reclaiming Popular Documentary: Fast Festivals and the Private Interest Documentary.' In *Reclaiming Popular Documentary*, Christie Milliken and Steve Anderson (eds.). Bloomington: Indiana University Press.

Winton, Ezra Forthcoming. *Buying In to Doing Good: Documentary Politics and Curatorial Ethics at the Hot Docs Film Festival*. Montreal and Kingston: McGill-Queen's University Press.

Zielinski, Gerald J. Z. 2008. 'Furtive, Steady Glances: On the Emergence and Cultural Politics of Lesbian and Gay Film Festivals'. PhD diss., McGill University.

16

'COMMUNIST INTERNATIONAL OF QUEER FILMS'

The radical culture of the Beijing Queer Film Festival

Hongwei Bao

Founded in 2001, the Beijing Queer Film Festival (BJQFF) is one of the longest running identity-based film festivals in the contemporary People's Republic of China (PRC).[1] Since its inception, the festival has undergone significant transformations: from being a student-led 'homosexual' film festival held on an elite university campus to now forming a part of China's independent film movement, from fighting 'guerrilla warfare' against police intervention in urban Beijing to its current form of the 'Beijing Love Queer Cinema Week' held annually at the cultural centre of a foreign embassy in Beijing.[2] The BJQFF plays an important part in China's queer movement; it also serves as a good example of how marginalised communities engage in media activism to contest illiberal neoliberalism in the Global South.

The BJQFF has been examined as a response to neoliberal governance in East Asia (Rhyne 2011) and cultural translation of sexual identities and politics in a transnational context (Bao 2017). So far it has not been studied in terms of its spatial politics, organisation forms, principles and practices, as well as how the festival can be seen as part of a broader, transnational radical film culture. In this chapter, I examine the history and organisation of the BJQFF, as well as the cinematic aesthetics and politics it advocates. In situating the BJQFF in China's historical transition from socialism to postsocialism, I interrogate how a postsocialist queer film event draws on socialist experiences to articulate a democratic, anti-authoritarian and anti-capitalist Left cultural politics.

'Radical films', encompassing both political and avant-garde films, are usually understood as films aligning themselves with the ethos of the political left – socialist, anti-capitalist, anti-fascist, anti-colonial, feminist and queer – they celebrate political engagement as well as aesthetic innovation (Radical Film Network 2019). Radical film culture is not exclusively Western or intrinsically Eurocentric, but it is often represented by political and avant-garde film practices from the Global North.[3] The Western bias of radical film culture is closely associated with unequal power relations in the world, where resources are distributed unevenly and information often fails to travel across linguistic and cultural borders.

This chapter addresses the Euro-American-centrism in the study of radical film cultures by examining cinematic and political practices in a non-Western context. It shifts radical film research's traditional emphasis on class to an intersectional approach that recognises complex interplays between different identities, including gender, sexual, class and national identities. I suggest that sexuality has an important role to play in radical politics, and that queer film festivals are important sites for radical film cultures to develop. Indeed, while neoliberal capitalism and the nation state often exert a powerful influence on queer film cultures transnationally, not all queer film festivals are radical, broadly understood as democratic, egalitarian, anti-capitalist and anti-normativity in this context (Richards 2016, 2017). If many queer film festivals in the Global North are seen as middle-class-serving, lifestyle-oriented and consumption-driven and have thus lost their critical edge, queer film festivals in many parts of the Global South are still charged with creative energies and radical potentials exactly because of state illiberalism and neoliberal governance, as my study of the BJQFF hopes to demonstrate.

In this chapter, I first trace a brief genealogy of the BJQFF with a focus on changing festival venues in order to see how the festival uses 'guerrilla tactics' to fight government intervention and contest neoliberal capitalism. Following this, I examine the various names that the festival has used, as well as the organising strategies of the festival, including organising principles, audience engagement and film dissemination. To conclude the chapter, I consider the political implications of the BJQFF in a transnational context by linking radical film culture to postsocialist cultural politics. I argue that radical film cultures represented by the BJQFF help us appreciate the value of some ideas and practices from socialist histories in the neoliberal, postsocialist present.

'Guerrilla warfare': the spatial politics of BJQFF

Yang Yang, one of the organisers of the BJQFF, made a documentary film in 2011 about the decade-long history of the BJQFF. The film featured a location map of the constantly changing screening venues, which were spread all over the city (Figure 16.1).[4] Yang named the film *Our Story: Ten-Year 'Guerrilla Warfare' of the Beijing Queer Film Festival.* The first-person plural pronoun ('our') and the rather militarist term 'guerrilla warfare' in the title capture what had happened in ten years – the unrelenting effort to build a queer community and the continuous struggles for survival – and ominously predict what would continue to be the case in the years to follow. Indeed, the BJQFF has been waging 'guerrilla warfare' on several fronts: against the authorities, a capitalist system, as well as middle-class dominated homonormative social values (Duggan 2003). This is not conventional warfare in which the fight is carried out in the open and on equal terms. Rather, it is a cultural-political war in which queer film activists are heavily outnumbered and outgunned, and therefore special tactics are required. That the BJQFF does not have a fixed event venue is one facet in this war; police intervention makes any commitment to a fixed venue difficult or even impossible. How the BJQFF organisers deploy a flexible spatial tactic to survive therefore makes a significant subject for analysis.

FIGURE 16.1 A DIY map of the BJQFF screening venues, 2001–2011. Courtesy of Fan Popo.

After the 'Jasmine Revolution' in 2011, Songzhuang, where the third and fourth iterations of the BJQFF took place, was no longer a safe haven for independent films. A young generation of film festival organisers – most of whom are queer-identified filmmakers – brought the festival back to the city centre. From the fifth year on, the BJQFF has been held at different venues – bars, clubs, bookshops, foreign embassies, community centres – in or near the city centre (Figures 16.2 and 16.3). The organisers have devised ingenious guerrilla tactics to deal with police intervention, including working with queer-friendly businesses such as foreign embassies and international

FIGURE 16.2 The Fifth Beijing Queer Film Festival panel discussion. Courtesy of Fan Popo.

FIGURE 16.3 A screening venue for the Fifth Beijing Queer Film Festival. Courtesy of Fan Popo.

cultural centres, minimum publicity before and during the event, multiple screening locations and alternative screening plans.[5] Different screening formats were used, including the onboard screening on a rented bus in 2013 and on a train in 2014. As Jenny Man Wu, co-director of the seventh BJQFF in 2014, recalls:

> On the morning of 18 September, we boarded a train from Beijing to Huairou from Beijing Railway Station. There were not many passengers on the train. The forty of us, including filmmakers, guests and volunteers, packed into a train carriage. We divided people into groups of two or three. Each group shared a laptop computer. We gave each group a USB stick with Yang Yang's film *Our Story*, a documentary about the history of BJQFF, on it. After arriving in Huairou, we travelled to a pre-booked venue by bus and held a Q&A there.
>
> *(Wu 2014)*

The onboard screening on a moving train showcases the rich imagination of the film festival organisers; it also pushes the limit of what a film festival can be like. While the Chinese government can censor queer films and ban queer film festivals, it cannot stop people from watching queer films on their own laptops in a public space. Watching *Our Story* under such an unusual circumstance undoubtedly inspired the participants, and this shared experience effectively bound the communities. Notably, a train carriage is not a typical queer space; it is owned by a state hostile to queers and run commercially. Although queers did not claim ownership of the train, they could still appropriate the train carriage at a particular time and make it a queer space. Like the poachers in Michel de Certeau's (1984) account, the BJQFF 'poaches' on the land it does not own and thrives on it. Indeed, flexible use of space is significant for such tactics. A tactic, according to de Certeau (1984),

> insinuates itself into the other's place, fragmentarily, without taking it over in its entirety, without being able to keep it at a distance. It has at its disposal no base where it can capitalise on its advantages, prepare its expansions, and secure independence with respect to circumstances.
>
> *(xix)*

Space, in this context, becomes an important site of contestation where the weak can fight against the powerful. The BJQFF's appropriation of public spaces as contingent festival venues has transformed these spaces into queer spaces; 'guerrilla warfare' is key to such a transformation.

Homosexuals, comrades and queers: what's in a name?

In a country where the state tries to regulate the use of language through linguistic and cultural policies as well as media censorship, how the BJQFF names itself is significant. The BJQFF has used many names for itself in the past, and the name has been constantly changing. What terms to use for queer, film and festival respectively corresponds to the gender, sexual and cultural politics that the festival advocates.

The BJQFF started as 'China Homosexual Film Festival' in its inaugural year, although the project proposal that the student organisers submitted to the Youth League, the youth branch of the Chinese Communist Party, for approval called the event a 'Comrade Cultural Festival'. 'Comrade' (*tongzhi*) was an honorific for revolutionary subjects in the Mao era, and it has come to be used by sexual minorities in the Chinese-speaking world for self-identification in the post-Mao era (Bao 2018). As the sexual connotation of the term 'comrade' was little known outside the queer communities at the time, the event was able to gain official approval from the university authorities. This was only possible once and its experience could not be replicated in the following years. Indeed, as is true with many tactical challenges, tactics cannot develop in a more linear fashion and must keep innovating as the state adapts its own strategies. After the event proposal had been approved, the BJQFF changed the term 'comrade' to 'homosexual' (*tongxin-glian*) to gain more media and public attention. This unfortunately led to state intervention and early closure of the festival, and the young organisers thus learned an important lesson about the use of language in a politically sensitive environment. The term 'homosexual' was soon discarded after the second iteration of the festival due to the political sensitivity of the term in the eyes of the authorities, as well as its negative connotations associated with histories of criminalisation and pathologisation.

'Queer' (*ku'er*) has been used in the name of the BJQFF since the third edition (2008) onward. A transliteration of the English term 'queer', *ku'er* was a term little known to the public and therefore could successfully bypass political sensitivity. Devoid of its stigmatised connotation in the Western context, *ku'er* (literally 'a cool kid') celebrates youth and difference and invites identification from the younger generation. Perhaps more importantly, *ku'er* rejects a homonormative gay identity politics and celebrates an inclusive and intersectional non-identitarian politics. Admittedly, the BJQFF was one of the first advocates to use the term *ku'er* in mainland China's queer communities, and the concept has significant implications for the aesthetics and politics of the festival programming (Bao 2017).

Although the English term 'film festival' remains in the BJQFF's title, the translation of the term in Chinese varies. The first two years used the most literal translation *dianying jie* ('film festival') and learned a hard lesson: in China, only the government has the right and authority to host a *dianying jie*; any individual's or NGO's use of the term immediately poses a potential challenge to the Party state. This partly accounted for the direct police intervention in the first two years of the festival. From the third BJQFF on, *dianying* ('film') becomes *yingxiang* ('moving image') to reflect the use of digital technologies in video and film production; and *jie* ('festival') becomes *danyuan* ('unit'), *zhan* ('exhibition') or even *zhou* ('week'), effectively making the event seem less ambitious and politically sensitive. The most common name for BJQFF in Chinese therefore translates literally as the Beijing Queer Moving Image Exhibition (*Beijing ku'er ying zhan*). This tactic has proven effective. It also signifies a more pragmatic attitude to festival organisation by focusing more on community building and less on fame and glamour.

Digital video activism: the prefigurative politics of the BJQFF organisation

We should not dismiss the festival's name change as simply a 'language game'; that is, playing with words to circumvent government censorship. The use of language also reflects on the profound change of the festival's organisational forms and politics. If a *dianying jie* ('film festival') is often characterised by glamour, prestige and hierarchical modes of organisation, *yingzhan* ('moving image exhibition') celebrates difference, diversity, and experience sharing. The BJQFF does not give awards to films and filmmakers; nor does it privilege one style over others. As BJQFF organising committee member Cui Zi'en remarks:

> I have come to a new understanding in the last couple of years. I don't think art is superior; nor can art be separated from politics. I think that the most important artworks are all politically oriented, and they are created to liberate or suppress certain groups of people. The boundary between politics and art is rather blurred. The best artworks are not those exhibited in museums or art

galleries for the privileged few, who have time and money to enjoy these artworks; they are the ones that can have an impact on, or even liberate, repressed people at a particular time and place.

(Cui in Zhao 2009)

Cui's philosophy of art is undoubtedly rooted in China's historical experience: it echoes Mao Zedong's Yan'an Talks on Literature and Art delivered in 1942 and articulates a strong grassroots-based socialist politics. To encourage local and grassroots production, the BJQFF has lowered technical and aesthetic barriers significantly: any submission from mainland China will be screened at the festival, regardless of its length, format, technical and artistic qualities. I have seen some rather long and tedious films made by amateur filmmakers at the BJQFF, some of which lasted several hours. The sacrifice of technical and artistic qualities for more diverse queer representations has been under constant scrutiny and debate among the BJQFF organisers, but the principle of encouraging diversity has been relentlessly upheld. As committee member Yang Yang states, 'Every film, every director, every audience member, every member of the festival organization committee has their own viewpoint. The only thing the film festival stands for is that everybody who participates can freely voice their opinion' (Yang 2011: 7).

In terms of its organisational structure, the BJQFF practises a prefigurative politics common in anarchism and the alterglobalisation movement. Carl Boggs (1977) identifies prefigurative politics as the desire to embody 'within the ongoing political practice of a movement [...] those forms of social relations, decision-making, culture, and human experience that are the ultimate goal' (100). The BJQFF has a loosely structured organising committee made up of about eight core members. Most important decisions are made collectively, either by in-person voting or expression of opinion in group emails. The festival does not have a lifelong director; committee members take turns in directing different editions of the festival. As old members drop out, new members join in and they inject new energies and ideas into the group. While most of the core members are queer-identified filmmakers themselves, many are not: some are NGO workers, others are cinephiles, and not everyone identifies as gay or lesbian. It is a shared mission that has brought all the people together: to keep the BJQFF running despite all the obstacles.

University students, young professionals and queer community members make up a large majority of the film festival audience and volunteers. In 2009, I attended the 4th BJQFF as a researcher, a community member and a volunteer. In the remote and rural Songzhuang village, organisers and volunteers lived, ate and slept together for a week. People watched the films together and had lengthy post-screening discussions about queer identities, communities and activism in China. There was a strong sense of friendship, camaraderie and solidarity during and even in the aftermath of the festival. In these unforgettable moments, the two meanings of *tongzhi*, both as 'comrade' and as queer, converged and conflated, and a socialist, egalitarian and democratic political culture emerged at the grassroots level.

'Go to the people' and the 'Communist hypothesis'

The film festival organisers have drawn upon slogans and tactics from China's revolutionary era to justify their practices: the Maoist slogan 'go to the countryside' was used when the BJQFF had to shift its screening venue from the Peking University campus to the Songzhuang Artist Village. At Songzhuang, 'surrounding the city with the countryside' became the slogan. These catchphrases, originating from China's socialist era, at once capture a sense of exile and a determination to continue fighting against all obstacles, and are a humble gesture from filmmakers to leave the academic 'ivory tower' and learn from the people. The brief experience at Songzhuang has made BJQFF organisers reflect critically on their own middle-class and intellectual privileges and consider how gender and sexuality intersect with other social issues, such as class, poverty, uneven regional development and social injustice. Apart from gender and sexual minorities, queer filmmakers have also cast their eyes on other marginalised social groups including migrant workers, homeless children and people living with disability.[6] Here, 'queer' ceases to be a term denoting the sexual orientation of a minority group – of which the most visible are often middle-class – and becomes the basis for an intersectional and coalition politics for all the people in a society. As Yang Yang describes in the preface to the fifth BJQFF catalogue:

> A queer film festival is not an event only open to the 'marginalised people' who come to escape the darkness of mainstream society. A queer film festival is a platform devoid of prejudice, a place where people can freely express, show, explore themselves and where they can enter into meaningful dialogues […] This has a huge significance not only for the queer communities, but for the whole society as well.
>
> *(Yang 2011: 7)*

These statements deliberately avoid making explicit political demands for human rights; they use the humanistic rhetoric of cultural diversity instead. They also demonstrate that most BJQFF organisers see the festival as a part of the collective struggle for democracy in China and as an experiment of a more inclusive form of grassroots-based political culture. As such, the political implication of the BJQFF is evident:

> Although this is a cultural event originated within the sexual minority community, it's hard to overlook the political connotations of the queer film festival. The festival lives in Beijing, the political and cultural centre of China – it explores freedom and plurality in human relations and lifestyles amidst a red climate drenched in Communist ideology […] Our greatest value and our ultimate goal as a queer film festival is to challenge and oppose these mainstream ideologies.
>
> *(Yang 2011: 7)*

Here, communism is seen as a state bureaucracy that stifles human freedom and creativity. However, the 'communist hypothesis' (Badiou 2010), understood as a different way of collective organisation that liberates human potentials, underpins many of the BJQFF's organising principles and practices. Values such as egalitarianism, direct democracy, social justice, freedom and anti-authoritarianism certainly are featured both in anarchist and communist philosophies; they also characterise the BJQFF organisation. Situated in a postsocialist context, the BJQFF serves as a type of postsocialist cultural politics that at once recognises the relevance of socialism to the neoliberal present and a critical reflection on the distinction between communism and socialism, and between communist bureaucracy and communist hypothesis.

Travelling queer film festivals

Apart from the Beijing-based and now-annual festival itself, the core members of the BJQFF organising committee have also made efforts to engage a diverse audience as they took films to different parts of the country. In past years, the BJQFF has sponsored audience members from smaller cities and remote regions in China to travel to Beijing to attend the BJQFF. Core members of the BJQFF have also brought queer films to different parts of the country in a project called the China Queer Film Festival Tour (CQFFT) (Figures 16.4 and 16.5). Between 2008 and 2011, the CQFFT visited two dozen cities and hosted over ninety screenings before a combined audience of 7,000 people (Fan 2015: 81). The move aimed to address the urban-centrism of queer activism, and to take film-focused queer activism to less developed parts of the country. In the process, the BJQFF collective collaborated with local queer organisations, community centres and queer friendly businesses and built a national network for queer films and activism.

FIGURE 16.4 A screening venue during the China Queer Film Festival Tour. Courtesy of Fan Popo.

FIGURE 16.5 A university campus screening during the China Queer Film Festival Tour. Courtesy of Fan Popo.

For Beijing-based filmmakers, this was a precious opportunity: in bringing their films to the communities, they obtained first-hand feedback from the audience; experiencing the life outside metropolitan cities also widened these filmmakers' horizons and enriched their understanding of Chinese society. These experiences and knowledge fed back into their filmmaking practice and generated more socially relevant films. As queer filmmaker Fan Popo reflects:

> Some audience members complained that some films were 'too arty' for their taste; they tended to relate more to documentary films that depicted the lives of Chinese LGBT people. Feedback of this kind generated immediate adjustments back in Beijing, including revising which films would be recommended and revising descriptions of the films so that future local organisers would have a clear idea about what to expect.
>
> *(Fan 2015: 84)*

Apart from the adjustment of screening programmes based on the audience feedback, community responses have also impacted on the content, style and aesthetics of the films the filmmakers make, as they continue to explore what types of films would best speak to their queer politics and to the needs of the communities. This is not an anti-intellectual position; nor does it compromise the experimental style and critical edge of the films produced. It is, rather, a recognition of the entwined relationship between films and society, and between community filmmakers and the communities they work with. During the tour, Fan collaborated with the queer organisation PFLAG (Parents and Friends of Lesbians and Gays) China and made several documentaries featuring queer people and their parents, including *Chinese Closet, Mama Rainbow* and *Papa Rainbow*. These films display diverse styles and distinct experimental features. As 'organic intellectuals' (Gramsci 1982), these community-based filmmakers have worked closely with the communities to create stylistically innovative and politically engaged films.

The 'communist international of queer films'

Both Ragan Rhyne (2011) and Luke Robinson (2015) note the extremely cosmopolitan nature of Chinese queer films and film festivals; that is, these films and festivals draw on a wide repertory of contents, styles and aesthetics from different parts of the world; as a result, they appear intrinsically international and cosmopolitan. The festival also has a strong emphasis on Asian and Sinophone queer films. For example, the fourth and fifth BJQFFs featured panel discussions on queer cinema in Hong Kong, Taiwan and other parts of Asia, and Genya Fukunaga from the Kansai Queer Film Festival guest curated the Japanese section of the 6th BJQFF. This suggests the BJQFF's acute awareness of constructing its cultural identity based on a decolonial approach informed by 'Asian as method' (Chen 2010), 'queer Asia as critique' (Chiang and Wong 2017) and 'queer Sinophone cultures' (Chiang and Heinrich 2014). With an international perspective and a specific focus on Asia, the BJQFF articulates a strong sense of queer internationalism based on people-led cultural exchanges at the grassroots level, a form of 'minor transnationalism' (Lionnet and Shih 2005) that goes beyond the hegemonic mapping of the nation state and transnational capital.

In a public speech, Cui uses the phrase 'communist international of queer films' to describe the circulation of queer films through piracy, gift-giving and grassroots cultural exchanges across national borders (Cui and Liu 2010). Cui juxtaposes this type of transnationalism with two other forms of state-led transnationalism: first, the spread of Communist bureaucracy after the Second World War; and, second, the 'strategic promotion of Americanism' worldwide (Cui and Liu 2010: 418). While the latter are hegemonic forms of transnationalism that often reinforce power relations across the world, the queer-led and film-centred transnationalism on the grassroots level is more liberating. 'I rejoice at this kind of globalisation' (423), Cui concludes. Indeed, the BJQFF participates actively in and contributes significantly to the minor transnationalism of queer cultures and radical film cultures.

At this point, it should be clear that the first decade of the BJQFF should be seen as an integral part of the radical film cultures and media activism in a transnational context. It reminds us of the transnational nature of the queer struggles and the importance of international solidarity. It also suggests the significance of gender and sexuality to radical film culture and media activism. Many queers and queer film festivals in the Global North may have lost some of their radical edge via the capitalist incorporation of a 'pink economy' and neoliberalism's homonormative identity politics. Yet in the Global South, exciting struggles are going on right now. They articulate queer intersectional and coalition politics, manifest a strong geopolitical consciousness, and deploy ingenious guerrilla tactics. Socialist comrades may have disappeared in the post-Cold War era, but postsocialist queers have kept up their good work by drawing on experiences from the socialist past and by giving socialism new meanings. Radical film cultures are an important part of this picture.

Notes

1 I wish to thank Steve Presence and Jack Newsinger from the Radical Film Network (RFN) for their feedback on the English version of this chapter. A German-language version appeared as 'Guerilla-Taktiken. Das Beijing Queer Film Festival und radikale Filmkultur' in *Montage AV* 28 (2) and I thank Chris Tedjasukmana and Stephen Lowry for their help and support. This chapter is the result of my long-term participation in and engagement with the Beijing Queer Film Festival and other forms of queer community culture in China. I am grateful to all the friendship, help and camaraderie I have received from the queer and radical film communities in China and transnationally. Special thanks go to Fan Popo for granting me permission to use the pictures from past BJQFFs to illustrate this chapter.
2 This chapter primarily focuses on the first decade of the Beijing Queer Film Festival. Since 2015, the festival has been rebranded as the Beijing Love Queer Cinema Week and hosted by the Institut Français of Beijing. Many old committee members have left Beijing since then, and the organising principles of the Beijing Love Queer Cinema Week differ from those of the Beijing Queer Film Festival. Notably, the Beijing Love Queer Cinema Week appears more urban and elitist in programming and audience participation, and it therefore deserves a separate analysis elsewhere. In this chapter, I have limited my analysis to the first seven iterations of the Beijing Queer Film Festival (from 2001 to 2014).
3 This represented a complaint from some Radical Film Network (RFN) members at the RFN Conference that took place in Dublin in 2018. The RFN meeting in Berlin and the Transnational Radical Film Cultures Conference in Nottingham in 2019 made special efforts to include more filmmakers, artists and scholars from the Global South. The author of this article was one of the co-organisers of the Transnational Radical Film Conference (with Danial Mutibwa). For more information about the RFN conferences, see https://radicalfilmnetwork.com/conferences/ (accessed July 22, 2019).
4 Most of the names I use in this chapter are real unless otherwise specified. The queer filmmakers and activists I mentioned in this chapter have consented to the use of their real names in media and academic publications. I use the *hanyu pinyin* form of transliteration and follow the Chinese convention in presenting names: surname first, followed by first names.
5 The BJQFF events are mostly financially supported by non-governmental organisations (NGOs). These events do not sell tickets, and most are open to the public free of charge.
6 For instance, Cui Zi'en made two documentaries, *We are the … of Communism* and *Night Scene* – one about migrant workers' children and the other about sex workers – during this period.

References

Badiou, Alain. 2010. *The Communist Hypothesis*. London: Verso.
Bao, Hongwei. 2017. 'Queer as Catachresis: The Beijing Queer Film Festival in Cultural Translation', in *Chinese Film Festivals: Sites of Translation*, edited by Chris Berry and Luke Robinson. London: Palgrave Macmillan, 67–88.
Bao, Hongwei. 2018. *Queer Comrades: Gay Identity and Tongzhi Activism in Postsocialist China*. Copenhagen: NIAS Press.

Boggs, Carl. 1977. 'Marxism, Prefigurative Communism, and the Problem of Workers' Control'. *Radical America* 11: 99–122.

Chen, Kuan-Hsing. 2010. *Asia as Method: Toward De-Imperialisation*. Durham, NC: Duke University Press.

Chiang, Howard and Heinrich, Ari Larissa, eds. 2014. *Queer Sinophone Cultures*. New York: Routledge.

Chiang, Howard and Wong, Alvin K. 2017. 'Asia is Burning: Queer Asia as Critique'. *Culture, Theory and Critique* 58 (2): 121–126.

Cui, Zi'en and Liu, Petrus. 2010. 'The Communist International of Queer Films'. *Positions: East Asia Cultures Critique* 18 (2): 417–423.

de Certeau, Michel. 1984. *The Practice of Everyday Life*. Berkeley CA: University of California Press.

Duggan, Lisa. 2003. *The Twilight of Equality?: Neoliberalism, Cultural Politics, and the Attack on Democracy*. New York: Beacon Press.

Fan Popo. 2015. 'Challenging Authorities and Building Community Culture: Independent Queer Film Making in China and the China Queer Film Festival Tour, 2008–2012', in *Queer/Tongzhi China: New Perspectives on Research, Activism and Media Culture*, edited by Elisabeth L.Engebretsen and William F. Schroeder, 81–88. Copenhagen: NIAS Press.

Gramsci, Antonio. 1982. *Selections from the Prison Books*. London: Lawrence and Wishart.

Lionnet, Françoise and Shih, Shu-mei. 2005. 'Introduction: Thinking through the Minor, Transnationally', in *Minor Transnationalism*, edited by Françoise Lionnet and Shu-mei Shih, 1–23. Durham: Duke University Press.

Radical Film Network. 2019. https://radicalfilmnetwork.com/about/

Rhyne, Ragan. 2011. 'Comrades and Citizens: Gay and Lesbian Film Festivals in China', in *Film Festival Yearbook 3: Film Festivals and East Asia*, edited by Dina Iordanova and Ruby Cheung, 110–124. St. Andrews: St Andrews Film Studies.

Richards, Stuart James. 2016. *The Queer Film Festival: Popcorn and Politics*. New York: Palgrave Macmillan.

Richards, Stuart James. 2017. '"Would You Like Politics Like That?" Queer Film Festival Audience as Political Consumers', in *Activist Film Festivals: Towards a Political Subject*, edited by Sonia Tascon and Tyson Wils, 229–245. Bristol: Intellect.

Robinson, Luke. 2015. '"To Whom Do Our Bodies Belong?" Being Queer in Chinese DV Documentary', in *DV-Made China: Digital Subjects and Social Transformations After Independent Cinema*, edited by Zhen Zhang and Angela Zito. Honululu, HI: University of Hawaii Press, 289–315.

Wu, Man Jenny. 2014. '"Bimu zhici: ku'er zhong de ku'er"' [Closing speech: the queer in queer], www.bjqff.com/category/7thfestival/%e8%87%b4%e8%be%9e-preface-7thfestiva l/ (accessed July 12, 2019).

Yang, Yang. 2011. 'Zhici' [Preface], *The 5th Beijing Queer Film Festival Catalogue*, 6–7.

Zhao, Ke. 2009. "*Cui Zi'en: Zhongguo de tongxinglian dianying hai chuyu zifaqi*" [Cui Zi'en: China's queer films are still at an initial stage]. www.fridae.asia/tc/gaynews/2009/07/25/8695.cui zienzhongguodetongxingliandianyinghuanchuyuzifaqi (accessed September 1, 2017).

17

STAR AND SHADOW CINEMA AND BEFORE

Radical screening culture in Newcastle upon Tyne

Christo Wallers

Star and Shadow Cinema (S&S) is a volunteer-run, horizontalist[1] space for cinema, music, art and alternative culture in Newcastle upon Tyne, UK. A grassroots evolution of DIY activism, it formed in the Amber-owned Side Cinema in 2001, alongside expanded cinema happenings at Waygood Gallery. It then moved, renamed and reconstituted itself in a derelict Tyne Tees TV set-building workshop on Stepney Bank in 2006. Given notice once again, the group embarked on three years of extraordinary effort, pulling off a small miracle by negotiating the community purchase of an empty furniture showroom on Warwick Street in 2015, inside which they self-built a state-of-the-art screening space and music venue, which opened in 2018. The purpose of this chapter is to present an overview of S&S's activity since 2001, situating it in the historical context of radical screening practice in national and international currents in alternative film exhibition. Defining such a practice is thorny, considering the historical tensions between radical form and content. In this context, 'radical screening' focuses on exhibition modes that 'imply an […] activ*ist* connection to social experience' (Andrews 2014, 118). While these activities have been voluntary, collaborative and collectivist, this is only one participant's account of the different social, political and cultural points of negotiation and change that inform the S&S history.

Since the mid-1990s, grassroots places have often provided a space for media, arts and social or political activism to intersect. The proliferation of social centres, emergent in the early 2000s as part of new environmental and anti-capitalist social movements, have used film screenings as triggers for discussion or action (see Hodkinson and Chatterton 2006). The DVD distribution culture of Schnews and Undercurrents connected audiences with activism in the late 1990s and early 2000s. As a reaction to the staid and institutionalised avant-garde film scene, a more anarchic exhibition culture emerged in London in the 1990s with Exploding Cinema, Omsk and Halloween, who embraced a carnival spirit of performative, participatory film screenings in underground spaces. More recent groups have concentrated their activities in fixed, multi-arts spaces with a strong emphasis on cinema like the Cube in Bristol, Star and Shadow Cinema in Newcastle, Liverpool Small Cinema, and Deptford Cinema in London. These examples collectively constitute a culture of DIY cinema exhibition in the UK. Commonly used to describe alternative, grassroots music and publishing scenes, DIY has become a way of resisting and 'circumventing the power of capitalist structures, while at the same time creating substantive alternatives' (Holtzman, Hughes, and Van Meter 2007, 54). I offer a definition of DIY Cinema, based on personal experience and further research. DIY Cinema is a *resistant* practice. Operating outside of the logic of both the commercial film industry and the state film institution, it resists the dominant narrative of exchange value and the top-down pedagogy or taste 'distinction' of the art establishment. Organised non-hierarchically and programmed on a participatory model, it is a *democratic* practice, creating a real-world public sphere where communities can explore ideas through cinema and dialogue. Whether fixed in a single building or itinerant, DIY Cinema is a physically located, *spatial* practice committed to providing a refuge for participants to 'stage a difference' (Schober 2013). Finally, DIY Cinema is a *reflexive* practice. It draws attention to the constructed and mediated nature of the cinema screening and its surrounding discourses by foregrounding the human in contrast to the professional. Furthermore, DIY Cinema, like other DIY practices, reflexively explores the utopian method as a 'complex process, whose failure and struggles are as important as success' (Cooper 2014, 4).

In his study of DIY culture in 1990s' Britain, George McKay wryly notes the ahistorical disposition of those involved, suggesting there is 'surprisingly little writing, especially from within, that starts "Are we? Is this new?"' (McKay 1998, 2). This simplification unfairly renders activists of the time as disconnected from previous struggles. It does however point to an epistemological break between the oppositional culture of 1968 steeped in Marxism, and those that politically came of age after the fall of the Berlin wall, or later still the anti-WTO protests in Seattle, 1999. Assessing points of connection over time and place is significant for how S&S understands and positions itself in a local and international historical context. Alternative approaches to film exhibition are by no means new on Tyneside. The Independent Labour Party Arts Guild convened a conference in June 1930 to discuss the possibilities of screening censored Russian films in private organisations (Hogenkamp 1986). This meeting failed to bear fruit, and there are no obvious records of a Workers Film Society on Tyneside. The Tyneside Film Society was actively promoting aesthetically progressive material, including a programme in December 1934 featuring experimental film *Tonende Handschrift* (Rudolph Pfenninger 1932) consisting of hand-drawn visualisations of soundwaves ('News from Societies'; British Film Institute 1934). The Tyneside Film Society formed in the Newcastle News Theatre in 1944, and by the 1950s it had become the largest film society in the country.[2] Throughout the 1960s, The Stoll, now renamed the Tyne Theatre, ran an idiosyncratic programme of X-rated and exploitation film alongside the type of continental film other commercial cinemas avoided by auteurs like

Alain Resnais and Luchino Visconti (Manders 1991). The Newcastle News Theatre ran into financial difficulties in the late 1960s and the BFI seized the opportunity to open it as Tyneside Cinema, one of their flagship Regional Film Theatres (RFTs),[3] operating it directly from London. This arrangement soon became unsustainable and the cinema closed again in 1975, reopening the following year as an independent RFT. The turbulence felt by the Tyneside Cinema was being experienced elsewhere, as notions of film appreciation jostled with a more politicised use of film exhibition flourishing in the Northeast through the Workshop movement. The driving force behind this political turn was Amber Films, who were soon joined by Trade Films and a host of other workshops connected to the Independent Filmmakers' Association (IFA).

Conceived by a group of students from working-class backgrounds at Regent Street Polytechnic in 1967, Amber started as a film and photography collective committed to documenting traditional, regional working-class communities. The Northeast became their base in 1969, and the focus for their 'socially embedded' work in representing regional, working-class identity (Newsinger 2009). Located on Newcastle's Quayside, Amber developed a film production facility and photography gallery, to which they added a debate cinema as an exhibition point for their own productions complimented by historical and contemporary cinema they thought relevant. Programmed initially by Roger Buck, Side Cinema opened in 1977 as an example of 'post-RFT' exhibition venues (Christie 1981). Like Four Corners in Bethnal Green and the New Cinema, Nottingham, these were spaces dedicated to cinema as a social practice, consciously moving away from the BFI's top-down agenda of film appreciation to engage with audiences in a process of debate and discussion around class struggle and identity. Amber had already been experimenting with different approaches to film exhibition, with screenings in communities up and down the coast during the River Project in 1974. The Side Cinema afforded space to delve deeper into the ideologies and discourses permeating British film culture, for example the Writers and Audience Weekend in 1982. This event brought together working class and socialist media practitioners seeking opportunities to connect with working class audiences through the Workshop Franchise. Side Cinema became a space for feminist culture, activated by Amber members' attendance of the ACTT[4] Women's conference, which encouraged a fluidity within the film elements of the Women's Movement. Elaine Drainville brought to Side Cinema the Working Women's Travelling Cinema, a film production and screening project that had started at refuges for women who had experienced domestic violence. They ran a crèche in the office upstairs while screenings happened in the cinema space, and the social aspect of selecting, watching and discussing films together was considered a political gesture in itself. This heyday of activity was, however, unsustainable in the face of ideological cuts to public funding carried out by the Tory government, and in the late 1980s regular film programming stopped.

Throughout the 1980s, the publicly funded independent sector experienced the inexorable shift towards a new 'language of economic development' (Dickinson 1999, 82). An emphasis on efficiency and hierarchical management extolled by business consultants, backed up by the Tory's assault on the public sector, left a diminishing space for emancipatory politics. Grass-roots film screening on Tyneside seems to have entered a hiatus through the late 1980s and early 1990s. However, parallel to this demise, other forms of oppositional media were being explored through video activism, underground culture, and a post-punk spirit of party and protest, more focused on animal rights and environmentalism. By the late 1990s, there existed a lacuna between the 1970s independent film culture and the emergent alternative film scene, inspired more by open source and DIY activism. Out of this ferment, two groups simultaneously rediscovered Side Cinema in 2001, Cineside, and the Tyneside Radical Film Festival (TRFF). Adopting a critical and playful style, Cineside was driven by a thirst for alternative, experimental cinema, born out of hobbyist super-8 filmmaking and a DIY attitude to contemporary art, cinema and music. For Cineside, these values were best embodied in artist-run spaces and squats, free from New Labour's entrepreneurial cultural policies. TRFF was more connected to the direct action and anti-capitalist movement and saw the potential of film to inform and inspire action. A community had developed out of recent interventions in central Newcastle like the Reclaim the Streets action in September 2000, followed by the Eclectic City squat on Pilgrim Street in October 2000, and the highly organised, volunteer-run Newcastle Community Green Festival. They were more than vocally critical of dominant structures on grounds of environmentalism, the corporatisation of the city, and the relationship between big business and globalisation made plain in recent WTO summits.

The new arrangement at Side Cinema launched in October 2001 with 'Cineside Alive', a free week of features and shorts, based on a traditional film society model, but with films mostly projected on 16 mm. Starting with Amber's *Launch* (1973) and *L'Atalante* (Jean Vigo 1937), the week continued with Hans Richter's experimental drama, *Dreams that Money Can Buy* (1943), *Peeping Tom* (Michael Powell 1960), *Le Samouraï* (Jean-Pierre Melville 1967), *The Harder They Come* (Perry Henzell 1973), *Alice* (Jan Svankmajer 1988) and *Songs from the Second Floor* (Roy Andersson 2000). The tone of the project, while playful, was driven by a dissatisfaction with the conservatism of contemporary independent cinema, and a desire to explore the rich histories of film they had become accustomed to at student film societies, and in other cities, through events like Little Stabs at Happiness at the ICA. They were unaware of Exploding Cinema and the 1990s underground film groups like OMSK, or Club Rhombus in Bristol, but would soon feel part of a rhizomatic network of alternative screening spaces across the UK, Europe and the United States. The Side Cinema, with its history of film and dialogue, was the dream location for Cineside to screen, and their enthusiasm was met with good humour from the Amber Collective. TRFF started their weekly programme a fortnight later, with screenings about the anti-globalisation movement, police violence against black detainees, and the Zapatistas' fight for land reform in Chiapas, following up with a night celebrating squatting, with films about the Exodus Collective and Christiania.

Screenings were popular, and would always be followed by a mass decampment to the great pub next door, the Crown Posada. Soon Cineside and TRFF were joined by the 'Other Side', an LGBT group exploring gender and sexual identity through cinema, and the A-Side, focusing on tactics and strategies visual artists use to engage politically through film. The 'four sides' started to collaborate more and by October they had federated as the New Side Cinema Collective (NSCC) with a bank account and an office space, while retaining their distinct programming 'personalities'. Perhaps because of their shared commitment to this 'promising space', traditional tensions around aesthetics and politics were contained and mitigated by the everyday work of running the space, the 'ethos of maintenance, of digging in and getting things done' (Cooper 2014, 7). Funding was sought from Northern Film and Media, not to cover wages, but to meet the costs of the lease, travel for visiting filmmakers, publicity and screening rights. As months went on, screenings diversified. Other Side were jumping from Jarman to Riot Grrrl via films like *Mädchen in Uniform* (Leontine Sagan 1931) while A-Side introduced Guy Debord and Ursula Bieman, further contextualised by TRFF (now 'Radical Side') presentations of Oliver Ressler and Noam Chomsky. Cineside was solicited from further afield, hosting a retrospective of Karl Valentin films from the Goethe Institute, and delving into a history of avant-garde film helped by experimental film curator Mark Webber. Simultaneously the collective had a studio in an artist-run space, the Waygood Gallery, and members were using space there under the project Filmbee, experimenting with darkroom processes gleaned from zines (e.g., Hill 2001). With the beginnings of a small-scale lab for super-8 and 16 mm, they invited David Leister, an active member of the London Filmmaker's Co-op through-out the 1980s and 1990s. Leister had been running his Kino Club in London for years, recognised as a precursor to the 'new London Underground' exemplified by Exploding Cinema (Reekie 2007). Leister not only introduced Filmbee to a host of darkroom techniques, he also opened the door to an internationalist experimental film culture in the artist-run film labs network. Inspired by lab-culture, and recent trips to Amsterdam and Berlin art-squats, Cineside's approach was infused with an emancipatory zeal, expressed in 'Expanded Cineside', freeform happenings in the mouldy, abandoned nightclub underneath the Waygood studios. Looped, re-purposed wedding videography adverts sat alongside double-16 mm-widescreen film sandwiches and a super-8 version of *The Exorcist* (William Friedkin 1974) projected onto a slide of the Side Cinema auditorium. Unknowingly they were performing some of the styles and modes of address cut loose within the 'Volcano generation' (Leister et al. 2017), the collection of film groups screening in London through the 1990s. As an example, Exploding Cinema's legendary events at the Cool Tan squat in Brixton subverted the conventional short film screening format through a completely open programming policy, candid audience interaction and the heightened, illegitimate sense of occasion that only a squat could create.

Activities at Side Cinema bore resemblance to Microcinemas in the United States, and Cineside played host to stalwarts of that scene on their UK tours, including Echo Park, Jack Stevenson, Noel Lawrence and founder of The Other Cinema, Craig Baldwin, who swung by to screen recent films in June 2003. It was through Sneha Solanki, a local artist experimenting with open source programming and web streaming, that the collective made proper contact with an inspirational model on its own shores, the Cube Cinema in Bristol. Kate Rich, one of the Cube's organisers, hosted a research trip for the 'four sides'. The Cube had been on their radar as another stop for touring DIY filmmakers, along with Ben Rivers' project at the Brighton Cinematheque, and the Horse Hospital in London. Cube had re-occupied the old Bristol Arts Centre, a focal point for independent cinema in the Southwest throughout the 1970s. They called it a Microplex in contrast to the proliferating multiplexes across the country. It was a formative trip and pivotal for NSCC's belief in what might be achievable. Up until early 2005, the collective had grown, with new programmers actively encouraged through publicised requests for suggestions, and post-screening discussion with audiences. A community was growing around this screening culture that cared about the dialogue, the off-the-wall programming, the cinema's smallness and informality, that it was cheap and, as one respondent suggested, 'the fact that the people who run it are just people – like the audiences'. They loved screening in the Side Cinema, and Amber was a source of continuous inspiration both in the way it was organised and in its slate of productions and projects. The NSCC were young, however, and had been exposed to a different set of ideologies around the social function of cinema, so understanding the occasional opaque comments from Amber founder Murray Martin about the end of dialectical filmmaking took more time than he perhaps had patience for. The café at the front could never quite see the opportunity to collaborate more. Getting bits of funding from Northern Film and Media was stressful as a voluntary group and they wanted to have more space for dialogue and play, not to mention the promise of financial self-reliance through a bar and performance space. The NSCC didn't fit into Amber's mould, formed in the years of the workshop movement, but it came as a surprise to be told that the lease wouldn't be renewed at the end of their summer 2005 programme. Programming the Side Cinema became the prerogative of Amber once again, and the NSCC looked for other options.

The 2005 G8 gathering was scheduled for Gleneagles. Dissent!, an international anti-capitalist network organising in opposition to the summit, facilitated the advancement of local groups around the UK, with small grants of around £10,000. Local activists put energy into preparing for actions, and co-ordinating a convergence centre, an inspirational base camp made of 'barrios' assembled by specific groups, and based on direct democracy. The UK had a growing infrastructure of autonomous social centres, in legalised spaces. The act of going 'above-ground' was energised by the J18 Reclaim the Streets action in London in 1999, and the simultaneous rise in police repression of squatting (Hodkinson and Chatterton 2006). The desire for an autonomous social centre in Newcastle coincided with the NSCC losing their Side Cinema home. In April 2005, a meeting was hastily organised at the artist-run performance space Bookville to tentatively explore the possibility of setting something up in the warehouse building as a larger collaboration between a mixture of Northeast artists and activists. To talk of 'artists' and 'activists' as separate entities simplifies the fluidity between these two groups, but it does point to the historical tension between aesthetics and politics. Some artists were concerned that their aesthetic ambitions would be curtailed under an exclusively political definition, while other activists doubted the potential of avant-garde aesthetics to speak to a wider audience. The shared history at the Side Cinema, where these competing currents had run alongside each other and often merged, added to by the pragmatism of having greater numbers involved, meant the group focused on what they had in common. The mutual vision of a decentralised organisation formed from the four programming groups of the Side Cinema, with an artist-run film lab and media centre all built around a social centre structure was still a shared aspiration. Twenty-seven people showed up and at least another twenty-one had expressed an interest. Arguably this was the meeting that defined the character of the soon-to-become Star and Shadow Cinema. Experienced in direct democracy from the anti-globalisation movement, activist participants proposed a set of guiding principles around consensus decision-making; no hierarchies; working groups feeding back to general meetings; financial self-reliance as opposed to dependence on subsidy and a general attitude of open participation. The focus was clearly on how a building might be run, rather than what might happen in it. These meetings continued, strengthening the DIY spirit from Side Cinema days and contributing to a sense of confidence that there would be enough people involved for a project of this scale to work. Always last on the agenda was what to call the new cinema. Among a long list, two were standing out more than any others. For some, the favoured name was The Star, maybe because it signified political struggle, or Newcastle Brown Ale, or possibly as an ironic *détourné* of Hollywood celebrity. Others wanted to call it The Shadow, perhaps because it suggests the disguised, the unconscious, the irrational, the hidden and because it conjures the apparatus of the cinema as a form of spectatorship in thrall to the shadows. Consensus was reached with silent nods when Noah Fisher suggested the two together: Star and Shadow. It sounded like a public house, and could provide a dialogic 'holder' for the mutually agitating forces of politics and aesthetics contained within the expanding group, while at the same time sounding familiar and approachable.

Options for a separate autonomous social centre were kept open by activists connected to Dissent. Meanwhile a core group formed with the immediate urge to get a screening space up and running. There was no time to lose and they set to work straight away negotiating the lease on the warehouse at Stepney Bank, taking a 38 per cent stake in the building. The New Labour vision of regeneration through the arts had been spectacularly embodied in the gentrified Gateshead Quayside. On the opposite bank of the Tyne, a small development trust envisaged a new 'cultural quarter' in the Ouseburn. Important during the Industrial Revolution due to its connection to the river Tyne, by the early 2000s it was a mixed cohabitation of scrap yards, garages and green spaces supplemented by Lime Street artists' studios, a community stables and a city farm. A large empty warehouse at the top of the valley had once been a set-building workshop for Tyne Tees Television, but, surplus to their requirements, had fallen into disrepair for nearly a decade. The symbolic rescue of a space from television into the arms of cinema was wryly noted.

This new collective's inexperience could have set off alarm bells to decision-makers, but they shared a huge amount of self-belief garnered from their own experience at Side Cinema and from the DIY activism movement. Their utopian vision was further catalysed by members attending the 2005 Rencontre de Labos meeting at Nova Cinema, a venerable, volunteer-run space for 'different' cinema operating in the heart of Brussels since 1997. Like Cube, Nova was built around an auditorium and a bar, with the atmosphere of a free arts space. The participants at the artist-run film labs meeting, who had come from all corners of Europe, provided a great sounding board for the plans back in Newcastle. On return, the group set about planning a building festival, to which the film labs were all invited. The festival revolved around an open call for people to come and physically build the cinema. Participants would teach each other practical building skills, watch and discuss films, consider alternative working models and eat together, while constructing an improvised cinema and bar. Building work commenced the day they were granted access, April 10, 2006. In attendance were fifty or more volunteers made up of European filmmakers and DIY cinema activists from Hungary, Portugal, Belgium, Germany and France alongside folk from Edinburgh, London and the Northeast. The festival launched with an open forum on site to define the vision for the space, what might be screened, and who could help make it happen. Huddled around a gas brazier in what would become the auditorium, forty or more listened, participated and signed up to working groups, including residents from the housing association flats across the road.

Enthusiasm waxed and waned as two weeks turned into two months and cinema was nowhere near built. Embroiled in planning, licensing and building regulations, progress slowed. They were film programmers teaching themselves every aspect of design and build. It did not stop them programming. In June, amidst rubble, they hosted legendary collector Jack Stevenson from Copenhagen's Husets Biograph, followed by the second edition of Projectile Anarchist Film Festival. In the autumn an appropriately ascetic screening of Béla Tarr's *Werkmeister Harmonies* (2000) was presented in the bare skeleton of the new auditorium. By March the following year, the plan for an independent social centre had dissipated. With the success of events like Projectile and the Films without Borders festival within the S&S programme, it made sense for all efforts to be focused on the one entity. For eight years, the open, participatory film programme and music culture facilitated a dialogic conversation of emancipatory politics and aesthetics at S&S, carried by a unique fluidity between audience and programmer. Events included live 16 mm performances by John Smith, Guy Sherwin, Sarah Pucill and punk experimentalists Gaëlle Rouard and Etienne Claire from Atelier MTK in Grenoble. Les Blank's *Garlic Is as Good as Ten Mothers* (1980) screened with live frying of garlic. Partnering with AV Festival they hosted Lav Diaz marathons, and the audience have programmed early films of Michael Winner, Lucrecia Martel, Fred Wiseman, Anna Biller and Agnès Varda. Events were organised with the Tyneside Claimants Union, the Anti-Cuts Network, mental health activists, a conversation group for asylum seekers and refugees, and fundraisers arranged for the Zapatistas, and the

Indigenous communities of the Peruvian Amazon. Space was made available for a host of DIY activities around zine making for film seasons, feminist film and music culture and banner-making for Occupy Newcastle. Organised through open meetings, email working groups, consensus decision-making and a wiki for centralising information, volunteer numbers rose into the hundreds. Star and Shadow evolved into a democratic, participatory space for grassroots creative and political engagement, with cinema providing the pretext for this activity.

On June 4, 2014, S&S got the bad news they had been preparing for, that their lease would be terminated and the site redeveloped. The gentrification process around the Ouseburn, which S&S had been both inadvertently part of and resistant to, had slowed briefly in the aftermath of the financial crash, but was picking up pace again with student and yuppie flats earmarked for development in an expanding zone around the Ouseburn. By the end of 2014, the collective's ambition was clear, to resist the exploitative logic of gentrification by owning its own building. Following in the footsteps of their forebears Amber, and more recently Cube, S&S set themselves the goal of buying and building a cinema as a long-term new home. The site of the new S&S is an old furniture showroom, built on a Victorian landfill site, and neighbouring a large residential part of Shieldfield. Between 2015 and 2018, the S&S collective were absorbed in a second building festival, to construct a high-spec cinema and music space for the commons. This version has been more expensive, higher profile, and bound by more restrictive regulation, qualities that bear down on S&S's DIY mode of organising. Furthermore, algorithmically controlled social media and online viewing patterns have obscured the importance of a real-world social space for screening and discussion. The terrain has changed but so has S&S. Designed according to the logic of 'with' not 'for', the channels of participation are opening up dialogic collaborations around film, music, politics, art, food and community. It is the DIY cinema as a resistant, reflexive, democratic space that facilitates this ecology, not exclusively the film text. The everyday utopianism of the project, which has persisted throughout the build and into the reopening, suggests it is worth fighting to prove that another way is still possible, and the collective space of cinema is as good a place to start as any.

Notes

1 Horizontalism is a term used by autonomous social movements concerned with direct democracy and non-hierarchical, participatory structures for organising. It stems from *horizontalidad*, exemplified in the neighbourhood assemblies the emerged during the popular rebellion in Argentina in 2001, to reject representative democracy (Sitrin 2012)
2 Over 1,500 members, according to the website of the Tyneside Cinema. 2018. The History of Tyneside Cinema (accessed June 5, 2018). https://www.tynesidecinema.co.uk/about-us/our-venue/heritage/tyneside-cinema-history
3 Regional Film Theatres (RFT) were a network of screening spaces subsidised by the BFI, to roll out the type of programming at the National Film Theatre to the regions (see Nowell-Smith and Dupin 2012; Selfe 2007).

4 The Association for Cinematograph, Television and Allied Technicians was the trade union for the film and television industries from 1933–1991, and one of the architects of the Workshop Declaration.

References

Andrews, David. 2014. *Theorizing Art Cinemas: Foreign, Cult, Avant-garde, and Beyond.* Austin: University of Texas Press.

British Film Institute. 1934. 'News from Societies'. *Sight & Sound* 3 (11): 139.

Christie, Ian. 1981. 'Notes on the BFI and Regional Film Culture', in *Reel Practices: A Directory of Independent Film from the Northeast.* York Film, 7–8. York: York Film.

Cooper, Davina. 2014. *Everyday Utopias: The Conceptual Life of Promising Spaces.* Durham: Duke University Press.

Dickinson, Margaret, ed. 1999. *Rogue Reels: Oppositional Film in Britain, 1945–90.* London: BFI Pub.

Hill, Helen. 2001. *Recipes for Disaster – A Handcrafted Film Cookbooklet.* New Orleans: Author.

Hodkinson, Stuart, and Paul Chatterton. 2006. 'Autonomy in the City?: Reflections on the Social Centres Movement in the UK'. *City* 10 (3): 305–315. doi:10.1080/13604810600982222

Hogenkamp, Bert. 1986. *Deadly Parallels: Film and the Left in Britain, 1929–1939.* London: Lawrence and Wishart.

Holtzman, Ben, Craig Hughes, and Van Meter, Kevin. 2007. 'Do It Yourself... and the Movement Beyond Capitalism'. In *Constituent Imagination: Militant Investigations//Collective Theorization.* Oakland, CA: AK Press.

Leister, David, Duncan Reekie, Jennet Thomas, Steven Eastwood, Philip Ilson, and Tai Shani. 2017. 'Roundtable Discussion: The Volcano Generation: London Film Groups in the 1990s'. *The Moving Image Review & Art Journal (MIRAJ)* 6 (1): 226–237. doi:10.1386/miraj.6.1-2.226_1

Manders, Frank. 1991. *Cinemas of Newcastle: A Comprehensive History of the Cinemas of Newcastle upon Tyne.* Newcastle upon Tyne: City Libraries et Arts.

McKay, George, ed. 1998. *DiY Culture: Party & Protest in Nineties Britain.* London; New York: Verso.

Newsinger, Jack. 2009. 'The Interface of Documentary and Fiction: The Amber Film Workshop and Regional Documentary Practice'. *Journal of British Cinema and Television* 6 (3): 387–406.

Nowell-Smith, Geoffrey, and Christophe Dupin, eds. 2012. *The British Film Institute, the Government and Film Culture, 1933–2000.* Manchester: Manchester University Press.

Reekie, Duncan. 2007. *Subversion: The Definitive History of Underground Cinema.* London: Wallflower Press.

Schober, Anna. 2013. *The Cinema Makers: Public Life and the Exhibition of Difference in South-Eastern and Central Europe since the 1960s.* Bristol: Intellect. http://site.ebrary.com/id/10675237

Selfe, Melanie. 2007. '"Doing the Work of the NFT in Nottingham" – or How to Use the BFI to Beat the Communist Threat in Your Local Film Society'. *Journal of British Cinema and Television* 4 (1): 80–101.

Sitrin, Marina A. 2012. *Everyday Revolutions: Horizontalism and Autonomy in Argentina.* London: Zed Books. http://ebookcentral.proquest.com/lib/reading/detail.action?docID=1026923

PART IV

Interviews

18

ARTISTS' MOVING IMAGE

Oliver Ressler interviewed by Mike Wayne

Oliver Ressler is an Austrian artist and filmmaker who produces installations, projects in the public space, and films on issues such as economics, democracy, global warming, forms of resistance and social alternatives. By merging the fields of art and activism, Ressler's films and multi-media work seek to address political ideas, and observe progressive social processes and alternative ways of how to organise society. His latest film project, *Everything's Coming Together While Everything's Falling Apart* (2016–20), charts the climate movement's struggle to dismantle an economic system heavily dependent on fossil fuels. The following interview took place at 'RFN: NYC, A Global Gathering', the Radical Film Network conference in New York City in 2017.

MIKE WAYNE (MW): *How would you describe yourself and your work?*

OLIVER RESSLER (OR): I'm an artist and filmmaker. I deal with issues like democracy, economics, global warming, various forms of resistance and social alternatives. I work on films, on projects in public space and on installations in art exhibitions.

In general, I'm interested in finding out how social movements, how activists organise. The projects are a lot about the structures of non-hierarchical organised groups and movements. I'm interested to find out about how decision-making processes are being carried out and how people collaborate with each other under such relationships.

Over the years, I've focused on different movements. I focused on the alter-globalisation movement or the Bolivarian process in Venezuela. More recently on the climate justice movement or the Occupy and square movement. I establish different situations from where people speak and try to document the spoken word of the activists. Some years ago I was primarily recording single people speaking directly to the camera. I abandoned this a bit in the recent years as my work was about how democracy can be created. It's clear that this is something that has to be done in between people. Therefore, I prefer to establish situations where people talk to each other. This will be documented for the camera.

MW: *Can you tell us how your work is similar to, and distinct from, the video-activism that might be produced by the movements themselves?*

OR: I'm someone who has a formal education in an art university, and my work is primarily being presented in art exhibitions in biennials in museums. When I started with this work, the main problem was that those people who were part of the art scene did not regard this as art, what I was doing. They regarded it as an art activism and didn't see meaning, didn't see any sense in presenting this kind of work within the art world. It was a long process to get this work as an artistic practice into the art world. Generally, I did works which are very similar I think to work that has been done by activists. I was never so much interested to develop something that would create a clear distinction, which makes it clear for everyone that this is not a work of activism. I'm more interested in blurring these lines than in merging them.

I also have a film practice, which is kind of experimental in the sense that I apply different formats and there is a lot of variation in it. The most recent films I did, *Everything's Coming Together While Everything's Falling Apart* (2016– 20), is a cycle of at the moment two films[1] related to the resistance of the climate movement. The films combine visual material, the voices of activists recorded at mass civil disobedience activities with a narration – radical, political poetry, which has been established in a dialogue to the images. I think it's quite clear to people that this is not a typical work of activist art. It's a quite elaborated product, which goes far beyond that typical documentation of an event you might find on YouTube or on some other place online.

MW: *What does the aesthetic dimension to your work add to the material that progresses the political changes you want to see? What is the aesthetic doing politically in your work? What are you trying to stimulate for the audience or the viewer?*

OR: There's more than one answer to this because of the variety of different films and installations I've worked on over the past few years. On the one hand, for sure, there's an idea to inform about certain themes. On the other hand, there is this wish to bring certain communities that are very often not that much heard into the position to get a platform from where to speak. Also, to speak about audiences is always a bit complicated for me just because I'm also working with a diversity of different audiences. I mean, it can't be denied that my work is to a very large extent being presented within exhibitions within the art world. Therefore, this is a central audience for me. On the other hand, the works are also used a lot by the social movements themselves and, from time to time, are being presented within film festivals. Different audiences have different expectations and relate the work they see to different contexts.

MW: *How does the dominant media framing of a subject influence your approach? I was particularly struck by how radically* There Are No Syrian Refugees in Turkey *(2016) deconstructed some of the dominant European perspective on things.*

OR: Yes. I mean, if we look to the vast majority of films of refugees on TV, for example, then we realise that the refugees are being used as someone who has a story to tell. Then we can hear stories about the escape, the refuge or how to cross the borders and maybe about the difficulties to stay in a foreign country and to make a living there. But I think refugees also have a certain experience and a certain knowledge that they can also be asked questions that go beyond their personal experience. That was the concept from the beginning for this film. My main focus, was more or less on a political analysis of the European Union and of Turkey. To get it delivered from these people directly. This is, of course, directly related to the hegemonic model that exists in mainstream media.

MW: *Yes. It was a lovely critique of Eurocentrism. How does the question of funding shape what you can do, when and how?*

OR: That's a very good question. I mean, it shapes a lot of what I do, when and how. I produce my films through quite a wide range of different funds, which I put together. Some of my films are produced because I get a very specific invitation, usually from an art institution that offers me to produce something new for a very specific exhibition, although very often the money that I'm offered is not enough. Then I try to find additional money in order to get something done.

There are also works where there's no invitation where I just decide that this would be a great idea to do such a film. Then I try to raise the funding. In some cases, this can take years to get the funding together for such a film. There are numerous projects which I never produced because I never managed to receive the funding I was hoping to receive. In some cases, I received a very small percentage of what I hoped I would receive. Then I still take this money and do something with it, which is not what I wanted to do originally, but I'm able to adapt the concept. I also work with funding from political organisations, from foundations that are maybe for labour rights or whatever.

MW: *'Occupy, Resist, Produce' was something of a multi-national co-production, wasn't it? That must have been difficult to put together.*

OR: Yes. Altogether, there are about nine or ten sources of funding in it. I think Dario Azzellini and I were very successful to raise the funds for the first three films. Maybe too successful because we received money from all foundations and all governmental institutions you could approach for this. Now we're not successful any more to raise funding for the fourth or for the fifth film.[2] Our budget is still zero, so it's a bit in question if we will ever manage to produce a fourth or a fifth film. We are in a lucky situation that the workers in the factories that we would like to record are already waiting for us. They want to inscribe themselves into this international cycle of worker-controlled factories in Europe. Which I understand politically, but economically, I can only produce this film if there comes external funding just because I don't have the money otherwise. I still hope that at some point there's an email in my inbox that tells me that I will be given €15,000 or €20,000 for the fourth film in this cycle.

MW: *How much did you raise for those first three films out of nine or ten funding streams?*

OR: For these three films, altogether it was I think €45,000. I should add here that in this case, Dario and I decided both not to earn any money involved with it. We worked for zero for this. If we had paid ourselves, it would have been at least €60,000, €70,000 or €80,000.

MW: *Do you have another job or do you survive on your art practice?*

OR: I survive on my art practice. In this time, I received regular income through a research project I was directing on utopia. This time is now over and I'm trying to survive as a freelancer. I'm doing relatively well, I would say, just because at the moment, in the past few years, my work really got a lot of attention internationally. I usually participate in approximately thirty exhibitions per year, which is really a lot (and a lot of work). This, of course, also generates a certain amount of income. In some of these exhibitions, there is also money to put into production.

MW: *Okay. What are the ethical issues involved in working with various different subjects and how do you address those issues?*

OR: Ethical issues are embedded in all the questions related to the form and to the content of how these films look and how they are being produced. Which excerpts of interviews or conversations to take, for example, and which ones not to use.

Also, for example, in *Emergency Turned Upside-Down* (2016), the core decision to do an animation was related to analysis of how media use certain images. The reaction to this usage is also related to ethical considerations. It's a film on the so-called 'Balkan Route' when refugees, in the so-called 'summer of migration', moved through Turkey and Greece through former Yugoslavian countries to Germany, Austria and up more to the North. At the very beginning, I found these images of thousands of refugees crossing borders super inspiring. This is self-empowerment. Yet only days after, the same category of images were being used by the media and politicians to warn and to stop these refugees that would, 'Come to us and take away our jobs.' Therefore I decided to do the film *Emergency Turned Upside-Down* without using any of these images of refugees crossing borders.

MW: *What do you think determines your ability to get an exhibition in an art gallery in Poland, Italy, Greece or Switzerland? Is it context? Is it contacts? What determines your ability to get your work seen?*

OR: This is quite a complicated question. I started to work as a freelance artist in 1995. At that time, I didn't see myself as a filmmaker but I worked with public interventions and installations that included video as one of several elements. My work from the very beginning was dealing with more or less the same issues I'm still dealing nowadays. At that time, there were only a few projects in art exhibitions and museums that were dealing with such issues. In addition, there were almost no documentary formats in it. In 2000, I completed my first film, *Rote Zora*.

Among others, it was presented in an exhibition with other artists such as Ursula Biemann or Hito Steyerl, who were also using different strategies to work with the documentary format in the art scene.

At the beginning, it was really very hard. When I presented my work first in public talks in 1995, people would ask, 'Why is this art? Why should this be presented within the confines of art institutions?' It was very frustrating and disappointing, and took years before this kind of work began to be slowly accepted within the art field.

I think a major change happened when Okwui Enwezor did the *documenta* 11 in 2002. It was a *documenta* that had a clear theme, on post-colonialism, and also provided a space for a multiplicity of different documentary formats. Even though I was not part of this *documenta*, I felt in the years that followed that it was easier now to present this kind of work within exhibition spaces. There were also more and more exhibitions afterwards dealing with political themes. I'm not saying that these exhibitions did not exist before. When I studied, for example, there were exhibitions dealing with political issues but these were in relatively small institutions operating financially on a very low level. They also did not have a lot of visibility within the larger art scene. After the *documenta*, this shifted a bit.

MW: *What different experience of a project does a three-channel installation produce as opposed to a linear field? 'Occupy, Resist, Produce', that was a three-channel installation and a film. What does that do?*

OR: Many of my works have more than one format. When you show in art exhibitions, it's usually a group show. In a spatialized presentation it is much more likely to attract attention. These are films about occupation. Workers occupy a space and I think my work as an artist is also kind of an occupation. I'm occupying space within an exhibition site. Very often, I'm also in group shows, which are not really political group shows. They include a variety of different things. Especially in such exhibitions I regard it as super important to occupy as much space as possible with these political films in order to get an audience for it. To occupy the space to show that it's important to regard this as art and to present this within the art field.

MW: *In terms of films, what would you say your visual style is? What sort of things do you think you like to do with the audio in relation to the visual?*

OR: This question is hard to answer in general terms because my film works are so different from each other. What I heard often from critiques is that my works prioritise the audio, the spoken word. I think I can agree to that. When editing I often start with the text. It can be the spoken word of other people or the text I write myself but usually I start with the text. This does not necessarily mean that the images are of a lesser importance. Editing is a creative process and lots of things can be altered in this process. I might come back to the text, change the order, cut things out and include other ones. This work always relates to the images. I am not interested in developing a specific style. I am more interested in working in different styles at the same time. Every work deserves its own visual language, its own approach.

MW: *Finally, what artists, filmmakers and theorists have been important and influential to you?*

OR: I think the most important and influential artists and filmmakers were those who were about in my generation or working in the same fields, in the same topics, in the past twenty years. Some of them became good friends. I named already two, Ursula Biemann and Hito Steyerl. Both of them are very important as persons, as thinkers and as filmmakers for my artist practice. It's also people like Zanny Begg, for example, with whom I collaborated also on three films, who is a fascinating filmmaker, artist, teacher, writer, activist, etc. Or Marcelo Expósito, a Spanish filmmaker who also did films related to the alter-globalisation movement. Harun Farocki was always influential with the entire body of work he produced over his life.

In relation to certain projects, certain theorists became really central. Toni Negri and Michael Hardt, for example, were of a huge importance when I was working on the cycle of films on the alter-globalisation movement. David Graeber was important in the recent years. There are, for sure, more.

Notes

1 The cycle was later expanded to six films.
2 In fact the fourth film was later completed.

19

EUROPEAN FEATURE DOCS

Moviemienta/Aris Chatzistefanou interviewed by Jack Newsinger, Steve Presence and Mike Wayne

Introduction

Moviemienta (formerly Infowar Productions) was founded in Greece in 2010 by a group of journalists from various media outlets who were disillusioned both with the dire political and economic conditions in the country and the state of its journalism. The group's first feature-length documentary, *Debtocracy* (2011), began life as a short film intended for YouTube that sought to counter some of the misinformation about the Greek economic crisis – that it was a result of financial mismanagement, for instance, or caused by an unproductive labour force – which began circulating in the mainstream media following the 2008 financial crash. However, after a successful crowd-funding campaign that generated €8,000 in just ten days, the ambitions for the film increased and *Debtocracy* developed into a feature-length documentary. The film was released online under a Creative Commons license in April 2011, where it quickly received almost 1 million views – one of the most successful crowd-sourced films about the crisis yet produced.

Moviemienta has since released four subsequent feature documentaries. *Catastroika* (2012) studied the history and consequences of deregulation and privatisation around the world in the context of the major privatisation programme demanded by Greece's debtors, including the European Union (EU) and International Monetary Fund (IMF). *Fascism Inc* (2014) addressed the rise of neo-fascism in Greece and Europe and the historic and contemporary links between fascism, capitalism and the economic elite. *This is Not a Coup* (2016) focused on Greece's relationship with the EU and the undemocratic nature of European Central Bank's (ECB) financial interventions in countries such as Italy, Ireland, Portugal, Cyprus and Greece. Following Infowar Production's change of name in 2019 – discussed below – Moviemienta released *Make the Economy Scream* (2019), which focuses on Venezuela and the consequences of the 'constant economic warfare' subjected to the country by the United States. All of these projects were crowd-funded – with all bar the latter released for free online – and have together been seen by several million viewers, making Moviemienta one of the most successful producers of crowd-funded radical feature documentaries in the world. This interview was conducted with Aris Chatzistefanou, co-founder of Moviemienta and director of all its feature films (except *Debtocracy*, which was co-directed with his former colleague and radio journalist, Katerina Kitidi).

STEVE PRESENCE (SP): *Can you tell us a little bit about the state of radical film and media culture in Greece? What other organisations are operating there and how do they survive?*

ARIS CHATZISTEFANOU (AC): After 2009–2010, when the great crisis started, because many people found themselves out of work, many professional journalists came together and created new media that was directly controlled by them. For example, we have a newspaper called *Efimerida ton Syntakton* – 'The Editor's Daily' is the translation in English – which is something like *Liberation* in the first days in France, which was controlled by its employees. There are many initiatives from the citizen journalist point-of-view – Omnia TV was a current affairs web-TV initiative.

In terms of how they fund themselves, it's very difficult – even for us. Of course there are many people who want to follow our example by crowd-funded projects [but] I would say we are the most successful example, as far as the amount of money we managed to collect. But it was difficult for us – it doesn't pay the bills, so I imagine it must have been much more difficult for smaller groups to survive.

MIKE WAYNE (MW): *How would you describe what it is that you're trying to do? What are your aims?*

AC: We are trying to give, to the widest possible audience, the arguments they need to understand what's going on in their daily lives. When we started *Debtocracy* [2011], the main idea was to explain to the Greek people that they weren't lazy. Because the media managed to persuade a lot of people that a guy who worked twelve hours per day was lazy and therefore responsible for whatever happened in Greece. We were trying to investigate the structural problems of the world financial system, and especially of the Eurozone. We don't deny, of course, that the Greek economy is a mess and that it had some structural problems – but you cannot find yourself with a debt of €360bn just from that. It's not a coincidence that at the same time, that you have the same crisis in Portugal, in Ireland, in different economies. The same crisis happening at the same time. So we wanted to explain these things.

With *Catastroika* [2012], when the first massive privatisations started, we wanted to bring examples from other countries where privatisation was a total failure for the population. So we came to Great Britain, we went to Russia, we were talking about trains, about water distribution systems, telecommunication or power networks in the United States. So, we were giving this information to the people for their everyday struggle. With *Fascism Inc*

[2014], we wanted to explain that fascism is just a historical part of capitalism; it's not something new. It's not a natural phenomenon that just happens – capitalist economics plays a specific role in promoting fascism. For *This is Not a Coup* [2016], we wanted to summarise the role that the European Union played, because we realised that the European Union was a common denominator to many of our problems: debt creation, massive privatisation, the rise of fascism and racism in many countries, especially in Greece. So we went back, and sought to explain the mechanism of the European Union and especially the Eurozone, making what Marx and Engels would characterise as 'the negation of the negation'. Our last documentary film, *Make the Economy Scream* [2019], is probably the 'odd one out' in the sense that we are leaving the Greek and the European crisis and focus on the recent events of Venezuela. We are trying to analyse the structural problems of the Venezuelan economy that led to economic collapse, like the so called Dutch disease (the dependence to the oil industry), several mistakes in the monetary policy but most importantly the constant economic warfare by the United States.

JACK NEWSINGER (JN): *Your films articulate some quite complex ideas about economics and finance and so on. How did you find a language to express these difficult arguments?*

AC: That was the most difficult part in some respects, because we had enough data to write several books but only eighty minutes of the documentary, and you have to make sure that people can grasp it and understand what is going on. So we had to kill most of that information and keep something like 10 per cent, and try to explain by using the language of image in a professional way. In *This is Not a Coup*, we even took some ideas from Hollywood, from *The Big Short* [2016], in the way that they're trying to explain more complicated issues about finance. We do the same thing but we have, for example, a hairdresser or someone cutting hair and we talk about haircutting the debt. We have a baby and we explain that ECB [European Central Bank] is like a mother towards her baby, who needs to provide liquidity in the milk or something, but without any conditions. If you are a mother, you cannot say, 'I will give you milk and keep you alive, but only if you accept these rules,' but the ECB is doing exactly that: it's imposing fiscal policy. All these idea that we have are out there, we are not saying that we bring something completely new. What we were trying to do was to sex it up, to make it accessible and understandable to a wider audience.

Make the Economy Scream is somehow different because the narrative is much more personal – I describe my journey from Europe to Caracas and then to the borders of Bolivia. I am using all these experiences in an attempt to make a political and economic analysis of the state and the society of Venezuela. So the end result might be similar but I am following a completely different path, as far as the narration and the aesthetics of the film.

SP: *You mentioned, can we just unpack that term 'professional' a little bit? You also talked about how you started from an amateur perspective. What do you mean by 'professional' when you use that term?*

AC: When we started our first documentary we were total 'amateurs', though I should clarify that our editor was professional, working in a big TV station, and so when he was getting our rubbish footage he was able to make something out of it. Year after year, or probably month after month, we've started understanding our equipment, we are using DSLRs and mirrorless cameras not only because of the cost, but because we can move around, just with a bag, and have the quality that ten or twenty years ago would have cost you hundreds of thousands of Euros. Then we started buying some more equipment, we got a slider, now we have a drone, because you cannot just put information – otherwise you could just write it down on big piece of paper and spread it in the middle of the square. We believe you need to follow the rules of professional filmmaking, and we are learning about that. I was a professional journalist, but I have no idea about moving images. Even though I've worked as a photographer, I knew how to frame things, but when things started moving inside my frame, I panicked. [Laughter.] 'Where should it stand? Why does it move that way?' So you can see, from documentary to documentary, we have developed a more cinematic approach.

MW: *Can you tell us more about how you fund your work?*

AC: So far we have made all our films using almost 100 per cent crowd-funding, and we explain to our audience that we will never take money from political parties or corporations or anything like that. We are also explicit about our ideological perspective on the subject, so people understand what we are going to say, and that we will not be balanced in the way that the mainstream media talk about being 'balanced'. We don't believe that journalists can be balanced. It should be serious, and not tell lies, but of course you will express a perspective at some point. We were saying to our audience, 'You have the other side of the story, you are listening and you are watching it every single day in the mainstream media. We will say something completely different, which will be news analysis, not just facts.' The reaction was tremendous. For the first documentary, we had something like eight or nine thousand Euros within a week, which for Greece was unique. Not only because of the amount but because there was no tradition of crowd-funding, no one really knew about it. Then we had some more money that allowed us to travel abroad. For example, in *Catastroika*, we got the money to travel to Russia and the United States. Every time it was just people or small unions or students' associations or things like that. But not big unions, because especially in Greece, big unions have their own bureaucracy and are connected in many ways with the government, with the state. So we wanted grassroots unions or movements.

Make the Economy Scream was also crowd funded and for reasons that I cannot still explain was the most successful. When we thought that people had lost interest in politics (because of the apathy that we were experiencing in Greece for several years) they showed to us that they need to understand the political and ideological background of a story that was unfolding on the other side of the Atlantic.

SP: *To what extent is that sustainable? One of the criticisms of crowd-funding for film production is that it's hard to replicate, so while it's very impressive that you've produced so many films this way, do you see that continuing in the future?*

AC: It's not totally sustainable, no. That's why after *This is Not a Coup* we are trying not to upload our films directly into the public domain, but to have a tour around cinemas and TV stations. Of course, we will at some point give it for free, because that's part of our philosophy. And for those that paid money towards it, these people first of all should take it and will have a password to access it online. But no, it is not sustainable and we cannot live from it – we do other work to survive.

SP: *Can you talk a little bit about the distribution and the exhibition of your work? How does that work, what's your strategy? Who is your audience, who's watching it?*

AC: For the first three documentaries, we just used the Internet: uploading on Vimeo and YouTube, giving people direct access. When we produced *Debtocracy*, it was not a coincidence but we were lucky that we had the Indignados movement in the square. In every single square in Greece there was a bigger or a smaller screen showing documentaries. So thousands of people managed to watch it either in public screenings or on the web. We now have more than 8 million views for our first three films. We also provided them for free to television stations. I'm proud to say that no mainstream Greek media accepted *Debtocracy*, even for free, and even though they were saying, 'Oh we have economic problems, we cannot afford to buy documentaries and this and that.' We said, 'take it', 'just broadcast it'. 'No'. But it was broadcast in many countries in Latin America and many other countries – even a public broadcaster from Japan showed *Debtocracy*.

SP: *And did they pay?*

AC: No, at that moment we insisted on not being paid because the idea was to have the widest possible audience. Now that we're going to cinemas, we ask for some money – which is not only about financing ourselves but because we realised we were losing part of the audience, because many television stations would never accept something that could be found on YouTube. We said again, 'Take it for free,' and they wanted to but said, 'That's in the public domain, I'm not interested.' So now we're saying 'okay, give us some money if you want the film'.

We were also losing cinema screenings, because cinemas would never dare show something the audience could find online. So although we are asking now for some money, it's not about the money – probably that's the last reason. It was because we were losing part of the audience.

MW: *Have you tried Telesur? Because they gave us a couple of thousand pounds for one of our films.*

AC: Yes, I've worked for them and they've broadcast all our documentaries. They helped us in different ways, because they then asked for some future stories that we made as a production company. So it was a way to say thank you in a sense, and also to do things that they wanted to do and we wanted to do.

JN: *Can you tell us about some of the biggest problems you've encountered? Have things gotten easier with each film or do the challenges remain each time?*

AC: Usually, the biggest problems are technical. I mean, for example for the last documentary, there's a section on European Central Bank which is in

Frankfurt. We should have spent weeks there filming but I had only four hours to take all the footage. I remember being alone, having a camera in front of me, and the drone above at the same time, and almost crashed into the building trying to do both. [Laughter.] There were some threats, especially for *Debtocracy*, our parents received some threatening calls, in the middle of the night, but we never really paid attention to those. Because what can they do? The main weapon that they have is, if you are a professional, you find yourself out of the job market. That was probably the worst thing could do and they did that already. My name is on a blacklist for the mainstream media, the big TV stations, for example, no one would ever let me work there. But the main thing was just that for what we were doing you should really have a group of twenty people, and we were just four.

SP: *Have things gotten easier as the budgets have increased – assuming they have increased?*

AC: The budget increased dramatically from *Debtocracy* to *Catastroika* because we started travelling. In *Debtocracy* we were just using footage that we could find online or even from other documentaries that would help. When we started travelling, I remember I was trying to get an interview with Naomi Klein for months – she called me on a Monday night, I was in Athens and she said, 'I will be in Wall Street on Wednesday morning, can you come for the interview that you asked?' So I said, "Yes, I can come,' but that was €2,000 just like that, because I only had twenty-four hours to make the journey. A rough estimate for that film is that for €20–30,000 we managed to cover all the expenses as far as travelling and equipment, and to give a symbolic amount to all the people that helped us.

Debtocracy cost about €8,000, but with that film we agreed to volunteer our labour. After that we said, 'no, we are professionals and should at least try to get a salary'. We understood that it wouldn't be a normal salary but it was a different model after *Debtocracy*. We were trying to find out if we could survive at some point, by doing that. Then we travelled a lot for *Fascism Inc*, too – to Germany, Italy, again Great Britain – the same for *This is Not a Coup*. It's about four to five countries per documentary that we are going to. And that also helps afterwards, because if you have more countries in the documentary, more people from these countries will be interested in it. But if this was a normal budget we couldn't have made it for less than €100,000 at least for a full-length documentary.

JN: *Can I ask about the politics a bit more? Obviously you've spoken about the political arguments in the film, but can you talk about your own political perspectives? Would you describe yourselves as socialists? Do you aim to appeal to a specific part of the left?*

AC: Of course, it's left politics, I would say that I have a Marxist analysis in the way that I understand the world and that means focusing mainly on the economic aspects. We're trying to understand society and even politics, by starting by the economics of it. Not staying only in economics, but we think that the main point of interest was economics. *The Guardian* once said that we've made the best Marxian analysis of the Eurozone crisis, which closed some doors for us but at the same time we were proud that we'd made the best Marxian analysis. [Laughter.] So, yes, it's a left-wing approach, trying to bring together different parts of the left, which especially in Greece splits like Monty Python's *Life of Brian*.

SP: *Okay, so finally, can you tell us more about the latest project,* Make the Economy Scream *[2019], and about the shift re-naming of your organisation from Infowar Productions to the Moviemienta? When did that happen and why? Is it still the same team as before?*

AC: The change in the name is an unfortunate and quite funny event. Infowar Productions was created more than ten years ago when the 'Infowars' radio show of Alex Jones, (a conspiracy theorist and personal friend of Donald Trump) was unknown in Europe. The name was just a coincidence but after Trump became president many people thought that we were somehow connected. I've almost lost an interview from a UN executive who thought that we were some kind of lunatics promoting conspiracy theories. So we thought it was time we got a name change.

So *Make The Economy Scream* was our first documentary to be released under the new name, which is Moviementa.com. The team and the ideas behind our production company remains the same.

20

VIDEO-ACTIVISM

Reel News

An interview with Shaun Dey by Eamonn Kelly

Introduction

Since it formed in 2006, Reel News has produced a newsreel on progressive movements and campaigns in Britain and around the world every two months, and as such is now the longest-running radical newsreel in British film history. The group is based in London and run by the founder and only full-time member, Shaun Dey, but the collective consists of a range of activists and individuals with skills in different media that contribute in different ways depending on the nature of the group's work and the campaigns with which it is involved at any given moment.

Financially, the group exists exclusively on donations and subscriptions to its newsreel from individuals and trade union branches, and does not apply for funding, sell its material to other news outlets or produce any other kind of filmmaking to subsidise its video-activist work. Moreover, the entirety of Reel News' output is also made available online for free, and is accessible both via its own website (http s://reelnews.co.uk/) and its YouTube channel (https://www.youtube.com/user/ ReelNews/). While this approach arguably restricts the capacity of the collective to expand or cover more campaigns, the group argues that its financial independence is the key to its political independence, and that Reel News has maintained such a regular volume and rate of production level for so long is testament to the effectiveness of its model. Perhaps equally unusual among video-activist groups is Reel News' fundamental commitment to class struggle. Or, as former union organiser Dey puts it, 'seeing as central the class basis of society and seeing that as the means to fight back'.

Upon their return from a three-month tour of North America making their American Climate Rebels series – a collection of eleven films that explore grassroots community-based struggles around climate change – Eamonn Kelly spoke to Dey about the experience of fourteen years of radical filmmaking.

EAMONN KELLY (EK): *Who are the audience for Reel News, and what methods do you use to publicise and distribute content?*

SHAUN DEY (SD): It's quite an interesting time to be asking that question particularly in terms of social media as things are changing quite quickly, but I would say our core reach is mainly based on subscribers and trade union branches, and activists who keep in touch constantly. By that I mean people who look us up online, have got a subscription, or are actively interacting with us on social media. Our subscription level is not that high, but when you look at who it is that maintains subscriptions, they tend to be grassroots trade union branches, quite a few are people who receive the DVDs as they are passed around, or the downloads, as we started distributing these about two years ago. The feedback we get from the latter includes many more people than who we send them out to. In terms of social media, it's becoming difficult to tell – for example we have over 13,000 people follow us on our Facebook page, and around 2,500 on our YouTube channel.

Our approach has always been that our aim is to get people in the same physical room, so that you have a chance to watch the film and then have a discussion, which can hopefully inform some type of action. That has always been the core of what we do, so we have a regular Reel News night in London, and we have other nights as part of tours more occasionally, and in other countries as well. We also screen at UK festivals in the summer.

But the change over time has been the use of social media to reach people, I'm thinking here of the Arab Spring, the Occupy and Black Lives Matter movements in Europe and the US, the movements in Spain and in Greece. All of these used social media to build their protests, to get people along to them and to give out information – we along with a lot of other people were using social media extensively as time moved on to do the same things. Everyone who is involved in this sort of thing is facing quite a big challenge.

Since 2018 Facebook in particular have changed all of their algorithms and this made it much more difficult to get this stuff out there, now it means people don't automatically get the material on their own feed. So, we're in a place where the reach online is shooting down, and everyone is trying to work out what to do about that, as it becomes more difficult to link on social media. I think that what is coming out of that is in order to have a major presence on social media and to get through to people you are going to have to share your stuff a lot more and have a lot more networks sharing each other's stuff – you can't do it on your own in the way that you did before.

The next thing which is happening is the formation of more specifically news media networks and cooperatives, so now in the UK, there is an alternative media cooperative called The Media Fund (themediafund.org) that is made up of about forty-five organisations. That would include people like

The Canary, Novara Media, Union News – quite a range of independent left media. I think we are now in the state where the ruling class is looking at social media and realised that there is far too much organising going on, far too many recent revolts using it and there is a squashing down. The clamp-down on 'Fake News' has been the rationale for it. Facebook say publicly on their adverts that they are making it easier for you to just chat to your friends and not have all of these annoying companies get in your way of that. The reality of what Facebook are actually doing is making it more difficult for people to see your feeds. The alt-right sites like Breitbart who put out blatant lies about things and get to reach a lot of people – they've got the money to still reach a lot of people, whereas the effect has been is to clamp down on grassroots activist media none of whom, like ourselves, have the money to advertise to people to encourage them to see our posts. We may have the production and some distribution, but we still don't have the money to pro-mote the output. Whereas before on social media we didn't need that kind of money to get heard, I think that's the main difference that is happening.

EK: *What has been the impact of Reel News and how this can be measured? What is your ability to change anything by making videos?*

SD: What we have learnt doing Reel News is that you only need a few thousand activists to see a video for it to have some type of impact in terms of changing the course of a dispute or a campaign. So three or four thousand people who are watching the video and who are all people likely to do something with that information – that can have quite an effect in terms of activism.

The first example where we began to realise the power of video, and what our job should be within that, was the BESNA dispute in 2011, where a few years into austerity, multinational building companies like Balfour Beatty had obviously decided to take advantage of the situation by trying to impose a 35 per cent cut in pay rates to electricians, so they were tearing up national agreements that had been in existence since 1968, and that was the frontline attack amongst others.

I was contacted by the chair of London construction workers at the time who said that they had suddenly got a meeting of 150 people when they normally only got fifteen. He asked us if we could get involved and film actions taking place and get them up on the Internet as quickly as possible, and they would use these to build further actions. From that point of view, it was quite easy to quantify the effect that we were having at the time. Partly from views we were getting on YouTube, but more importantly from the feedback that we were getting with people mailing us to say they saw the stuff and inviting us to come and film their actions taking place around the country. People were watching what was happening in London and this increased confidence to carry out their own activity. So, we were involved in helping spread the action by using the videos as a tool to inform and build further action.

Another aspect of that is that they sent them out to the building workers union in Australia, and after the dispute won, these guys came over for the victory celebrations. We got introduced and I said, 'Have you seen any of our videos?', and he replied, 'Seen them? Me and nearly every other building union member – how do you think we managed to collect AUD $20,000 and then send it to the action committee, and not the union bureaucrats?' It was a lesson to us in how the work could be used both as a fundraiser and also to spread news and confidence. The other issue is that the dispute was won with no mainstream news coverage at all – it simply wasn't reported. It is clear that you can win disputes as long as you produce your own material and, crucially, use it to help build activity. This is when I learnt, that we could go beyond just publicising disputes to seeing video as a tool, as a weapon to help organising. A similar thing happened with British Airways cabin crew who were striking over a living wage campaign. They also contacted us, to help them reach their own members and crew on other airlines. The early videos were watched with 10–20,000 views and the last ones by about 200,000. It became clear from talking to the activists, the union reps, that the videos were being watched by cabin crews across the different companies. Also, in terms of simple publicity, video can make a difference, small numbers of people can take action, even a token occupation, and know that it can help publicise a campaign. Once the pictures and video go online, it can have an impact beyond the small number of participants.

Internationally, the best example is Catalonia, where myself and photographer Guy Smallman travelled over to cover the Independence referendum and protests in 2017. What we decided to do on the day and during the general strike two days later, was to post short bits of video streaming action as often as possible throughout each day. We found that after an hour or so, the shares were going up and this continued to build over the following days. One of the general strike videos reached nearly quarter of a million views, obviously a 'view' can be short, but these clips were short, and so probably were watched. Later we organised a TU [trade union] delegation, and I think we were able to do this because we were able to highlight the grassroots activism that was an important feature, and I think this helped inform the debates on the left about it.

EK: *What is your approach to film screenings and how you mount them?*

SD: At first we thought we had to get lots of people to these screenings, as time has gone on we have realised that actually the optimum amount of people is between twenty and forty. You need enough people to create a lively discussion and enable people to more easily contribute and engage with each other. We also ensure these are very, very informal. There is usually a bar and people are free to wander around the screenings as well as talk. The other thing we have learnt is not to show too many films. We used to try and show lots of films, but now we keep it down to two to three shorts about different campaigns, and then inviting people from the campaigns along to talk about them. Importantly, these campaigners get to meet each other as well, and so the screenings work very effectively as an informal meeting space to catch up, and not let things get too big. We do big events, but these are a very different thing that more resemble a performance. We were invited to take part in 'The Disobedient Objects' exhibition at the Victoria and Albert Museum in London in 2014. They staged an open evening with a bar, and thousands attended. We had one of the best attended sections with people coming and going all night – at these events we cut out discussion and staged campaign films accompanied by the most charismatic and lively activists from campaigns. That provided a template for what we do at numerous music festivals each summer such as Glastonbury, and others that we appear at, about four or five each year including the labour movement festival at Tolpuddle. We still do speakers and discussion here, but in the evenings we have a space with DJs where we screen visuals, overlay films etc.

I think a lot of the time the collective aspect of Reel News is in the way that I and other members work with the campaigns involved. The ideal of that was the campaign with the striking cleaners at London University who watched the rough cut of our films in their union meeting; they had a collective discussion about it, and then told me what changes they wanted. I would then make those changes, and when everyone was happy with it, that's when it would go out.

EK: *Reel News has been quite distinctive from lots of left media in consistently giving prominence to the Climate Emergency over quite a long period of time. How did that come about?*

SD: Similar to many of our ideas, like starting Reel News, it came out of Latin America. We were over there in 2001/2002 when the uprising occurred in Argentina – we visited social movements all over Latin America, and part of that was going to the World Social Forum in Port Alegre, and we met the members of the Brazilian Landless movement based in the Amazon who explained to me there the logging and mining operations that were taking place there, and that was taking away a crucial part of the eco-system which was going to bite everyone on the bum quite quickly. It was the first time really that I began to understand the full impact – I was vaguely aware about it through the anti-capitalist movement of the time, but this changed when I met a lot of the front-line communities who were directly affected. It was coming into direct contact with these movements in the global south who educated me in the severity of what was really happening and from then on, we realised that this was going to be a major issue, and especially for working class and vulnerable communities.

It has taken a long time for the left in the global north to really catch up. When we started Reel News in 2006, the writer George Monbiot was explaining that emissions needed to be cut by 90 per cent and the implications of that, and that if we don't get a handle on this, then the people who always end up paying worse for this, working people, are going to end up paying again. So, at that point we became more aware of which groups internationally were fighting to combat this and those who had a class perspective on it. We saw it as important in identifying the issue and integrating it into everyday struggle, and from this point on more widely there became a push around the world for this to happen as well. We've been steadily covering this for over thirteen years, and now in the last year it's been great to see how this has arrived as a central issue to fight over.

EK: *How has your experience of being involved in Reel News impacted upon your political outlook over this period?*

SD: It has impacted a lot. Because Reel News being a very campaign driven thing, and is driven by people who get in contact with us, I think I get exposed to a larger variety of ways of organising and a wide variety of different political outlooks than maybe a lot of people would. Particularly as a result of the international engagement of Reel News where we have travelled to cover international campaigns where we possibly can, I get a lot of different ways of looking at things, and organising, and that has definitely changed my attitude over the years. I couldn't say precisely how it has, apart from the fact that I'm not sure I would automatically put a label on myself like 'I'm an anarchist' or 'I'm a revolutionary socialist'. I tend to absorb lots of different ideas and traditions and have a strange mix in my head. But at the bottom there is something that never changes, which is seeing as central the class basis of society and seeing that as the means to fight back.

21

COMMUNITY ACCESS

Echo Park Film Center/Paolo Davanzo and Lisa Marr interviewed by Steve Presence

Introduction

Echo Park Film Center (EPFC) is a non-profit media arts organisation in Los Angeles that is committed to providing equal and affordable community access to film and video resources. Established by Paolo Davanzo and two friends in 2001, EPFC is now almost twenty years old, making it one of the longest-running organisations of its kind in the world. The interview below was conducted at EPFC's premises in July 2019 with Davanzo and Lisa Marr – Davanzo's life partner and one of EPFC's longest-standing members. It builds on an article, 'Sell your TV and come to the cinema: how to start a film center',[1] written by Davanzo and published online in 2016, and should be read as a companion piece to that article, which includes a history of the organisation. In keeping with the focus of this book, the interview focuses on the strategies and tactics EPFC has developed to sustain itself and its work over such a long period, all the while maintaining its radical spirit and remaining true to the community it was set up to serve.

STEVE PRESENCE (SP): *I wanted to start by asking what's changed since you published the article – is EPFC still based on those five core activities – screenings, teaching, equipment rental, the mobile cinema and the residencies?*

PAOLO DAVANZO (PD): The five things are still there, but they're more robust, I would say. So, the community-curated cinema series does about 200 events a year, every Thursday and Saturday night almost without a miss. On Fridays, we allow people to four-wall the space, and it helps subsidise the organisation. Maybe it's stuff that the co-op wouldn't curate themselves, but maybe someone made an indie feature and they want to show it, right?

SP: *How much do you charge?*

LISA MARR (LM): It's $250 for four hours; that includes a projectionist. If you're non-profit, it's $200. Those rates haven't changed in years. It's the same with the cinema admission – it was $5 in 2001, it's still $5. And that's a suggested donation, no one's ever turned away for lack of funds. This is one of the ways in which we self-generate our income: every time someone steps in here, they're supporting all our free programming by coming to a movie, or by renting a piece of gear.

PD: Yes, because for most of the screenings, the filmmaker doesn't pay – we pay them. It's a $5 donation at the door, and we always split that 50/50. Though we're just talking about the Friday nights, sometimes, people just want to four-wall it. The cinema's a huge part of EPFC and what many people know us for. The education part, which is paramount in what we've been doing from the beginning, is always free for youth, always free for seniors. I think now we're up to 10,000 young people we've taught, you know, all over the city and all over the world. So maybe you work at the grocery store, you're raising a family, you want to tell a story but you don't have that access. So, it's like, $20, $30 for a class to learn digital editing and you can rent a camera for $20. It's giving people access.

LM: But we pay the teachers. So, again, any of the tuition, when people do pay for the classes, it goes to the teachers and the other half goes to sustain our organisation. So, it's always a profit-sharing model. That's how it started: school, cinema, store. Then in 2005, we started the residency programme, where emerging or established filmmakers from around the world come and spend a month here. We give them a place to stay and a stipend and they have full access to everything in here, all the knowledge and equipment. Then they make something inspired by their time here, teach a youth class, the community members get to come and meet them, and then they do a presentation of their work. Now, we also do four two-month residencies for people from Los Angeles County, and that's been really successful as well.

SP: *The focus seems very much on experimental film and documentary. Is fiction explicitly something you don't do?*

PD: That's a good question. Partly, we don't teach narrative filmmaking because that's what this whole town is about, right? My desire and passion was documentary and experimental cinema, and I was, like, 'Okay, let's stop, you know, actors and car crashes and women in bikinis, let's get past that. Let's tell community stories, people stories.' We're lovers of narrative films, of course, but it's just not our mandate – though we do show narrative films on occasion.

SP: *And what about the Filmmobile, is that still running?*

LM: That's still rocking. It's birthed some children, actually. The bus is still amazing – still veggie oiled and solar powered – but now we also have the Filmcycle: a bike with a big box on the front. It's big enough to hold a generator and we've got a little homemade rear projection screen, so you can be peddling and projecting. These are just more ways to get to more populations and spread the word. We also have a modular trailer that can be used as a living space for artists in residence, or as seating for outdoor screening, but it's also a darkroom and cinema.

SP: *And how about the fifth activity — has the equipment rental declined with the advent of cheaper digital and mobile technologies?*

PD: DVD rental has, for sure — we use them more as teaching aids now. But this younger generation is super excited about the physicality of analogue film, the slowness, we call it the slow film movement, like the slow food movement. It's not super cheap — and we love the accessibility of being able to make a film on your phone — but there's also a beauty and a reverence to celluloid, and the analogue stuff has never been more popular. The courses sell out — there's a waiting list to get into them. It's fascinating.

LM: All the gear is always checked-out. Especially the 16 mm stuff. Nobody else is renting this stuff. So we're the only game in town in some ways.

SP: *Can you say a bit about how the organisation is run?*

PD: Sure, that's the biggest thing that's changed. In 2014, Lisa and I were getting more and more invitations to do work abroad, so we met with the few members that have really propelled the EPFC vision forward — filmmakers, educators, parents — and said, 'How can we be stronger? How can we really sustain ourselves and move forward?', and we became a collective co-op. Now, EPFC is run by about twenty co-op members, where everyone has an equal voice in decision-making.

LM: Many are former students, some work in the film industry and are doing quite well, others are single parents raising four kids by themselves, some are art school grads. But the common bond is that everyone found the Film Center, for some reason, at some point in their life, and everyone loves the Film Center mission for what it is. It's all very organic. There's no minimum hours or anything like that, and everyone's encouraged to do a little bit of everything.

PD: Sure. We have three part-time paid positions: Lisa, and I, and Andrew Kim are those. But we work, you know, eighty hours a week … and do other jobs for money. The rest of the co-op functions on a profit-sharing model. Once again, terms that are not radical or sexy by any means, but which allow you to function.

LM: Formally becoming a co-op was exciting, too. When you open the organisa-tion up to more participants and more voices, it becomes stronger and more dynamic in ways that we couldn't even have dreamed. Because every one of those twenty people have different interests, different skills, and they're bringing that all to the table.

SP: *As founders, did you find it hard to let go? Because you obviously have ideas about where the organisation should go, so to step back and let other people drive it could be a difficult thing to do. How was that?*

PD: I think it's healthy, and it was time. I mean, we're two college-educated, white, privileged people. We want to hear these other voices. You see it in here today, you feel the energy, the diversity of thoughts and ideas and perspectives and back-grounds of our constituents. So making space for other voices just felt natural.

LM: Sometimes it's hard, when you think, 'Oh, I wouldn't do it that way,' but it's healthy to take a step back, for sure.

SP: *You mention in the article that you're in Echo Park because it used to be a working-class neighbourhood and the rent was cheap. Can you talk a bit about that process and how the area has changed? Is gentrification a threat to the film center?*

LM: I'm from Vancouver, Canada, and ended up here by a fluke series of circumstances in 1997. I had participated in a film centre in Vancouver called The Blinding Light, but there was no real radical cinema space in LA at that time. It was weird to be in a place where movies were so important to people and there was so much conversation around film, not to have a more community-based centre to feed them. I lived in Echo Park, and was walking around one day and, you know, I walked in here and Paolo was here and he said, 'Oh, we're opening a Film Center today.' On the very first day.

But my story is the same story as everybody else who comes here. You walk through the door, you fall in love with the space, and the energy in the space, and you just want to be here. You want to help out, you want to be part of it, and then people just stay for years. I started as a volunteer and then [Paolo and I] fell in love, and it's been an amazing journey. But I see it every time, you know, someone new comes in the door and becomes part of the establishment.

SP: *How did you come to be here, Paolo?*

PD: I was born in Italy to an Italian father and a Canadian mother – I was seven when I came over to the US. They were super radical. My father would talk about the revolution and my mother worked in soup kitchens for the homeless and was a real radical activist. They died when I was very young, in my early twenties. I'm now almost fifty. Them dying was such a catalyst for me – I'd been political and in various organisations through my mum and through my own activism – but it was really just the spark that said, 'Hey, I need to do something bigger than myself,' so that's when we opened.

But the history of this neighbourhood is fascinating. The indigenous people of this area, the Tongva and the Gabrieleño were first here, then the Spanish came by and established the Mission in downtown – hence the name of the city, Los Angeles. Echo Park was one of the first suburbs after the wave of the gentry came, from the Europeans. It's had such a rich history since then, too. There was a huge Italian immigrant population, a huge Cuban population. During the 1980s, during the civil wars in Central America, a lot of people from El Salvador and Honduras came here.

LM: And a lot of lefties. By the 1940s and 1950s, it was super radical, it was known as Red Hill or Red Gulch, and a lot of people that were part of Hollywood Ten would hide-out here. Woody Guthrie lived here. There's also a rich film history here. Right down the street is where the Mack Sennett studio was.

We've done projects with the youth around these issues, because they carry though to this day with immigration rights and housing – it's still an activist neighbourhood in a lot of ways, even though it is gentrifying. Again, we recognise our own part in that. We are not saying we're outside of this wave. We've been here twenty years – the Film Centre for eighteen years – but we were still part of a wave that you can point to and say, 'Oh, this is when something started to change.' We like to see ourselves as an organisation that is of value to the community, is not just a capitalist enterprise. But you still need to recognise your place in this evolution of a neighbourhood, you know?

SP: *Does gentrification pose a threat to EPFC? Two of the leading radical community cinemas in the UK – the Cube Microplex in Bristol and the Star and Shadow in Newcastle – have recently bought the buildings they're based in. Am I right in thinking you rent the space?*

PD: That's right, we don't own this building, so with regards to the danger gentrification poses to us – there's no guarantees. This is a conversation we're having all over the world. There are no guarantees that you will have a physical space. We have had one for eighteen years, and it's always been this space, it just gets more and more crowded, and more and more things happen here.

But, you know, next time our lease comes up for renewal, there's no guarantee that we'll even be able to have a conversation around renewing it. It could just be, 'Please leave,' you know, 'Your time here is done.' Space in general in Los Angeles right now is rare, and it's contested. So, we need to be able to think about how we can continue to do our work if we're displaced or we need to move.

SP: *How would you describe the political nature of EPFC and the work that you do?*

PD: Everything we're doing is political in some way. Even here right now, some of our former students that are now instructors are teaching this class, Migration Narratives. They're undocumented and very defiant about their status, and wanting to educate people about what that means. The whole class is based around this notion of migration and borders, and who defines borders. Lots of our classes have these kinds of political themes. Inherently our curriculum is around these issues that we need to be discussing.

LM: We call ourselves cinema activists, and we talk about the cinematic revolution. We're not out there necessarily, you know, preaching about larger political issues, but the goal is to make a space where these conversations can happen. Again, we are not here to lead, we are here to make the space for other people to come and get involved and tell their stories.

Personally, I'm losing a lot of faith in the wider political system. I just see it as this stalemate that just gets into more and more deadlock every year. There's just so much noise around this stuff that, as I get older, I just feel like I can't engage on that level anymore, and I don't really want to. Until capitalism ends, I don't know how we're going to be able to move forward, and I don't know how we're going to get to that place. So I'm figuring out how can I be political and active in my daily life. For me, it's about connecting with a community that I can have a direct exchange with and, and see what they need, and try to help that.

PD: On a government level, it's frustrating. I haven't given up hope, but I also feel like, actually, the work is here. The work is local, the work is with every person that comes in, every screening we have. Because that, like, resonates much louder than one vote. I mean, we should vote, but it's been a catastrophe recently, yes? In your country and in ours.

LM: We don't like competition – that's a major thing with this place. A lot of places have youth film competitions and awards – we're very against that kind of thinking. We've never given prizes, we've never sent films to festivals. We really try to move beyond these hierarchies in everything that we do, in the way we teach, the way we work with the others in the co-op.

PD: There's no director, there's no producer. Like, everyone is just a filmmaker, everyone makes the work, makes the content. There are no titles.

SP: *So is it fair to say you're broadly anti-capitalist? Can you say a bit about how you negotiate with and secure funding from a capitalist context you're working in?*

PD: Yes, I would say that we are broadly anti-capitalist, and our funding is largely built on these foundations that are very old, blue blood organisations that I'm sure made their money in oil reserves and the stock market, so it's complicated. Every organisation needs to navigate this system in a way that makes sense to them, and which enables them to do good work at the end of the day.

LM: It's that old saying, 'Can you hold hands with your funder in public?' Obviously we try to be discriminating, but that's the system. There's a Robin Hood element to it, where taking the money is justified because of the good we do with it, but this is also why we try to self-generate a significant portion of our income, so that we can say it's coming from the community, for the community.

SP: *Just finally, do you have any words of wisdom to young people who might pick this book up and be thinking about setting up an organisation of their own?*

PD: I think you just have to live your passion, you know? If you have an idea and you want to do it, definitely do it. You know, you have nothing to lose. Just get out there and have that adventure. Really, at the end of the day, it's your passion that's going to carry you through. Money comes and goes, you can figure it out, you know, space, whatever, you can always get around that. But if you have that feeling in your heart and you are true to it, you will be fine. I think just do the work, you know?

LM: Yes, and it's important to know your community and invite your community to be a part of it, whatever it is.

Note

1 You can find the article on OtherZine's website here: www.othercinema.com/otherzine/sell-your-tv-and-come-to-the-cinema-how-to-start-a-film-center/

22

'WE NEED CRITICAL MAGAZINES, DEBATES, SPACES!'

Third Cinema in Morocco

Nadir Boumouch interviewed by Steve Presence

Introduction

Nadir Boumouch is a Moroccan filmmaker who first came into contact with the Radical Film Network as part of Guerrilla Cinema, a film collective that formed in Marrakesh during the 2011 revolutions and uprisings that swept much of North African and the Middle East as part of the so-called 'Arab Spring'. Like so many activist film collectives, Guerrilla Cinema was a short-lived initiative (though a record of the group can be found on the RFN's Directory – which includes a link to its work on its still-live YouTube page).

More recently, Boumouch has been working with the residents of Imider, a commune in southeast Morocco known for its ongoing successful resistance to the destructive social, economic and environmental impacts of Africa's biggest silver mine. The interview below – conducted in 2019 – situates Nadir's work within the tradition of Third Cinema and radical film in Morocco, explores some of the challenges involved in making collaborative, politically committed work in the current context, and explains why militant film practice must consist of more than content alone.

STEVE PRESENCE (SP): *Can you tell us a bit about how you came to be making films – did you study filmmaking?*

NADIR BOUMOUCH (NB): I had the opportunity to study both cinema and political science abroad, in the United States. I would say it was both a blessing and a curse: a blessing because not many young people in Morocco have the opportunity to study abroad, and a curse because it was a very American/Hollywood-focused perspective on cinema. That's why I like to say that most of my formation was actually after I left the university and came back to Morocco. I've learned more about cinema from the peasant communities I have worked with since 2015 than the very technical Eurocentric and prescriptive approach I received in the United States.

SP: *You mentioned in Dublin that you work predominately with peasant workers – can you elaborate on that a bit? What is it that you try to do? What are your aims?*

NB: I tend to focus on what the colonial state had called 'useless Morocco' – the most marginalised regions of the country which are often perceived as empty 'backlands' but which are actually the richest in natural resources. More importantly, I am interested in these regions because not only do they make up the majority of the country, but because they are home to a still-massive peasantry which has increasingly come under attack by the neoliberal state. The state has ravaged these communities – eroding the solidarity within their social fabric; pulling apart the collective-ownership systems that characterised their tribes and replacing them with privatisation; undermining everything that had made them more-or-less autonomous in the past, and destroying the environments in which they live. Droughts have been ravaging harvests in the southeast, fish are becoming rare in Ihahan country and lands are being expropriated left and right to make room for private mega-projects, often encouraged by the World Bank. Yet the social and environmental destruction which has come with the incursion of capital into these communities has been almost completely ignored in Moroccan cinema. In most Moroccan films, peasants tend to be caricaturised and mocked as backwards, ignorant people – either to be laughed at or condemned. Through my filmic and photographic work, I try to offer an artistic medium through which peasants and seasonal workers can express and represent themselves as directly as possible.

You could say that my aim is to shed light on and provide counter-propaganda for the various resistances against the neoliberal state while highlighting the beautiful and empowering aspects of our indigenous popular culture – which the state has long worked to erase in favour of 'modernisation', nationalism and obedience to authority. Concepts like 'tiwiza' (mutual aid), enacted during harvests; autonomously managed community projects like traditional canals and irrigation systems, which bring life to arid regions without hurting the environment; or non-hierarchical organisational formations like 'agraw' (our indigenous general assemblies). These are the foundations for a future society, they are my biggest influence and inspiration and they must be documented before they're completely destroyed so that they can inspire others.

SP: *Guerrilla Cinema were one of the first groups outside Europe and the US to affiliate to the RFN. Can you tell us a bit about that experience and about activist film culture in Morocco more generally? Are you in touch with or do you work closely with any other groups?*

NB: Militant film culture goes back several decades in Morocco. Actually even in Morocco, very few contemporary filmmakers realise that the pioneers of Moroccan cinema came from a progressive leftist tradition with filmmakers like Ahmed Bouanani or Mustapha Derkaoui. At the time there were thousands of militant ciné-clubs in both urban and rural areas as well as many cultural and cinema magazines (like Cinema 3, which was inspired by the Third Cinema manifesto) which produced a wealth of knowledge. After the beginning of the counter-revolutionary period in the 1980s – which was led by King Hassan II's authoritarian state, economically reinforced by the IMF and politically invigorated by the Islamists, the left in Morocco was weakened significantly. It became increasingly rigid and authoritarian, before it shot itself in the foot by retreating from culture and the arts. This allowed for a massive takeover of cultural production by liberals who found themselves reinvigorated by neoliberal policies and tons of funding from French institutions. Now they're just making whatever films might make them money in France, with not much thinking involved. The results on our society have been catastrophic: individualism and greed have completely replaced the generosity and solidarity our grandparents tell us about.

Anyway, this is just a summary of the historical context to explain how we came to the dire situation we were at when we decided to form the 'Guerrilla Cinema' collective amidst the February 20 uprising in 2011. We were all young people, mostly Anarchists between sixteen and twenty-three years old who refused to ask for obligatory permits to make films. We saw in our cinema a form of direct action. Unfortunately, that experience failed and I became more and more disillusioned with working in urban areas …. As I mentioned earlier, today I prefer to work in rural areas where I can work directly with marginalised communities. Since 2016, I have worked with the Movement on Road '96 and we formed the Local Film Committee of Imider (LFCI), a temporary film collective consisting of unemployed youth, peasants, rural university students and seasonal workers from Imider. Imider is a commune in southeastern Morocco known for its resistance against Africa's biggest silver mine – the main shareholder of which is the Moroccan Royal Family. The mine began draining water away from agricultural lands since the 1980s, and the community has been engaged in struggle against it ever since – occupying and shutting down the water pipeline to the mine to protect and irrigate their land. Working in Imider has been a much more fulfilling experience. We've produced two shorts and one feature so far in addition to organising two editions of the clandestine 'Environmental Justice Film Festival of Imider'. Now we're trying to expand this experience by sharing our knowledge with other communities to begin their own autonomous film production groups.

SP: *How do you fund all this work?*

NB: It really depends. Most of my previous work was self-funded or crowdfunded, and begging my parents was not out of the question, especially since I was still a student when I made my first work. My latest and first feature film, *Amussu* [2019] was shot with almost no budget. I had my own equipment and two friends, a sound recordist and a cinematographer, who volunteered to help shoot the film. The rest of the costs were relieved by the villagers of Imider who provided us with a place to sleep in the protest camp, and when we were really low on funds they provided us with bread and olive oil to get through … there were at least two occasions when we only had some dry bread for the day, not even olive oil!

We also trained the villagers and so they were able to act as camera and sound assistants, so that removed a lot of the cost. In other words, Tiwiza (mutual aid) was the main basis for the work and it is precisely that which eliminated the need for the large amounts of money usually required to fund a three-year long project. By the second year of filming we finally began to receive grants from abroad and these helped us compensate our volunteers for their enormous, until then unpaid, efforts and more importantly to fund our post-production. For grants, we employed a 'No-France' policy, even though France is the biggest funder of North African films … they give tons of money. But for us, besides the colonial past that would mark such a relationship, the reason for our refusal of French grants in particular is the paternalistic attitudes French funders take vis-à-vis African cinema. They want to control us and tell us what to do, what will make them money in France, and we just can't accept that. So we stay selective and only take grants that do not impose any conditions.

SP: *Can you describe some of the main political and ethical issues involved in this kind of filmmaking?*

NB: I could go on for a long time trying to answer this question, but to be more succinct I would say there are three inter-related axes which I try to address: content, form and mode of production. Today, most contemporary militant or revolutionary film practice seems to satisfy itself with content alone. That is, many appear to be satisfied with doing nothing more than just simply filming what they determine to be 'revolutionary content' (whatever that means). I profoundly disagree with this approach. If we are looking to confront capitalism, we must rethink how we make films. Our modes of filmic production must reflect our dedication to constructing a more equal, just and free society liberated from the hierarchies of capital and state. This objective goes far beyond content, it becomes a way of showing people what is possible. This is why I think we should experiment with how cultural production would look like in a future society where authority and economic inequality no longer exist – the participatory school of architecture established by Italian anarchist Giancarlo De Carlo could teach us some lessons in this regard.

Personally, in my practice alongside the community of Imider, we have developed a bottom-up means of production which makes the peasants and workers both creators and producers. Compare this with the usual approach film collectives take by organising themselves separately from the marginalised classes they seek to film. Our collective mode of production and creation pits itself against this avant-gardist approach. As a film professional and intellectual, I do not believe I should work exclusively with other intellectuals or artists to make art about people, but with people. This ultimately has formal implications, since revolutionary forms will emerge organically out of the interaction between revolutionary content and revolutionary modes of production. In our case, by organising 'agraws' – indigenous Amazigh general assemblies which function through direct democracy – including the 'agraw for filmic writing', the 'agraw for film production' and the 'agraw for montage' – we have facilitated the emergence of formal suggestions which would have never emerged from an individual, no matter how proficient or knowledgeable in cinema.

This collective mode of production has managed to break the authority of the 'auteur' and that flagrant imbalance of power between those standing behind the camera with those standing in front of it. In our case, the peasant is no longer a passive 'subject' who is 'subjected' to the 'genius' eyes of an 'auteur', but an active decision-maker and creator of her own representation. What is bizarre is that we don't have any problems thinking this way in regards to fields like pharmaceuticals, for instance, by imagining a world where medicines are produced democratically, based on people's needs and not on profit. Or in urbanism, by imagining a world where the structural organisation of our cities and towns is determined by the communities who live in them rather than real estate corporations and states that seek to control our movement and consumption. But what if we applied these concepts to art? What wonderful possibilities could exist if art was not the individualist endeavour the bourgeois conception has made it to be?

SP: *Has a particular aesthetic emerged from the work? Do you see yourself as working in an aesthetic context as much as a political one?*

NB: I'm glad you ask this question since it permits me to speak to something I haven't had the chance to address yet. In a word: decolonisation. Since I am working in a colonised or formerly colonised context I often find myself confronted with the domination of European aesthetics, something which often tends to push my African colleagues into a 'copy-and-paste' approach to cinema. We don't actually explore our own languages and cultures and how they materialise in unique forms and aesthetics. African content, European aesthetic – it's no wonder many of us laugh even in those scenes supposedly designed to make us cry. It's so absurd and unreflective of our realities, so alienating that we can only laugh. This mimetic tendency in the cinemas of the colonised world has also largely meant a uniformity, an increasing homogeneity of aesthetics in the name of this disingenuous 'universalist' ideal which does nothing more but erase the specificities and beauty of cultural plurality. You could say there is a McDonalds-ification of world cinema. If you compare post-2000 Senegalese cinema with post-2000 Tunisian or French or Argentinian cinema you'll find very similar aesthetics and forms. This isn't to say there are exceptions, but you could say there is a general tendency towards homogeneity in aesthetics and form.

But to get back to Eurocentric tendencies in African cinema, I wouldn't just blame contemporary liberal film institutions for this, even the Euro-American left with its modernist obsessions has been responsible for a massive erasure in the past. Perhaps this has to do with the Marxist-Leninist obsession with the proletariat and implicit hatred for the peasantry as a 'reactionary' class. I bring this up because the historic foundations of our culture was formulated within peasant and nomadic societies, not industrialism or modernism. It is there, I think, that the decolonisation of aesthetics can find its foundation. Luckily, some pioneers of African and Latin American cinema have left us with a lot of questions and answers around the decolonisation of cinema. Not coincidentally, their ideas emerged from rural popular and indigenous culture – not from urban areas where alienation, both economic and cultural, was already underway. Unfortunately, the liberal take-over I referred to earlier has effectively erased the memory of these pioneers – people like Bouanani in North Africa, Sembene in West Africa or Sanjines in Latin America. Today, I find their ideas of great importance and relevance.

SP: *Okay. Aside from funding or sustaining the work, can you describe some of the main problems you face as a radical filmmaker?*

NB: I am having enormous difficulty finding other North African filmmakers or film professionals who share my radical views on cinema. My aim isn't to just take a radical position for the sake of it: I seek to contribute to radical social change and this is something that requires a widespread effort by many filmmakers and cultural workers in the region I work in. We need a radical cultural movement, and at this point I still cannot see one forming. So it can sometimes feel constraining to be a radical surrounded by liberals, capitalists or outright monarchists in your 'professional community'. How is one supposed to develop or revise ideas without a community engaged in constant discussion, dialogue and knowledge production? We need critical magazines, debates, spaces! This can't happen if the 'professional community' lacks even a drop of intellectual reflection. They're just too invested in the capitalist system for them to withdraw or even think about withdrawing themselves from it. This is precisely why I have decided to start focusing on building relationships with film students and giving workshops to children and teenagers interested in cinema. I think it may be too late for the generations who are already producing films right now.

SP: *Finally, can you tell us a bit about your future plans? Are there any immediate issues or problems you want to focus on? In what ways does the wider political context impact on your work?*

NB: Well, for one, the environmental question is extremely urgent, and poses an enormous risk for the future existence of our species on this planet. Furthermore, the first who have suffered – and who I think will begin to suffer in far more horrendous ways in the future – are the poorest social classes, especially in the Global South. So seeing the quasi-non-existence of environmental debates in North Africa, I feel a responsibility to focus on environmental, land and water justice … without forgetting their relationship to food sovereignty and thus, autonomy. These questions are deeply political, to the extent that I would say that climate change and extractivism are the most elemental challenges ahead of us today. As one friend put it: the next big revolutions in North Africa will be about climate change and water. In many ways, this is already the case. Very few people realise that the 2011 revolutions in our region began in the most polluted, water-scarce mining regions of Tunisia. Some have even called the Syrian revolution, now a counter-revolution, the first climate change war.

INDEX

FILM INDEX

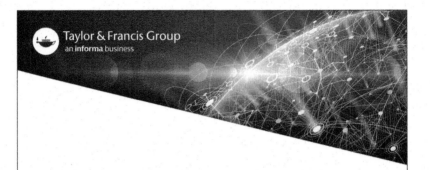